REPOSITIONING SHAKESPEARE

Repositioning Shakespeare offers a far-reaching assessment of how the Bard has been appropriated within postcolonial contexts, especially in the United States. Thomas Cartelli explores how Shakespeare is repositioned as postcolonial cultures seek to renegotiate Shakespeare's standing as a privileged site of authority within their own national formations.

Cartelli provides innovative readings of texts and events that position themselves in relation to Shakespeare, such as:

- polemical essays by Walt Whitman
- the nineteenth-century play, *Jack Cade*, commissioned and staged by the first major American Shakespearean actor
- an essay on labor-management reform by social activist Jane Addams
- novels by Aphra Behn, Ngũgĩ wa Thiong'o, Michelle Cliff, Tayeb Salih, Nadine Gordimer, and Robert Stone
- the 1849 Astor Place Riot
- films by James Ivory and Gus Van Sant
- a Shakespeare tercentenary masque performed on the campus of the City College of New York in 1916.

Repositioning Shakespeare makes an original contribution to debates about the cultural uses of Shakespeare, as well as to the question of what counts as postcolonial.

Thomas Cartelli is Professor of English at Muhlenberg College. He is the author of *Marlowe, Shakespeare, and the Economy of Theatrical Experience*, which was awarded the 1991 Hoffman Prize for Distinguished Publication on Christopher Marlowe.

REPOSITIONING SHAKESPEARE

National formations, postcolonial appropriations

Thomas Cartelli

London and New York

First published 1999
by Routledge
11 New Fetter Lane, London EC4P 4EE

Simultaneously published in the USA and Canada
by Routledge
29 West 35th Street, New York, NY 10001

© 1999 Thomas Cartelli

Typeset in Baskerville by Routledge
Printed and bound in Great Britain by Creative Print and Design (Wales),
Ebbw Vale

British Library Cataloguing in Publication Data
A catalogue record for this book is available from the British Library

Library of Congress Cataloging in Publication Data
A catalogue record for this book has been requested

ISBN 0–415–19134–3 (hbk)
ISBN 0–415–19498–9 (pbk)

TO MY MOTHER AND IN MEMORY
OF MY FATHER

CONTENTS

CONTENTS

ACKNOWLEDGMENTS

This book had its start in the essay, "Prospero in Africa," that was first published in 1987 in *Shakespeare Reproduced* and is reprinted in revised form here. An opportunity to build upon this piece was provided when the Shakespeare Association of America invited me to deliver a paper on Shakespeare and postcolonialism at its annual meeting in Kansas City in 1992. The result, "After *The Tempest*: Shakespeare, Postcoloniality, and Michelle Cliff's New, New World Miranda," was later revised for publication in *Contemporary Literature*, Volume 36, No. 1 (1995), and has been once more revised for inclusion here as a companion-piece to "Prospero in Africa." It appears by permission of the University of Wisconsin Press and the Board of Regents of the University of Wisconsin System.

I might never have heard of Michelle Cliff were it not for my long-time friend and colleague, Jim Bloom. Jim later successively acquainted me with Percy MacKaye's *Caliban by the Yellow Sands*, Jane Addams's "A Modern Lear," and Robert Stone's *Children of Light*, while adding immeasurably to my understanding of Nadine Gordimer's *My Son's Story*. Jim also offered to read the entire manuscript, which he did with his usual impatience for slack thinking and pretentiousness. I owe him the store.

An early version of Chapter 1 was presented at the 1994 annual meeting of the SAA in Albuquerque in a session on "Shakespeare and Democracy" which I organized with Michael Bristol. The chapter on *Othello* and *Oroonoko* owes mightily to earlier work done on these texts by Margie Ferguson among others, and not a little to the resources of the Folger Library. The subject of Chapter 7, Tayeb Salih's *Season of Migration to the North*, was first brought to my attention by Michael Neill during our own season together at the Folger, though my primary debt here is to Jyotsna Singh, whose essay on the novel helped show me what more might be done with it.

What Jim Bloom has been to the American studies section of this book—source, resource, and inspiration—Ania Loomba has been, in a less obvious way, to its "Third World" postcolonial side, though more in the way of conscience, articulator, and example. She sets the standard for intelligence, honesty, and rigor in this field where Shakespeare and postcoloniality cross.

Others who have heard or read portions of the book, and have commented on them in one way or another, include Mary Fuller, Coppélia Kahn, William Carroll, James Shapiro, Barbara Bowen, Tom Berger, John Drakakis, Martin Orkin, members of the Columbia University Shakespeare Seminar, and my wife Jackie Miller. I talked through much of this material with Alan Sinfield, Jonathan Dollimore, and Nick Visser at a conference in Johannesburg hosted by Martin Orkin in the summer of 1996. Thanks are due to Alan for practical advice regarding circulation of the manuscript, and to Nick Visser for his intellectual generosity and boundless hospitality. Nick's untimely death leaves us all diminished.

I owe special debts of gratitude to Terry Hawkes, who encouraged me to submit the project to Routledge and became its first official reader, and to Talia Rodgers, whose enthusiasm for my writing helped me keep the faith. Sophie Powell has been an indefatigable facilitator and correspondent, and patient audience for my anxieties.

Muhlenberg College has been unusually supportive of me and my projects. Much of the work I've done on this book has been under-written by the year's leave I enjoyed as Class of '32 Research Professor, a series of generous summer research grants, and a crucial sabbatical leave in the spring of 1996. Thanks in particular to Curtis Dretsch for sending me to South Africa that summer.

I've taken more time away from my family to complete this book than should be allowable. I promise to return what I owe with interest to Philip and Gregory.

A final word of thanks to Harriet and Israel Miller, and to Carol Proctor, who in different ways continue to make many things possible.

Lines from E.K. Brathwaite's "Didn't He Ramble" are drawn from *The Arrivants*, London: Oxford University Press, 1973. They are quoted by permission of Oxford University Press.

Passages from Ngũgĩ wa Thiong'o's *A Grain of Wheat*, London: Heinemann, 1968, are reprinted by permission of Heinemann Educational Publishers, a division of Reed Educational & Professional Publishing Ltd.

Passages from *Season of Migration to the North* by Tayeb Salih, translated by Denys Johnson-Davies, are reprinted with permission of Lynne Rienner Publishers, Inc.

Unless otherwise noted, all quotations from Shakespeare are drawn from David Bevington's fourth edition of *The Complete Works*, New York: HarperCollins.

INTRODUCTION

1.

This book's primary aim is to explore how Shakespeare is repositioned, as emerging or residually postcolonial cultures seek either to respond critically to the depredations and misrepresentations of colonialism, or to renegotiate Shakespeare's standing as a privileged site of authority within their own national formations. Given the preoccupation of postcolonial cultures with the representational practices of their colonial period, and Shakespeare's implication in their development, the book's concerns extend to appropriations of Shakespeare that are undertaken during, as well as after, the official period of British political control over a geographically specific place or polity. The Shakespeare that emerges from these acts of appropriation may thus be construed as the repositioned product of a complex of social, cultural, and political factors that variously combine under the pressure of colonial, postcolonial, and more narrowly national imperatives.

These repositionings of Shakespeare may be negotiated through the medium of established interpretive practices, of individual texts like Tayeb Salih's novel, *Season of Migration to the North* (1969), or of events like the 1849 Astor Place Riot and the 1916 Shakespeare tercentenary masque, both of which were "produced" in New York at different moments in America's evolving relationship with Shakespeare. They may be expressly oppositional in orientation, as are, for example, many of Walt Whitman's recorded comments on Shakespeare; contestatory of Shakespearean drama's underwriting of class-based or imperialist agendas; or merely critically or creatively responsive to the force or authority exerted by texts like *The Tempest* in fixing the relationship of master and slave, colonizer and colonized, lord of culture or capital and immigrant laborer. The Shakespeare reproduced by these texts and events is not directly answerable to the evaluative or interpretive criteria

1

that apply to an understanding of Shakespearean drama at its moment of production. As Jonathan Bate notes with respect to English responses to Shakespeare in the eighteenth and nineteenth centuries: "The history of appropriation may suggest that 'Shakespeare' is not a man who lived from 1564 to 1616 but a body of work that is refashioned by each subsequent age in the image of itself" (Bate 1989: 3). This tendency becomes even more pronounced when "Shakespeare" is "refashioned" outside the national boundaries of British culture and society "in the image" of cultures and societies seeking either to establish their independence from imperial influence or to identify, define, and assert their own national values or priorities. Hence, this is less a book about Shakespeare than it is a book about what becomes of Shakespeare's work in its translation from early modern playtext to colonialist pretext to postcolonial target, preoccupation, or objective.

Rather than readings of specific Shakespearean texts, then, this book will instead offer assessments of texts and events that position themselves in relation or response to Shakespeare: polemical essays by Walt Whitman; a nineteenth-century play entitled *Jack Cade* commissioned and staged by the first major American Shakespearean actor; the 1849 Astor Place Riot; an essay on labor-management reform authored by the social activist Jane Addams; novels by Ngũgĩ wa Thiong'o, Michelle Cliff, Aphra Behn, Tayeb Salih, Nadine Gordimer, and Robert Stone; films directed by James Ivory and Gus Van Sant; and a Shakespeare tercentenary masque performed on the campus of the City College of New York.

The body of the book is divided into three parts or sections. Part I, "Democratic Vistas," ranges over approximately ninety years of U.S. encounters with Shakespeare, and focuses specifically on responses to Shakespeare's alleged anti-democratic bias on the one hand, and his more consistent positioning as "author" of "the father to the man in America" and, hence, as a virtual founding father on the other. This section of the book is broadly concerned with how the ambivalence of America's relationship with British culture—and the persistent filial deference to Shakespeare of U.S. writers and social critics—repeatedly compromise efforts to develop alternatives to established models of social and textual organization constructed in Shakespeare's name.

These U.S. transactions with Shakespeare specifically witness the failure to develop models of democratic subjectivity that could be said truly to break from the critically established heroic, individualist, and paternalist bias of Shakespearean drama. The expressly anti-aristocratic play of 1841, *Jack Cade*, cannot finally imagine a hero whose individuality is an extension, rather than a supersession of, the collective aspirations of the common man. Nor can its sponsors, authors, and chief actor work free of the canonically naturalized textual formats of Shakespearean drama that characteristically privilege the burdens of leaders at the expense of those who serve them. The economy of this transaction is partially re-enacted in Jane Addams's 1894 essay, "A Modern Lear," when Addams cannot commit herself to a "plot" that must finally exclude the claim of paternalistic lords of capital to a continuing role in determining the lot of largely immigrant labor. The 1916 tercentenary masque, *Caliban by the Yellow Sands*, ritualizes this recuperative process by modeling the future of an increasingly multicultural republic on the immigrant Caliban's surrender to the guiding hand of a Shakespeare who, at the end of the pageant, takes Prospero's place onstage and assumes the role of infallible sponsor of an embattled Anglo-Saxon power elite's claim to moral and cultural leadership and authority. Although they do not themselves operate in a distinctly postcolonial field of engagement, "A Modern Lear" and *Caliban* significantly complicate and redirect *Jack Cade*'s oppositional approach to British culture by deploying Shakespeare as a reconciling mediator of divisions *within* the United States between capital and labor, on the one hand, and the new metropolitan center and its immigrant "colonies" on the other.

The opening chapter of Part II, "Prospero's Books," charts the development of colonialist paradigms derived from Shakespeare's staging of the relationship between Prospero and Caliban in *The Tempest*, explores their application to British imperialist ventures in Africa, and examines in greater detail Ngũgĩ's repositioning of these discursive formations in *A Grain of Wheat*, a 1968 novel focused on the aftermath of Kenya's struggle for national emergence. The next chapter broadly discusses the network of relationships that continues to tie West Indian writers to the Western canon, but focuses on Michelle Cliff's effort to develop a postcolonial subjectivity and textuality that extend beyond the orbit-plot of *The Tempest*. The emphasis throughout this section falls on how African and Caribbean writers (and the characters they put into motion) attempt to free themselves from "the so-called dependency complex of colonized peoples" (Fanon 1967) embodied in the Prospero/Caliban configuration and the plantation model of social (and textual) organization it suggests.

The third section of the book treats the colonial afterlife and postcolonial career of the "Othello Complex." The first chapter explores Shakespeare's formative construction of racial difference or Otherness in the context of evolving racial paradigms of the seventeenth and eighteenth centuries. It specifically focuses on Aphra Behn's recuperative refashioning of Shakespeare's arguably "intractable" Moor in *Oroonoko* (1688) under the pressure of New World colonialism and plantation slavery, and considers the influence exerted by *Oroonoko* on a host of texts it spawned, beginning with Richard Southerne's 1695 stage adaptation. The second chapter focuses on Tayeb Salih's *Season of Migration to the North* (1969), a Sudanese novel that examines the disintegrative effects of the Othello complex on Arab-African identity formation. My concern here is with how Shakespeare's racial and ethnic constructions are elaborated and "fixed" by repositionings of *Othello* that are negotiated under the influence of New World slavery on the one hand, and British imperialism on the other. This section, however, ultimately focuses on the vicissitudes of *internal* or *subjective* colonization and on what could be termed the economy of postcolonial self-fashioning.

The book's Conclusion shifts interpretive ground to conceive, and consider, the possibility of a decolonized or decommissioned Shakespeare, relieved of his obligation to circulate as a fixed object of scorn or emulation in the orbit of postcolonial applications. It specifically offers a comparative assessment of Shakespeare's relegation to the pastoral margins of contemporary South African experience in Nadine Gordimer's *My Son's Story* (1990), and of the case for Shakespeare's intertextual viability which Robert Stone makes in *Children of Light* (1986). Stone's novel, which dramatizes the evolution of a self-identified Rosalind figure into a veritable Queen Lear and portrays the chronic Shakespearizing of its male protagonist as a form of late imperial substance abuse, suggests that the prospective closing of Shakespeare's career as a source and medium of struggles for political and cultural self-definition may allow his plays to circulate more freely, unconstrained by their overextended afterlife as adjuncts to British imperial resolve and postcolonial rage and resentment.

2.

The field of postcolonial literary studies is, at this stage of its development, very broadly—some would say, badly—defined. As identified by some of its most articulate theorists, its purview would appear to be material produced in or about recently emergent polities of the developing world during the postwar/post-independence period, and its politics expressly anti-colonial in orientation. In practice, however, the field remains preoccupied with the social, educational, and political institutions of the colonial period (see, e.g., Viswanathan 1989 and Singh 1996), and with literary works produced after independence that take as their subject matter not only the depredations of colonialism (see, e.g., the early work of Achebe, Soyinka, and Ngũgĩ) but also the succeeding depredations of indigenous power elites (see, e.g., the later work of Achebe, Soyinka, and Ngũgĩ).[1] This is not only predictable but inevitable, given the continuities that run through the official divisions of the colonial and the postcolonial. As the authors of *The Empire Writes Back* observe in their own Introduction: "We use the term 'post-colonial'... to cover all the culture affected by the imperial process from the moment of colonization to the present day. This is because there is a continuity of preoccupations throughout the historical process initiated by European imperial aggression...In this sense this book is concerned with the world as it exists during and after the period of European imperial domination and the effects of this on contemporary literatures" (Ashcroft *et al.* 1989: 2). One could, in fact, argue that the term "postcolonial" is the primary source of misconceptions about the field since most so-called postcolonial societies are *post*colonial in name only insofar as they remain subject to the economic exploitation, political influence, military intervention, and social and legal constructions of the officially withdrawn colonial power or of its foreign and domestic surrogates or successors.

The failure of officially postcolonial nations to break decisively with the language, institutions, influence, and control of the imperial "center" should not, however, be taken as a counter-indication of their postcoloniality since, even under the best conditions, the long-sustained regime of colonialism may be said to produce for itself both an inescapable history and an afterlife in the postcolony. As Stuart Hall observes, the postcolonial is not "one of those periodisations based on epochal 'stages', when everything is reversed at the same moment, all the old relations disappear for ever and entirely new ones come to replace them." According to Hall, "disengagement from the colonising process" is always "a long, drawn-out and differentiated affair, in which the recent post-war movement towards decolonisation figures as one, but only one, distinctive 'moment'" (Hall 1996: 247). In most cases, then, what we are speaking of when we speak of post(-)coloniality is the liminal space between freedom and subjection, independence and dependence, that is demarcated in the dash between prefix and noun. It is within this space that a continuing engagement with colonialism takes place as the postcolony attempts to negotiate a sense of national and cultural self-definition that may, as it were, *post*date the colonial connection and situate it in a past from which the former colony has now presumably emerged.[2]

One of the arguments of this book is that such a space existed and such negotiations took place in the postcolony of the United States in the nineteenth century and for some time thereafter, and that this connection became postdated only when new models of social formation (and new ways of describing them) emerged that superseded the prevailing postcolonial framework. One of the ironies of this development is (as I discuss below) the establishment *within* the United States of relations between capital, on the one hand, and labor and immigrant communities, on the other, that work within a recognizably colonial model of human relations: one that situates immigrants and laborers in the position of "Caliban types," who are as congenitally unequipped and unready for self-governance as the subject peoples of the British empire. Another is the U.S.'s own twentieth-century embrace of an imperial destiny made intermittently, if inexorably, manifest in the nineteenth: a transaction that has made the very idea of an American postcoloniality difficult to sustain in a discursive climate focused on clear-cut distinctions between First World and Third World, dominator and dominated, oppressor and oppressed. As Lawrence Buell notes, "even mildly liberal academics will suspect the possible hypocrisy of an exercise in imagining America of the expansionist years as a postcolonial rather than proto-imperial power, as if to mystify modern America's increasingly interventionist role in world affairs" (Buell 1992: 411).[3]

Certainly, any notion of postcoloniality I might apply to U.S. experience in the nineteenth century will need to be clearly differentiated from the ongoing struggles of contemporary "Third World" societies to contend with the material legacies of colonialist exploitation, and will need to account for the development of colonizing impulses within America itself. Yet, as others have noted, the nineteenth-century U.S. struggle for social, cultural, and political self-definition serves, in many respects, as a proving ground for more recent efforts to establish a sense of national identity in such postcolonies as Nigeria and Kenya, Trinidad and Jamaica, Australia and New Zealand. As Ashcroft and company write:

> perhaps because of its current position of power, and the neo-colonizing role it has played, [the] post-colonial nature [of the U.S.A.] has not been generally recognized. But its relationship with the metropolitan centre as it evolved over the last two centuries has been paradigmatic for post-colonial literatures everywhere. What each of these literatures has in common beyond their special and distinctive regional characteristics is that they emerged in their present form out of the experience of colonization and asserted themselves by foregrounding the

tension with the imperial power, and by emphasizing their differences from the assumptions of the imperial centre. It is this which makes them distinctively post-colonial.

(Ashcroft *et al.* 1989: 2)

The reluctance to sanction the inclusion of America in a discursive category that largely embraces the literary productions of so-called Third World countries is understandable given the highly politicized nature of the category itself, and has often been extended to the literatures of other "settler colonies" like Canada, Australia, and New Zealand which developed as "filial" and "affiliated" extensions of the "mother country." Unlike so-called "invaded colonies" like India or Nigeria or the "slave colonies" of the West Indies, the settler colonies may be said to have "grown up" in a responsive relationship with the mother country and to have "separated" upon their maturation without the violence and loss of life that attended, say, the "separation" of Kenya or India from England. Indeed, as Vijay Mishra and Bob Hodge observe of countries like Australia, "which, historically, has always seen itself as part of the Empire, ever ready to follow, uncritically, in the footsteps of the Mother Country," the "settler colonies provided the manpower, the support systems for colonialism to flourish" (1991: 400).[4] Although Mishra and Hodge would no doubt quarrel with my conclusion, arguments like their own that consign settler colonies like Canada or Australia to the category of the "complicit postcolonial" indirectly underwrite the U.S.'s claim to inclusion in the larger body of postcolonial states, since no other settler colony can be said to have endured a more violent passage to independence.[5] The expressly anti-colonial positioning of much U.S. writing of the post-independence period, some of which took direct aim against Shakespeare, lends further ballast to the claim to inclusion. As Robert Weisbuch observes:

I find enmity the keynote of Anglo-American literary relations in the mid-nineteenth century. There was a war, after all; indeed, there were two for the generations of Americans directly preceding Emerson. There was a quarrel of nation and colony, and another of nation and nation...enmity is the keynote because American writers chose to dramatize difference and to devalue agreement.

(Weisbuch 1986: xviii)

Weisbuch, however, also argues that this enmity was primarily directed against contemporary British writers, and finds "very few instances of an American writer alluding to Chaucer, Spenser, Shakespeare, or Milton in such a way as to challenge that writer's vision" (1986: 18).[6] The fact that American anti-colonial writing demonstrates less critical force and unanimity in its assessment of Shakespeare and other major canonical figures indicates the singular space that nineteenth-century U.S. culture occupies in the category of the postcolonial: a space between what Mishra and Hodge designate as the "complicit" and the "oppositional" postcolonial (1991: 407) that may, as it edges into the twentieth century, extend to the category of the "emulative" or neo-colonial. The fractiousness of the break with England, and the revolutionary democratic principles that informed it, established a clear-cut opposition between the two societies. But the continuities of language, religion, culture, and custom, enforced by 170 years of British colonization and by the post-independence succession of a largely Anglo-Saxon ruling elite, fostered a rapprochement with the "mother country" that, for the most part, extended its embrace to Shakespeare.

The Shakespeare that American writers of the nineteenth century "inherit" is, as Michael Dobson has noted, very much the product of the series of literary and social processes that eventuated in his canonization and enshrinement "as the transcendent personification of a national ideal" in England (Dobson 1992a: 14). This is certainly the Shakespeare that Emerson responds to, and attempts to annex in the form of a more universal theme, in his famous essay on "The Poet" in *Representative Men* (1850). This is also the Shakespeare that as late as 1916 the Anglophilic American poetaster, Percy MacKaye, will seek to celebrate as the embodiment and exemplar of all things bright, beautiful, and civilized in his tercentenary masque. Yet, as both Dobson and Bate are careful to note, the "official" canonization of Shakespeare that was transacted in 1769 in Garrick's Jubilee should not imply that "anything about Shakespeare was settled once and for all" (Dobson 1992a: 13). Although Whitman, and the democratic militants who collaborated in the 1841 production of *Jack Cade*, appear to be critically responding to this conflation of Shakespeare with British national ideals, even Whitman was awake to what Bate describes as "a strand in Bardolatry which turns Shakespeare against the power of the State and repossesses him in the name of liberty" (Bate 1989: 7). This "strand in Bardolatry" was also available to the social reformer, Jane Addams, when she "repossessed" Shakespeare in 1894 as a voice opposed to the power of paternalistic feudalism in both family and industrial relations. Yet it is, in part, a symptomatically American deference to power and private property that also informs Addams's inability to resist the long-cultivated sense of Shakespeare's devotion to balance, order, and proportion, and that impels her to issue a call for moderation and endurance which softens and constrains her critique.

By contrast, it is the understandable reluctance of contemporary postcolonial writers to enlist Shakespeare's collaboration in the work of decolonization that most distinguishes Third World from nineteenth-century U.S. constructions of Shakespeare. Yet, as I hope to demonstrate, this sympathetic attachment to Shakespeare has not been maintained uncritically, without regard for its inconsistency with America's national ideals. As Dobson has observed:

> The presence of Shakespeare's plays in the culture of the United States of America—a nation descended, according to its principal founding myth, from seventeenth-century Puritans who fled England to avoid (among other things) Renaissance drama—has always been attended, understandably, by a certain ambivalence, even on the part of the most bardola-trous, and given the turn toward politics visible in much contemporary criticism, it is not surprising that some American scholars have begun to wonder whether the very existence of a Shakespeare industry on their side of the Atlantic may be a sign of the ultimate failure of the American revolution.
>
> (Dobson 1992b: 189)

The "ambivalence" Dobson attributes even to "the most bardolatrous" is, of course, hardly comparable to the unqualifiedly anti-colonialist stance taken to plays like *The Tempest* by such overtly oppositional post-colonial writers like Ngũgĩ, and indicates both the weakness of, and difference in, the claim for postcolonial convergence. The claim for convergence is, however, strengthened by the series of attacks on Shakespeare's alleged pro-aristocratic bias I examine in this book's first chapter, as well as by the U.S.'s symptomatically postcolonial "mental dependence on England [which] continued long after its civil allegiance had ceased" (Alger 1877: 1:193).[7] It is strengthened further by a factor that Mishra and Hodge fail to acknowledge in their otherwise instruc-tive effort to purify the dialect of the postcolonial. While they are right to insist that "an undifferentiated concept of postcolonialism over-looks...the unbridgeable chasms that existed between White and non-White colonies" as well as "the very radical differences in response" to "Mother Country" and "imperial centre," respectively, they neglect to note the comparative uniformity of the "center" or

"Mother Country's" condescending assessment of the cultures of "White and non-White" postcolonies alike and the role that assessment played in shaping what are often highly analogous responses (Mishra and Hodge 1991: 408).

Postcolonial U.S. culture was repeatedly discredited and disvalued by British commentators on the subject throughout the nineteenth century. As Buell has noted:

> Foreign visitors denied American refinement...Nineteenth-century travelers on the notorious American practice of tobacco chewing and spitting, for instance, sound like V.S. Naipaul on Indian shitting. European travelers acknowledged American skill at practical calculation...but tended to depict Americans as more irrational than rational, as an unphilosophical culture whatever its legislative genius, as hasty and slapdash nation builders...They even denied the Americans language in the spirit of Rudyard Kipling's remark that "America has no language," only "dialect, slang, provincialism, accent, and so forth."
>
> (Buell 1992: 417–18)

The delegation to American culture of a rough, uncultivated, and barbarous quality both by condescending visitors from England like Kipling, Dickens, Trollope, and William Macready, and by equally condescending American brahmins like Henry James, has analogues in James Froude's influential book about the English in the West Indies (1888)—with its famously dismissive assertion that "There are no people there in the true sense of the word, with a character and a purpose of their own"—and in our own time in the delegation of similar qualities to Third World cultures by Naipaul and condescending Americans like Saul Bellow. And the responsiveness of Third World writers to such mischaracterizations have, for all their manifest differences, demonstrated a corresponding host of connections. Indeed, the revulsion felt by James, and later by expatriate writers like T.S. Eliot and Ezra Pound, for the secondariness of U.S. culture, resembles in many ways the postcolonial self-hatred that besets Naipaul and impelled him to let Froude's assertion stand as the epigraph to *The Middle Passage* (1962), his book about five Caribbean societies. The fact that many of the best-known contemporary postcolonial writers (Naipaul, Selvon, Rushdie, Okri, Lamming) are expatriates headquartered in London or its environs indicates, moreover, that a sympathetic attraction to the cultural productions of the "imperial centre" is not the exclusive heritage of writers drawn from the former "settler colonies." While exile can hardly be considered a matter of choice for African writers like Ngũgĩ, Achebe, and Soyinka, who live in the condition of political expatriates, the fact that a great many other Third World artists and intellectuals choose neither to make their homes, nor to take their stands, on native grounds, while they continue to focus almost exclusively on the postcolonial condition in their works, establishes further this sense of shared dependence on the metropolitan or imperial center.

It might, of course, be argued that the decisive break with England effected by the American Revolution, and the prospect of infinite space and possibility generated by the succeeding westward expansion, encouraged U.S. culture to develop along its own lines, despite the influential ties of language, race, religion, and custom that continued to bind the U.S. to Great Britain and helped forge the American national identity.[8] Henry Clay Folger's construction of his Shakespeare Library in triangulated relationship with the U.S. Capitol Building and Supreme Court may, in this respect, be read as a triumphant act of counter-colonial appropriation. But the Library itself may also be construed as a well-endowed neo-colonial outpost, founded in the spirit of cowed emulation to mark the continuing influence of Shakespeare—and of feudal British culture—over great stretches of the American imagination. Mishra and Hodge would no doubt argue that if this *is* postcolonialism, it is of the *complicit* variety and is firmly rooted in America's sense of itself as the progeny and inheritor of the British imperial mandate.[9] There would be more than a grain of truth in such a contention which would, moreover, help explain why America has become the target or objective of Latin American restagings of the Prospero/Caliban confrontation.[10] Yet even this convergence of a counter-colonizing and imperializing America, at once playing Caliban to Britain's Prospero and Prospero to Cuba's Caliban, makes clear, as Peter Hulme has emphatically observed, that "the field of postcolonial studies *needs* to find a place for America"; that "the inclusion of America will, and should, affect the shape and definition of the field"; and that "many of the misgivings about the role of America in post-colonial studies…are misplaced" (Hulme 1995: 119).

That said, it is, nonetheless, also clear that Third World writers are better positioned to conduct oppositional transactions with Shakespeare and the Shakespeare myth, and to bring to them alternative models of social and textual organization. The systematic exploitation of native populations of black and brown peoples, their reduction to the status of subjects in their own homelands during the colonial period, and the difficulties their societies have subsequently experienced in establishing political and economic stability render the material conditions that obtain today in the Indian subcontinent and in the former colonies of Africa and the West Indies incomparable to the conditions that obtained in the rich, expansive, and underpopulated confines of the post-independence United States. The preoccupation of postcolonial U.S. writers with developing a national literature independent of British models was, for all its fractiousness, a largely intramural debate engaged in by native speakers of English. Since all Third World postcolonies represent examples of "invaded" or "slave" as opposed to "settler" colonies, the "official" use of English is the direct consequence of enforcement or imposition and has failed to disable the production of vernacular literatures. In the West Indies English was more successfully naturalized only because the population was either enslaved or brought to bay through indentured servitude. In all these areas, literary or cultural issues did not initially loom as large as political or ethnic concerns; independence brought to the fore matters more pressing than the development of a national literature. When time and space did allow for the development of an indigenous literary culture, it was the long-sustained reign of dispossession enforced by colonialism, the humiliations of mimicry, emulation, and cultural erasure—not merely, as for Whitman, the burden of influence—that primarily preoccupied the literary imagination and provided the grounds for the work of appropriation. This is nowhere more graphically apparent than in Achebe's groundbreaking *Things Fall Apart* (1958).

For such reasons among others, the Third World postcolonial generally "foregrounds a politics of opposition and struggle, and problematises the key relationship between centre and periphery" (Mishra and Hodge 1991: 399). That such a relationship is "key," much less a problem, is, however, not a consensus view uniformly distributed across all the divisions of what I have termed the Third World postcolonial.[11] Several of the "invaded" postcolonies of Africa and the Indian subcontinent are engaged in acts of cultural recuperation that will presumably result in a remapping of "centre and periphery" and supersede the compulsion to challenge or oppose an imperium emptied out of power, authority, and influence. Others, like Kenya, Nigeria, and the Sudan, are so immersed in internecine struggles within their own boundaries that a problematizing of such relationships is a luxury only expatriates can afford. The struggle with and against the "centre" remains a more vexed and contentious matter in the West Indies where the battle is joined on fronts foreign (against the U.S. and Britain) and domestic, and conducted in competing forms of the same language. As Derek Walcott writes:

Our bodies think in one language and move in another, yet it
should have become clear, even to our newest hybrid, the black
critic who accuses poets of betraying dialect, that the language
of exegesis is English, that the manic absurdity would be to
give up thought because it is white. In our self-tortured bodies
we confuse two graces: the dignity of self-belief and the cour-
tesies of exchange. For us the ragged, untutored landscape
seems as uncultured as our syntax.

(Walcott 1970: 31)

Even here, as Walcott's caustic reference to the black critic's espousal of
dialect or "nation language" indicates, little that is uniform can be
ventured or maintained. Like the "Third World postcolonial," the
"West Indian postcolonial" is a multiform and multivalent thing, differently rendered in and across its expressive register. Racially tied to
Africa and India, historically bound to Europe, geographically
connected to both North and South America, and differently preoccupied with the formative events of New World history, it has, however,
consistently laid claim to hybridity as a social and cultural characteristic, to appropriation as its primary medium of cultural exchange, and,
as I hope to demonstrate below, to a leading role in reshaping the plot
(and repositioning the politics) of *The Tempest*, a play that has for so long
spoken in its name.[12]

This tension between the different and the same, the general and the
specific, the global and the local, besets everything I have heretofore
broached in the name of the postcolonial and postcolonial studies. At
the same time, it functions as the enabling condition that allows one to
address a multiform thing that is not entirely identifiable with, or
reducible to, its constituent parts. For Walcott, the espouser of hybridity,
the tension is fertile and creative, and leads as much from margin to
center as from center to margin, effectively dissolving the claim to
priority of either. For E.K. Brathwaite, espouser of a "nation language"
that is the hybrid product of master and slave, colonizer and colonized,
dialect is betrayed by and in "English," hence hybridity or "creolization" must take another, avowedly "negative" direction, both back and
on to "blackness" where what is now margin can become center
(Brathwaite 1977). This debate is itself only one location, one formation, of the West Indian postcolonial, and can only be said to echo, not
replicate, debates in Kenya about the use of English or Gikuyu, or in
India about English and a host of competing vernaculars.

There is yet another side to the debate that would consign the postcolonial itself to the category of a proscribed term, rendered

unthinkable on the grounds that, so long as it is thought, the condition it describes will continue to cast a distorting and disabling spell on its adherents. As Anne McClintock incisively writes:

> [The] term postcolonial...is haunted by the very figure of linear development it sets out to dismantle. Metaphorically, the term postcolonialism marks history as a series of stages along an epochal road from "the precolonial," to "the colonial," to the "postcolonial"—an unbidden, if disavowed commitment to linear time and the idea of development...Metaphorically poised on the border between old and new, end and beginning, the term heralds the end of a world era but by invoking the same trope of linear progress which animated that era.
>
> (McClintock 1995: 10)

In short, for McClintock, "Colonialism returns at the moment of its disappearance" (1995: 11).[13]

I am of the opinion that only history, not a change in discursive preferences or models, will make colonialism disappear from view, though not even history is liable to check or monitor its continued circulation in the political unconscious where it may continue to operate long after the material effects of colonization have ceased to resonate. It is through this back door of the return of the repressed that I would like to bring this section to conclusion by reiterating that, despite the provenance of the prefix "post," the characteristic space of the postcolonial (at least as the term is deployed here) is not the "after-ness" of linear development but the "between-ness" of historical indeterminacy. This is the case because the postcolonial is, in the end, less an experiential than a discursive category or construction: more an interpretive grid laid on experience than a fixed or determinate phenomenon. The postcolonial retains its descriptive force so long as the state of process or between-ness it describes maintains itself as a prominent "form of talk" in a given culture. It loses its descriptive force when this kind of talk, or what gives rise to it, ceases. As Bill Ashcroft observes: "words such as 'post-colonial' do not describe forms of experience but forms of talk about experience...Once we see the term 'post-colonial' as representing a form of talk rather than a form of experience we will be better equipped to see that such talk encompasses a wide and interwoven text of experiences" and hinges on "a grammar of multiple intersections" (Ashcroft 1996: 26). One of the most well-traversed sites of intersection for this form of talk, I submit, is Shakespeare: a site most often approached through the "grammar" of appropriation.

3.

As Michael Dobson and Jonathan Bate have demonstrated in books devoted to the periods 1660–1769 and 1730–1830, respectively, the history of Shakespearean appropriation is both long and eventful within the bounds of England itself, and embraces from the start borrowings from, allusions to, and comprehensive adaptations of Shakespeare that have obvious social and political force. Indeed, I would argue that the first overt appropriation of Shakespeare on behalf of a clear-cut social agenda was Ben Jonson's critical response to *The Tempest* in his 1614 play *Bartholomew Fair* (see Cartelli 1983). There is, moreover, a crucial difference between what Jonson does in selectively carving out a point of contention with Shakespeare and demonstrating an alternative and, say, what an adaptor does in using the plot of *King Lear* to structure a novel set in the American heartland, or in setting an otherwise faithful film version of *Richard III* in a "Nazified" vision of 1930s London. What differentiates the act of appropriation from these acts of adaptation is that the one is a primarily *critical*, and the other a primarily *emulative* act. Appropriation as I understand it here both serves, and works in, the interests of the writer or group doing the appropriating, but usually works *against* the avowed or assigned interest of the writer whose work is appropriated. Although, as Michael Dobson has noted, comprehensive adaptations like Dryden and Davenant's *The Tempest; or The Enchanted Island* (1667) also constitute clear-cut acts of appropriation (see Dobson 1992a: 38–61), most adaptations are interested merely in adjusting or accommodating the original work to the tastes and expectations of their own readership or audience. Since successful adaptations generally feed off the fame or prestige of their originals, they also may be said to exist in a consciously tributary relationship with the work they enlarge upon, reorient, and emulate. Although the acts of appropriation and adaptation are equally opportunistic, the former tend to serve social or political as opposed to primarily literary or commercial agendas. Works that combine the two actions, like Brecht's *Threepenny Opera*, may be said to serve both.

In his own discussion of the terminology of appropriation—which he opposes to "accommodation" not, as here, "adaptation"—Jonathan Bate states that he "prefer[s] the term 'appropriation' because it suggests greater activity on the part of the appropriator…and because it has stronger political overtones than 'accommodation'" (Bate 1989: 5). Recognizing that the simultaneous vagueness and capaciousness of the term encourages one too easily to assume that "all interpretations are appropriations," Bate later adds that if this is indeed the case "then a special value should be attached to those that acknowledge themselves as such" (1989: 207). Through these formulations Bate effectively defines the act of appropriation as a self-conscious activity engaged in for an at least *implied* political purpose. Although I work within Bate's terminology and preference, I also think it necessary to note that appropriation is not always an activity initiated or undertaken by a self-identified appropriator. As Dobson has noted:

> For some, Shakespeare's texts [may be said to] appropriate their readers—as in [Marjorie] Garber's work, where Freud, Nietzsche, Delia Bacon, and others prove to be dutifully playing out the unconscious of the First Folio. For others, individual readers either misappropriate Shakespeare's texts (if they are bad readers), or both appropriate them and are appropriated by them (if they are good readers)—as in Bate's work...For others still, the hegemonic discourse of the ruling oligarchy appropriates both Shakespeare's texts and his readers, effortlessly co-opting all concerned in the interests of the state—as in the work of [Terry] Hawkes, [Graham] Holderness, and, to a lesser extent, [Gary] Taylor.
>
> (Dobson 1992a: 11–12)

Like Dobson, I will draw "to different extents on each of these models" in the body of this book, but I will also demonstrate how the models themselves "interact" and change when applied by and to radically different acts of appropriation. We will note, for example, how in the hands of a writer committed to decolonization like Ngũgĩ an act that might seem an obvious example of *mis*appropriation to one interpretive community may be construed by another as an entirely accurate assessment of a given text's effects and consequentiality. We will also note how even the most ambitious acts of appropriation may be compromised by an overarching deference to constructions of Shakespeare that are themselves the product of a previous age's appropriations.

Before moving on to consider examples like the above, I would like to pause for a moment longer over what remains for me a vexed case of terminology. Like Bate, I prefer the term "appropriation" for the sense of self-constituted agency it suggests. I find it particularly applicable to the cases I examine because of its additional associations "with abduction, adoption and theft," with what Jean Marsden calls "the desire for possession." As Marsden adds, "Appropriation is neither dispassionate nor disinterested; it has connotations of usurpation, of seizure for one's own uses" (Marsden 1991: 1). These connotations have obvious pertinence to appropriations of Shakespeare that are undertaken under the sign of colonialism; indeed, they seem scripted to describe the impulses that preoccupy Caliban in *The Tempest* and have similarly preoccupied a generation of postcolonial writers in Africa and the Caribbean. But, as Dobson instructively notes, appropriation is not the one-way street some might like it to be; even self-constituted sponsors of Caliban bent upon acts of linguistic or cultural usurpation may be sucked into the vortex of the Shakespearean unconscious and made subject to a colonization of the mind. For these reasons among others, it is useful, however briefly and reductively, to consider further some of the different shapes appropriation may take in critical and creative practice.

I would begin by claiming that as a selectively predatory act, appropriation, unlike adaptation, does not seek to reproduce in any faithful or sustained way what it "abducts" from its objective. Possibly the most extreme example of this kind of selective predation is the *satiric* appropriation, embodied in the many full-length travesties or burlesques of Shakespeare that were particularly numerous in the nineteenth century which tend deliberately to fracture and fragment an array of Shakespearean texts, unmooring them from their established contexts and reassembling them in ways that render them absurd.[14] An equally selective and predatory appropriative mode is the *confrontational* appropriation which directly contests the ascribed meaning or prevailing function of a Shakespearean text in the interests of an opposing or alternative social or political agenda. Examples would include Aimé Césaire's and Ngũgĩ's critical confrontations of the ascribed highmindedness of Prospero in *A Tempest* (1969) and *A Grain of Wheat* (1968), respectively; Gus Van Sant's subversion of the royalist bias of the *Henriad* in his film *My Own Private Idaho* (1991); and Robert Taylor Conrad's corrective rewriting of Shakespeare's alleged betrayal of the common man in *Jack Cade* (1841). Confrontational motives also inform contemporary feminist appropriations of Shakespeare like Michelle Cliff's recasting of *The Tempest* in *No Telephone to Heaven* (1989), and often surface in an older tradition of woman-centered appropriations and rewritings.[15]

A less directly confrontational mode is the *transpositional* appropriation which identifies and isolates a specific theme, plot, or argument in its appropriative objective and brings it into its own, arguably analogous, interpretive field to underwrite or enrich a presumably related thesis or argument. Examples we will examine or touch on include Jane Addams's "A Modern Lear" (1894), O. Mannoni's *Prospero and Caliban: The Psychology of Colonization* (1950), and George Lamming's *The Pleasures of Exile* (1960). *Transpositional* appropriations may be distinguished from *proprietary* appropriations which, however much they also may be indebted to an enabling critical bias or theory, involve the application and elaboration of an avowedly "friendly" or reverential reading of appropriated material. The entire "script" of Garrick's 1769 Jubilee would fall into this category, as would other periodic celebrations, encomiums, and pageants such as Percy MacKaye's 1916 tercentenary masque, *Caliban by the Yellow Sands*.

The last appropriative mode to have a bearing on the subject of this book is the *dialogic* appropriation which involves the careful integration into a work of allusions, identifications, and quotations that complicate, "thicken," and qualify that work's primary narrative line to the extent that each partner to the transaction may be said to enter into the other's frame of reference. Works that transact this form of appropriation include Robert Stone's *Children of Light* (1986), Nadine Gordimer's *My Son's Story* (1990), Aphra Behn's *Oroonoko* (1688), and, most notably, *Season of Migration to the North* (1969), Tayeb Salih's critique of the Orientalist afterlife of *Othello* in England and the Sudan.

I engage in this inventory of appropriative modes because without such specification the term cannot sustain the range of applications performed in its name. As in the case of the *postcolonial*, the term "appropriation" has generally come to signal some form of subversive or oppositional intervention in an established discourse. It has, in short, been "appropriated" to serve an exclusively counter-discursive function. Yet, as Michael Dobson and Michael Bristol have demonstrated in their histories of the development of the British and American Shakespeare industries, respectively, appropriation, particularly in its proprietary mode, has been the favored practice of parties devoted to the nationalization, domestication, naturalization, and institutionalization of Shakespeare. The publication of the First Folio in 1623, the editing project of Malone, Garrick's 1769 Jubilee, the building of the Folger Library, all constitute acts of proprietary appropriation and could be afforded additional subcategory definitions in an expanded inventory of appropriation (as could a host of other activities, beginning with the practice of quotation). I have chosen, instead, to categorize and define only those forms of appropriation with which the present work is concerned. However, since acts of appropriation like those listed above have more than occasional effects, we need to add one last word to our critical vocabulary.

One reason why the term "appropriation" has been so restrictively applied is because its effects have been interpreted as largely pertaining to the specific appropriative act or intervention. But, as Mishra and Hodge note, and as I have tried to demonstrate, appropriation actually "gathers under a single term a large and diverse set of strategies involving both accommodation and compromise, whose political meaning is highly dependent on specific historical circumstances" (1991: 401). What gives an appropriation political significance is the fact that it is transacted not only in relation to specific Shakespearean texts, but in relation to specific *constructions* of Shakespeare that are themselves the products of earlier appropriations and have thereby acquired a political significance of their own. For example, when Whitman states that "Shakespeare's comedies are non-acceptable to Democracy," he is responding as much to a construction of Shakespeare as a poet of aristocracy that had been collaboratively developed by a group of fellow democratic nationalists as to Shakespeare's comedies themselves. By contrast, when Jane Addams claims that *King Lear* offers an incisive critique of paternalistic feudalism, she may be said to be writing against the grain of a construction of Shakespeare promoted by Whitman himself in his identification of Shakespeare as a defender of the "feudal institutes" (see Chapters 1 and 2 below). The commonplace Third World postcolonial construction of Shakespeare as a poet of empire or imperialism is clearly rooted in its advocates' experience of, or reflections on, colonialism. But it also developed in reaction to a valorization of Shakespeare as the quintessential national poet which, as a tenet of colonial literature instruction, was vigorously promoted by scholars like G. Wilson Knight in the 1940s, and was the product of conflations of Shakespeare and the British national identity that may be backdated to 1769 and the Garrick Jubilee (see David Johnson 1996 for a related discussion of Shakespeare's deployment in the classrooms and exampapers of South Africa).

Appropriations of Shakespeare are not, moreover, transacted solely in relation to prevailing literary or cultural constructions. They are also the product of a host of ancillary practices and informing conditions that may be said to shape the form a given appropriation takes. In the following chapters, we will, for example, explore individual and successive acts of appropriation in their relation to broader social and institutional circumstances including, but not limited to, constructions of Shakespeare. It is this same kind of process Roger Chartier has in mind in his more overtly historicized understanding of appropriation:

> In my own perspective, appropriation involves a social history of the various uses (which are not necessarily interpretations) of discourses and models, brought back to their fundamental social and institutional determinants and lodged in the specific practices that produce them. To concentrate on the concrete

conditions and processes that construct meaning is to recognize, unlike traditional intellectual history, that minds are not disincarnated, and, unlike hermeneutics, that the categories which engender experiences and interpretations are historical, discontinuous, and differentiated.

(Chartier 1995: 89)

While I hesitate to make the same claims for thoroughness and comprehension as Chartier advances, I too will be attempting to demonstrate the "involvement" of appropriation in specific "social and institutional determinants" in what follows. So it is that I will concentrate less on Aphra Behn's conscious attempt to rewrite *Othello* in my chapter on *Oroonoko* than on her text's responsiveness to the seventeenth-century institutionalization of plantation slavery. In a similar vein, I will situate MacKaye's 1916 tercentenary masque in closer relation to other contemporaneous responses to the immigration crisis in turn-of-the-century New York than to prevailing literary constructions of the Prospero/Caliban configuration. The production of an alienated "native" intelligentsia by imperial British educational institutions will partially underwrite my discussion of Tayeb Salih's appropriation of *Othello* in *Season of Migration to the North*. And the late nineteenth-century emergence of the semi-emancipated college woman from the wraps of the paternally centered American family will serve a similar function in my chapter on Jane Addams's "A Modern Lear."

4.

As the selective nature of my subject matter indicates, this is not a book that attempts to offer a comprehensive assessment of Third World appropriations of Shakespeare, or of how Shakespeare has been accommodated to U.S. national formations over the course of two centuries; that will attempt to do for Canada or Australia what it does for the United States, for India what it does for the West Indies. It is, instead, a book that seeks to put a number of different encounters with Shakespeare in responsive relationship with one another while working within several more obviously unified fields of engagement. The amount of time and attention given to U.S. constructions of Shakespeare will no doubt be construed as an appropriative gesture in its own right: an attempt to usurp the prerogatives of "more truly" postcolonial cultures and to "colonize" postcolonial theory itself (see Kaplan 1993: 21 n. 17). My answer to such objections would be threefold: the first premised on the already established symptomatic (as opposed to paradigmatic) nature of the United States' evolving "relationship with the metropolitan centre" (see Ashcroft *et al.* 1989: 2), particularly with respect to that relationship's development in the nineteenth century; the second on the exclusivity of the objectors' position for whom the postcolonial is more a specific temporal, spatial, and political category and identity theme than a discursive construction of flexible application.[16] My third response may well seem patronizing and disingenuous, but fastens on my deployment of the professedly "more truly postcolonial" as a bridge to the recovery (at least in words) of the U.S.'s lost anti-colonial potential.

I have myself returned "home" after a long scholarly sojourn as a Shakespearean, and a shorter, but more intense, period as a student of the so-called new literatures in English. Tutored in the dialects of decolonization by writers like Ngũgĩ and Soyinka, Brathwaite and Césaire, and in the more rueful strains of postcolonial dispossession by Walcott, Lamming, and a younger V.S. Naipaul, I have been struck as much by the venturesomeness of the writing as by its richness and complexity. Witness Walcott again on the language question:

> Pastoralists of the African revival should know that what is needed is not new names for old things, or old names for old things, but the faith of using the old names anew, so that mongrel as I am, something prickles in me when I see the word Ashanti as with the word Warwickshire, both separately intimating my grandfathers' roots, both baptising this neither proud nor ashamed bastard, this hybrid, this West Indian. The power of the dew still shakes off of our dialects.
>
> (Walcott 1970: 10)

As in Whitman's "Song of Myself," new possibilities emerge with each word Walcott puts on display, with each crossbred experience he annexes to the Caribbean cultural imagination. The democratic spirit of Whitman's New World Adam is particularly strong within Walcott's celebration of a "mongrel" subjectivity that extends beyond both pride and shame.

Yet always and ever there is in the West Indian the swerve into and against history, the raised hand meeting the closed door or mind or fist, the sound of blade against cane, whip against back. Newness is beset, belittled, belated, turned against itself, rendered shallow, rootless, void of substance, pedigree, depth. Caliban the would-be poet is repeatedly transposed into bond-slave, servant, peasant, vagrant, nomad, thief. As in Brathwaite's "Didn't He Ramble":

So to New York London
I finally come
hope in my belly
hate smothered down
to the bone
to suit the part
I am playing

That summer was fine
newspaper notices
variety acts
what the heart lacked
we supplied with our hips
and the art
of our shuffle shoes

But with the winter I knew
I was old. Poor
Tom was cold. Feet
could no longer walk the fallen
gold of parks...

(Brathwaite 1973: 22)

And there in the dark backward and abysm of time the last best hope of
Whitman stands unmasked, making slaves of its neighbors, kings of its
gentry, beggars of its poor, girls of its women, boys of its men.

"New World" like "America" was once a name to conjure with. I see
the promise of the name restored in the writing of Walcott and
Brathwaite, of Michelle Cliff, Erna Brodber, Wilson Harris; even the
younger V.S. Naipaul, who could make the language of Trinidad sing
before he took on the geriatric pose—and prose—of the English
garden. Informed by that promise, I have turned the pages back to
dissident strains in the U.S.'s embrace of its self-proclaimed manifest
destiny. What I have found there is not always pretty; for every plain-
speaking Whitman, an Edwin Forrest, more demagogue than democrat;
for every blue-blood lover of immigrants and the dispossessed like Jane
Addams, an apologist for the Anglo-Saxon "biologic stream" like Percy
MacKaye. But there is also the strain, the struggle to hold onto, maintain, the presumably originary difference, now displaced to the domain
of late imperial romance where Robert Stone's wandering gringos play
disaffected witness to the "other" America's struggle for bread, land,
and life.[17]

The late imperial moment may well serve to demarcate the space within which this book is written, frame the subjectivity of its writer, gazing through a screen of unassailable privilege at textual transactions in an Africa largely void of books, a Caribbean whose triumphs are largely discursive, disseminated by means of memorial reconstruction by poets resident in New York, Boston, and London. Prospero's book tells us, though, that nothing is forever, that this screen too will dissolve and leave not a rack behind, that these latter-day struggles for self- and national definition will have their day before they also fade to black.

In this, as in so much else, Shakespeare is arguably more help than hindrance, more outlet than obstacle, lending himself to "accents yet unknown," giving Brathwaite a "hook" for his poem: "Poor/Tom was cold." Although this is a possibility easier to entertain in the so-called First than the Third World, and even here no doubt appeals mainly to those who don't see their faces disfigured in the biased mirrors he held up to nature, the fact remains that Shakespeare is as inescapably bound up with history as history is bound up with him. A release may be in the offing when the postcolonial becomes more than "a splinter in the side of the colonial" (Mishra and Hodge 1991: 411), less a promise, projection, or "form of talk" than a new (and renamed) dispensation in its own right. Until then Shakespeare will continue to function as he always has: as an unusually charged medium of textual exchange.

Part I

DEMOCRATIC VISTAS

1

NATIVISM, NATIONALISM, AND THE COMMON MAN IN AMERICAN CONSTRUCTIONS OF SHAKESPEARE

1.

Gus Van Sant's 1991 film *My Own Private Idaho* boldly appropriates the Boar's Head subplot of Shakespeare's *Henriad* in the process of dramatizing the one-sided romance of two male hustlers and the rejection by one of them of his Falstaffian father-surrogate in the contemporary American Northwest. Van Sant's injection of mannered Shakespearean dramaturgy into a film that is more generally responsive to the edgier, inarticulate rhythms of contemporary urban life arguably imposes an inflated style and pattern of significance on a narrative that neither requires, nor is able to sustain, the effort. But by focusing its appropriative energies on the rejection of "Falstaff" by the film's Prince Hal figure—Scott Favor, the attractively prodigal son of the officious Mayor of Portland, Oregon—and by linking its sympathies and point of view with the narcoleptic hustler, Mike Waters, who is also cast off by Scott, the film makes Shakespeare function in the interests of its socially and sexually marginalized protagonists.[1] In the end, Van Sant offers a pointedly democratized—and homoeroticized—rewriting of Prince Hal's interactions with his criminal companions in the *Henriad*, one that conspicuously departs from Kenneth Branagh's conservative reworking of some of the same material in his own recent film, *Henry V*.[2]

As in the case of Prince Hal in *1 & 2 Henry IV*, Scott's belated reconciliation with his father is directly connected to his summary rejection of an array of transgressive practices, an act which the film, unlike the play, presents as an unambiguous indication of social and sexual betrayal. Having privileged throughout the interactions of the homeless

27

hustlers, and having favorably presented Scott's sensitive and protective relationships with them, the film casts a critical eye on his concluding transformation—which eventuates in Scott's emergence as a born-again heterosexual, Mike's wholesale abandonment and return to the streets, and—as in the *Henriad*—in "Falstaff's" death from the failed heart "Prince Hal" has killed.[3]

Probably the most significant aspect of Van Sant's appropriation of the *Henriad* is its clearly positioned critique of Hal's transformation. All manner of critics have had difficulty accepting Hal's reconciliation with his father, rejection of Falstaff, and assumption of the Lord Chief Justice as his father-figure. Yet most have been persuaded to accept the transformation as both morally and politically constructive.[4] *My Own Private Idaho* rejects this recuperative gesture because its social and sexual positionings stand opposed to the normative moral and political imperatives even revisionist critics have endorsed in the face of Falstaff's carnivalesque challenge to order and responsibility. Bringing to this material a sensibility that is at once romantic, individualist, and egalitarian, Van Sant revives a dissident strain in U.S. constructions of Shakespeare that has largely gone silent since the death of Walt Whitman. By restaging scenes whose resolution, both in criticism and in production, almost always privileges what Michael Bristol terms "the pathos of kingship," and having them instead record a shift of sympathetic identification from ruling class to underclass, Van Sant effectively repositions Shakespeare in terms that Whitman might well consider more "consistent with the institution of these States" (Whitman 1907: 249).

By effecting this departure from standard interpretations of Hal's transformation, *Idaho* brings back into focus one of the long-term "anomalies" of the American romance with Shakespeare. As Bristol writes:

> Shakespeare's centrality in American culture might be construed as a kind of anomaly in that it entails respect and admiration for an archaic world-consciousness deep inside the American project of *renovatio*. Why should a society whose founding actions entail radical separation from all institutions of hereditary privilege be devoted to a writer whose primary themes are the pathos of kingship and the decline of the great feudal classes?
>
> (Bristol 1990: 2)

Shakespeare's "centrality in American culture" has been convincingly demonstrated both by Bristol himself in his recent book on the institutions that have evolved to sponsor "the Shakespearizing of America" and by Lawrence Levine who, in his study of Shakespeare and American popular culture, concludes that "Nineteenth-century America swallowed Shakespeare, digested him and his plays, and made them part of the cultural body" (Levine 1988: 24). Neither Bristol nor Levine, however, address at any length the anomalous nature of the American romance with Shakespeare as Bristol describes it. Nor do they consider the admittedly exceptional, but recurring, voices that have dissented from the American consensus on the very grounds outlined by Bristol.

These voices may be heard with some consistency in the "national penchant for parodying Shakespeare" in the first half of the nineteenth century that Levine takes to be indicative of a widespread familiarity with Shakespeare in America (Levine 1988: 14–16) but that may also indicate Shakespeare's perceived irrelevance to American experience.[5] Like *My Own Private Idaho*, some of these parodies take a decidedly revisionist position toward Shakespeare, rewriting him in terms that are not only irreverent but consistent with the increasingly pluralistic nature of American society and the development of anti-authoritarian strains within it. In John Brougham's *Much Ado About a Merchant of Venice* (1868), for example, we find Shylock described as "a shamefully ill-used and persecuted old Hebrew gentleman," whose "character was darkened by his Christian contemporaries simply to conceal their own nefarious transactions" (Wells 1978: 5:78) and Portia represented as a Philadelphia lawyer who caustically derides the corruption of the contemporary judicial system (Wells 1978: 5:113).[6] Of course, the penchant for parody also embraced less savory aspects of American national interests, as the series of blackface travesties produced throughout the century demonstrate. One of these, John F. Poole's *Ye Comedie of Errours* (1858), includes several unflattering references to fugitive slaves, the underground railroad, and Harriet Beecher Stowe.[7]

In this chapter, I would like to re-examine the similarly qualified, but more seriously intentioned, dissent against the Shakespearizing of America that is recorded in the writings of Whitman and to explore in a more sustained manner the efforts on behalf of a national drama undertaken some time earlier in the nineteenth century by William Leggett, Edwin Forrest, and Robert Taylor Conrad that eventuated in their collaborative production, *Aylmere, or Jack Cade*. My intention is less to contest Levine's or Bristol's respective accounts of Shakespeare's naturalization and institutionalization than to provide a supplementary account of "American contestatory discourses and practices" (Murray 1994: 268) that may be productively connected to contemporary efforts to reposition Shakespeare both in America and in other former colonies of Great Britain.[8] As I will demonstrate, the defense of the common man advanced by Whitman and the collaborative "authors" of *Jack Cade* was qualified by a rhetoric of proud individualism and democratic self-congratulation modeled, in many respects, on the same kind of immersion in purported Shakespearean ideals that Levine and Bristol describe. Their efforts to defend the claims of American democratic subjectivity against foreign contamination were further qualified by a strident nationalism that often betrayed a marked nativist bias. The very mounting of this defense, and the record of dissent it supplies, however, indicate that for many nineteenth-century Americans Shakespeare was more "a site of cultural contest" (Sinfield 1992: 264) than of cultural consensus or accord, and functioned as a privileged medium through which a self-consciously postcolonial society could both address and construct its differences from the society that had produced it.

2.

While bardolatry generally prevailed on both sides of the Atlantic in the nineteenth century, Whitman, invested as he was in promoting a national literature freed from the grip of European feudalism, brought a contentiously critical approach to bear on his assessments of Shakespeare. Whitman's contentiousness was no doubt rooted in his close affiliation with the Young America movement of the 1830s whose "members sought to make a case for literary nationalism" (Bender 1987: 142) and called for the development of an "American Shakespeare" who would "condemn conventional distinctions of rank and wealth" and "affirm the brotherhood and equality of man" (Bender 1987: 150). This movement reached its productive zenith in the early 1840s in the pages of the *Democratic Review*, which Thomas Bender called "the most brilliant periodical of its time" (1987: 145), and to which Whitman began contributing in 1841. Whitman was drawn to the *Review* as much for its affiliation with the radical Locofoco wing of the Democratic Party, as for its literary aspirations. Whitman's artisan father was himself "a Locofoco Democrat, and like the son an admirer of William Leggett" (Bender 1987: 153) who was "the ideological patron saint of the *Democratic Review* and of radical Locofoco Democracy in New York" (Bender 1987: 147). Leggett, in turn, was the longtime friend and associate of the celebrated actor and radical democrat, Edwin Forrest, whose sustained attempt to establish a national drama would anticipate and influence Whitman's own commitment to literary nationalism.

Like Leggett's and Forrest's, Whitman's quarrel with Shakespeare—which may be more precisely construed as his objection to Shakespeare's operation as a model for American writers—almost exclusively focuses on Shakespeare's alleged degradation of the common people in his plays. As Whitman writes in *Democratic Vistas* (1871):

> The great poems, Shakspere included, are poisonous to the idea of the pride and dignity of the common people, the life-blood of democracy. The models of our literature, as we get it from other lands,…have had their birth in courts, and bask'd and grown in castle sunshine; all smells of princes' favors.
>
> (Whitman 1907: 218)

In the later *November Boughs* (1888), after contending that Shakespeare "stands entirely for the mighty esthetic sceptres of the past, not for the spiritual and democratic, the sceptres of the future," Whitman observes that:

> The low characters, mechanics, even the loyal henchmen—all in themselves nothing—serve as capital foils to the aristocracy. The comedies (exquisite as they certainly are), bringing in admirably portray'd common characters, have the unmistakable hue of plays, portraits, made for the divertisement only of the elite of the castle, and from its point of view. The comedies are altogether non-acceptable for America and Democracy.
>
> (Whitman 1907: 393–4)

No one familiar with Whitman's poetry will be surprised to learn that these decisive assertions do not represent his "last word" on Shakespeare.[9] Indeed, in the very same pages of the essay in which he declares the comedies "non-acceptable for America and Democracy," Whitman offers the following comparison of the avowedly "popular" poet, Robert Burns, with the allegedly elitist Shakespeare:

> [Burns] has been applauded as democratic, and with some warrant; while Shakspere, and with the greatest warrant, has been called monarchical or aristocratic (which he certainly is). But the splendid personalizations of Shakspere, formulated on the largest, freest, most heroic, most artistic mould, are to me far dearer as lessons, and more precious even as models for Democracy, than the humdrum samples Burns presents.
>
> (Whitman 1907: 399–400)

31

Rather than consider this merely another of Whitman's many celebrated contradictions, one would do well to notice that Whitman's
distinction pivots less on express political principles than on the relative
capacity for freedom and breadth of expression of Shakespeare and
Burns. Shakespeare is preferred to Burns largely because his alleged
positioning in the camp of the English aristocracy gave him imaginative
access to the freest, most powerful, and fully realized "personalizations"
of his age, on whom he modeled his own. Enjoying the same individual
freedoms the American common man of the nineteenth-century could,
presumably, claim as his birthright, Shakespeare's heroic princes
provide "dearer lessons" or "models for Democracy" than do Burns's
countrymen, who are still bent under their feudal, "old world" yokes.[10]

Whitman moves in a similar direction in *Democratic Vistas*. After
claiming that such master spirits as Shakespeare, Kant, and Hegel were
"grown not for America, but rather for her foes, the feudal and the
old," he asks them:

> but to breathe your breath of life into our New World's
> nostrils—not to enslave us, as now, but, for our needs, to breed
> a spirit like your own—perhaps, (dare we say it?) to dominate,
> even destroy, what you yourselves have left!
>
> (Whitman 1907: 233)

Specifically at stake here is the negotiation of an American shortcut to
greatness that might be achieved without payment of the "propor-
tionate price" which Whitman, in a more sober moment, knows that
"as for all lands" greatness should exact (Whitman 1907: 247). In the
end—at least at the end of *Democratic Vistas*—Whitman concludes that
the negotiation of greatness must finally involve neither the servile
mimicry nor the empowering absorption of ancient models, but,
instead, their appropriation and critical transformation:

> We see that almost everything that has been written, sung, or
> stated, of old, with reference to humanity under the feudal and
> oriental institutes...needs to be re-written, re-stated, in terms
> consistent with the institution of these States, and to come in
> range and obedient uniformity with them.
>
> (Whitman 1907: 249)

As citizens of a former "settler colony" still "tributary" to the
parent-stream of language and culture, American writers were at once
compelled to register the falseness of New World experience conveyed

in "Old World terms" and their continued dependence on the Old World for a defining sense of literary standards and values (see Ashcroft *et al.* 1989: 16–17, 133–8). Whitman and his fellow literary nationalists were keenly aware that early American efforts to "nativize" prevailing forms of English writing, more often than not, became the occupational victim of a poetics of emulation, as efforts at representing New World experience effectively recuperated the favored formats and authority of British models. Emerson's ambivalent musings on Shakespeare and his English literary successors demonstrate the extent of the American writer's difficulty in framing an adequate solution to this problem. Noting, for example, in *The American Scholar* (1837), that "Genius is always sufficiently the enemy of genius by over-influence" and that the "English dramatic poets have Shakspearized now for two hundred years" (Emerson 1971: 57), Emerson offers what appears to constitute a pre-emptively Whitmanian declaration of incipient American literary independence: "Our day of dependence, our long apprenticeship to the learning of other lands, draws to a close. The millions that around us are rushing into life, cannot always be fed on the sere remains of foreign harvests" (Emerson 1971: 52). However, a scant thirteen years later in *Representative Men* (1850), we discover that "literature, philosophy and thought are [now] Shakspearized," that Shakespeare's "mind" constitutes "the horizon beyond which, at present, we do not see" (Emerson 1903: 204). Looking closer still, we find that Emerson has actually attempted an act of wishful appropriation in which the (literary) model that cannot be superseded is annexed by the (political) model that supersedes. Emerson now speaks of Shakespeare as:

> the founder of another dynasty, which alone will cause the Tudor dynasty to be remembered—the man...on whose thoughts the foremost people of the world [namely, Americans] are now for some ages to be nourished, and minds to receive this and not another bias.
>
> (Emerson 1903: 202)

Although Emerson's transformation of Shakespeare into a virtual founding father might appear to operate as an early sign of the burgeoning imperialist American imagination, it may also be said to signal a premature surrender in the American struggle for cultural independence. Represented as the author of "the text of modern life," who "drew the man of England and Europe; [and] the father of the man in America" (Emerson 1903: 211), Emerson's Shakespeare effectively re-establishes American dependency on "the sere remains of foreign harvests" (Emerson 1971: 52). As Michael Bristol observes:

> It does not seem to have occurred to [Emerson] that the Shakespearization of America might entail a concurrent Europeanization of America, a recapture of the emergent social project of American democracy and self-government by supposedly abandoned modes of traditional privilege and domination.
>
> (Bristol 1990: 129)

A similar misgiving would pull Herman Melville up short in a letter written on 3 March 1849 (approximately ten weeks before the Astor Place Riot) to Evert A. Duyckinck, one of the founders of the Young America movement, in order to correct an earlier one in which he had celebrated his comparatively belated discovery of Shakespeare:

> do not think, my boy, that because I, impulsively broke forth in jubillations...over Shakspeare, that, therefore, I am of the number of the *snobs* who burn their tuns of rancid fat at his shrine. No, I would stand afar off and alone, and burn some pure Palm oil, the product of some overtopping trunk.—I would to God Shakspeare had lived later, & promenaded in Broadway...that the muzzle which all men wore on their souls in the Elizebethan days, might not have intercepted Shakspers full articulations. For I hold it a verity, that even Shakspeare, was not a frank man to the uppermost. And, indeed, who in this intolerant Universe is, or can be? But the Declaration of Independence makes a difference.
>
> (Davis and Gilman 1960: 79–80)[11]

In his insistence that a revolutionary democratic purity should characterize American literary productions, Whitman expressly dissents from Emerson's implicitly neo-colonialist summons to the "Shakespearizing of America" and registers the nationalist bias of his own position, confirming Melville's claim that "the Declaration of Independence makes a difference." This joint privileging of democratic and nationalist principles in Whitman's otherwise more qualified assessment of Shakespeare—who variously becomes a model best left unread (1907: 393–4), an authoritative critic of the manifold evils of feudalism (1907: 391), and an inspiration for the future creation of "sweet democratic despots of the west" (1907: 233)—is also characteristic of an earlier stage in the debate about literary nationalism, whose beginning may be traced to Edwin Forrest's efforts to encourage the creation of a national drama in the 1830s and whose end may be identified with the Astor Place Riot of 1849 and the nativism that was both its contributing cause and consequence.

3.

Forrest began his attempt to free the American stage from continued reliance on foreign sources by sponsoring, in 1828, a contest for prize plays written by and about Americans. The first contest explicitly called for "the best Tragedy, in five acts, of which the hero or principal character shall be an aboriginal of this country" (quoted in Moses 1929: 96) and led to the composition of *Metamora; or, The Last of the Wampanoags* (1829) by John Augustus Stone. *Metamora* was the first in a series of prize plays that, according to Montrose Moses,

> were all of the same tragic and romantic magnitude: they aimed for picturesque effectiveness of attitude, for well-rounded utterance of high-flown sentiments; they instilled the precepts of patriotic love of country and awakened a sympathy for the nobility of the oppressed.
>
> (Moses 1929: 98)

Moses adds, with a special pertinence to our discussion, that "their rhythm is familiar, their imagery stilted, and one meets in them many reminiscences of Shakespeare—many echoes of the Shakespearean line" (1929: 99).

Like most other examples of U.S. writing of the first decades of the nineteenth century, Forrest's prize plays were thoroughly derivative, and made little effort to disguise their grounding in the poetic emulation of five-act, heroically centered Shakespearean drama. As Moses observes:

> Forrest did not really want an *American* Drama; He wanted the *forensic* pose. This might not absorb those who looked for subtle art, but it would hold—and did hold—the masses. Forrest wanted character of a combative nature, which admitted of the grace of taut body, and the music of conflicting emotion— sarcasm, pride, hate, love, inspiration, ecstasy.
>
> (Moses 1929: 100)

While Moses finds *Metamora* "teeming with these qualities," he notes that it also "had what, in Forrest, was a consuming passion,—a realization of the prime greatness of his country in contrast with the littleness brought upon it by the white man's machinations" (Moses 1929: 100). In Stone's rendering the character Metamora is, significantly, "more a patriot than a savage, exhorting his warriors in the manner of Patrick Henry" (Mason 1991: 100). In other words, *Metamora* provided Forrest with an adaptable vehicle to express, through the native American's defiance of the colonizing white man, the nineteenth-century American patriot's defiance of the European.[12]

Although the prize plays lacked stylistic innovations commensurate with Forrest's strident nationalism, they were aggressively democratic in their ideological positioning and thematic orientation. Forrest's attempt to promote a democratic alternative to the aristocratic bias of Shakespearean drama achieved its most sustained expression in Robert T. Conrad's appropriation of the Jack Cade subplot of *2 Henry VI* in a play first composed and performed in 1835, which was later significantly revised in 1841 under the influence of Forrest and William Leggett.[13] This play, *Aylmere, or Jack Cade*, constitutes a full, frontal attack on Shakespeare's alleged misrepresentation of the historical Jack Cade in *2 Henry VI*, which Conrad addresses in both surviving versions of the play-proper and in the extensive notes attached to its two editions (1852, 1869).[14]

The efficacy of Conrad's appropriations will not, however, be immediately evident to those who know no more of the play than the following (abbreviated) synopsis reveals:

> When the play opens, Cade, now called Aylmere, has returned to England [from Italy] with his wife and child to avenge the killing of his father [by the evil aristocrat, Lord Say] and to lead a rebellion of the bondsmen...
>
> The rebellion is filled with horrors: Cade's mother is burned to death in her cottage; his child is killed; his wife is captured, abused by one of the nobles, and driven mad. Still Cade clings to his noble cause...
>
> The revolt finally succeeds. Cade kills Lord Say and in turn is mortally wounded by him. As Cade is dying, the charter declaring the bondsmen free is brought in. Cade seizes it, clasps it to his bosom, sinks to the floor, and dies.
>
> (Moses 1929: 198)

The synopsis describes a play prodigal in melodramatic premises and devices that transforms Cade into a populist prince of the people, a democratized composite of Hamlet and Robin Hood. Lord Say, who, along with Humphrey, Duke of Gloucester, is presented in *2 Henry VI* as a sympathetic aristocrat, becomes in *Jack Cade* the play's most extreme embodiment of ruthless aristocratic presumption, while the ample supporting cast of Shakespeare's play is pared down to serve the interests of a Manichaean combat between aristocrat and commoner, good and evil, right and wrong. Nominally set in Kent, Cade's historically specific stronghold, the play generally operates well beyond the bounds of material or, for that matter, temporal specificity in a loosely situated space and time.

The predominance of romance and melodrama in *Jack Cade*, along with Conrad's choice of a univocally poetic, Shakespearized English for the speeches of both "high" and "low" characters, is, of course, entirely consistent with *Jack Cade*'s moment of production in which the emulation of "foreign models" continued to inform efforts to develop a national literature. Emulation also haunts *Jack Cade*'s plot, which appears patterned on the disguised royalty plots of the "citizen drama" of the 1590s, a fact which compromises the lowborn Cade's positioning in the role delegated in the earlier plays to an aristocrat in hiding.[15] These predictable symptoms of emulation should not, however, distract us from the considerable interventions Conrad and Leggett effected with respect to Shakespeare's alleged pro-aristocratic bias in *2 Henry VI*. *Jack Cade* aggressively appropriates from *2 Henry VI* what that play relegates to the status of extended subplot, and makes it the primary matter of a production that displaces the formerly privileged interactions of Shakespeare's protagonists. It effectively counters Shakespeare's alleged demonization of Cade and his confederates both by heroizing them and demonizing their aristocratic opponents. More dramatically, as a reviewer from the (Irish) *Cork Examiner* observed after viewing a touring production of *Jack Cade* in 1846, the play "abounds with passionate appeals to liberty, withering denunciations of oppression, and stinging sarcasms, unveiling at a glance the narrow foundation upon which class-tyranny bases its power and usurpations" (quoted in Alger 1877: 1:405).[16]

As Leggett observes in a letter to Forrest of 25 October 1837, the prospect of advancing such revisionary ambitions on a field commanded by so influential an "antagonist" as Shakespeare was daunting:

> I have been turning over the "Jack Cade" subject but I confess I am almost afraid to undertake it. The theme is a grand one, and I warm when I think of it; but I must not mistake the ardor of my feelings in the sacred cause of human liberty for

ability to manage the mighty subject. Besides, the prejudices and prepossessions of the world are against me, with Shakspeare on their side. Who must not feel his feebleness and insignificance when called to enter the list against such an antagonist?

Leggett prefaced these remarks with a caustic comment on the subject of "that insolent patrician *Coriolanus*...[who] was not quite so much of a democrat as you and I are," adding the wish that

> Shakespeare, with all his divine attributes, had only had a little of that ennobling love of equal human liberty which is now animating the hearts of true patriots all over the world, and is destined, ere long, to effect a great and glorious change in the condition of mankind. What a vast and godlike influence he might have exerted in molding the public mind and guiding the upward progress of nations, if his great genius had not been dazzled by the false glitter of aristocratic institutions, and blinded to the equal rights of the great family of man!
>
> (quoted in Alger 1877: 1:324–5)

Such sentiments clearly played a defining role in shaping the oppositional stance of Conrad's play. It is, however, less easy to determine Conrad's success in distinguishing American assumptions of the post-revolutionary period from those of the "feudal institutes" he had obligated himself to supersede.

Like Shakespeare, Conrad takes manifest liberties with historical records, even the ones he prefers to those employed by Shakespeare. In addition to recording his own conflations of the risings of 1381 and 1450 (such as choosing to name one character "Jack Straw" and to have another, Friar Lacy, spout the doctrines of John Ball), he has Jack Cade anachronistically refer to the revolutionary stirrings of "free Italy" and "the rekindled fires of freeborn Rome" (Conrad 1852: 30/1869: 21) and offer conspicuously post-Enlightenment appraisals of liberty:

> Liberty gives nor light nor heat itself;
> It but permits us to be good and happy.
> It is to man, what space is to the orbs,
> The medium where he may revolve and shine,
> Or, darkened by his vices, fall for ever!
>
> (1852: 154/1869: 59)

At other times, as in Cade's response to Friar Lacy's remark that the commoners are already abusing the liberty they have gained—"Already they are struggling for their rank./All would be great, all captains, leaders, lords"—Conrad makes Cade sound more like Shakespeare's Henry V than like a self-styled "captain of the commons."

> Life's story still! all would o'ertop their fellows;
> And every rank—the lowest—hath its height
> To which hearts flutter, with as large a hope
> As princes feel for empire! But in each,
> Ambition struggles with a sea of hate.
> He who sweats up the ridgy grades of life,
> Finds, in each station, icy scorn above,
> >   Below him hooting envy.
> >   (1852: 154/1869: 59)

Indeed, in this passage Cade seems so caught up in the lonely burdens of leadership that beset Henry *IV* that one expects him to conclude, "Uneasy lies the head that wears the crown."

This presumably unintended echoing of Shakespeare is symptomatic of *Jack Cade*'s intertextual immersion in the ideological substructure of Shakespearean dramaturgy. One can assemble any number of passages from the play that testify to Conrad's commitment to democratic principles of social justice, many of which are marked by an egalitarian devotion to the cause of the poor and disenfranchised:

> The poor have no friends but the poor; the rich—
> Heaven's stewards upon earth—rob us of that
> They hold in trust for us, and leave us starveling.
> [They shine above us, like a winter moon,
> >   Lustrous, but freezing.]
> >   (1852: 25/1869: 19)

And Cade expressly identifies himself, and his own aspirations, with the downtrodden whom he only wishes to lead through the threshold of their own liberation:

> ...I seek not power:
> [I would not, like the seeled dove, soar on high,
> To sink clod-like again to earth.] I know
> No glory,—save the godlike joy of making
> The bondman free. When we *are* free, Jack Cade

Will back unto his hills, and proudly smile
Down on the spangled meaness of the court,
Claiming a title higher than their highest,—
An honest man—a freeman!

(1852: 132/1869: 56)

But even this deferral to the national mythology of the reluctant leader is dramatically underwritten by Conrad's attribution to Cade of a noble mind modeled on Shakespearean precedents, a textual transaction that suggestively resonates with Whitman's previously recorded preference for Shakespeare's noble "personalizations."

As Conrad's introductory note makes plain, the effort to redeem Cade's reputation from "the servile chroniclers of the past" produces a collateral transformation in Cade's social standing that distances him from the lives of the common people Conrad attempts to valorize. In a studied effort to redeem the historian Hall's "young man of a goodlie stature and right pregnaunt wit" from Shakespeare's alleged travesty of the historical Cade, Conrad argues, on the flimsiest of evidence, that "Jack Cade" was only a nickname strategically employed by one "Mr. John Aylmere, Physician" (Conrad 1869: 8). He insists elsewhere that "Aylmere, instead of being the ignorant, ferocious, and vulgar ruffian generally supposed, was a patriot eminently enlightened and discreet" (Conrad 1869: 9). Although these recuperations of the historical Cade are effected in order to free Cade from bondage to a history recorded by his enemies, they also seek to discredit the notion that a popular revolt could be led by a mere commoner.

A possible key for unraveling this complication in Conrad's professed commitment to the common man is provided by the word "patriot" which indicates the distinctly nationalist cast of Conrad's attempt to reconstitute Shakespeare. Like Shakespeare himself, who was often considered (most notably by Emerson) an influential precursor in the forging of the American sensibility, Cade has been appropriated by Conrad less to correct the historical record than to serve the interests of a later revolution, one not made by, or for, inarticulate bondmen alone. The connection between Cade and America's founding fathers is, in fact, the theme of the long peroration—itself an extended quotation of William Leggett—with which Conrad's introductory note ends. As Leggett writes:

If Cade was the wretched fanatic which it has pleased the greatest dramatic genius of the world...to represent him, how did it happen that twenty thousand men flocked to his standard the moment it was unfurled?…Hollinshed has recorded his list of grievances and stipulations of redress; and let those who think the term Jack Cade synonymous with an ignorant and ferocious rebel and traitor, examine it; let them compare it with the grievances which led our fathers to take up arms against their mother-country,…instead of the scorn of mankind, [Jack Cade] deserves to be ranked among those glorious martyrs who have sacrificed their lives in defence of the rights of man. The derision and contumely which have been heaped on Cade, would have been heaped upon those who achieved the liberty of this country, had they been equally unsuccessful in their struggle.

(Conrad 1869: 14)[17]

Leggett's informed positioning of the unsuccessful rebel's defamation offers a politically sophisticated corrective to those who are still too apt to universalize what they find in Shakespeare. His inspired assessment of the ideological distortions of servile historians is, however, colored by his own passionately ideological conflation of Cade's project with the American Revolution. In his eagerness to monumentalize Cade and his exploits, Leggett effectively exchanges one precursor for another whom he finds more adaptable to the American master narrative of revolutionary martyrdom and self-sacrifice.

Although Leggett's passionate republicanism inspired the efforts of Conrad and Forrest in ways that both were proud to demonstrate, the latter were not, finally, as profoundly committed to the cause of the common man as was the man whom "The Abolitionists regarded…as a knight in armor" (Moses 1929: 185).[18] For Conrad, the historical Jack Cade remains a remote figure whose steps do not often shadow those of the poetically licensed Aylmere, melodramatically endowed with a maddened wife, starved child, murdered mother, and personal vendetta with a Lord Say who is more a snarling stage villain made out of spare parts of Coriolanus and Richard III than a character rooted in history. And while Leggett's redemption of the historical Cade is given pride of place in Conrad's introductory notes, "reminiscences of Shakespeare" qualify the effort to translate noble deeds into distinctly populist terms in Conrad's play.

4.

Considerably more ominous contradictions inform Edwin Forrest's militant espousal of democratic principles in a professional life marked by a "growing sense of ideological identification" with an audience notable for its "volatile reaction to anything they considered condescending behavior, out of keeping with the unique nature of American society" (Levine 1988: 67).[19] For such an audience, "Anything even bordering on unpatriotic or aristocratic behavior was anathema" (Levine 1988: 60). This audience could become especially volatile when it was encouraged to make the kinds of connections between democratic interests and the American national identity that Forrest's increasingly hostile competition with the aristocratically condescending English actor, William Macready, was provoking immediately prior to the outbreak of the notorious Astor Place Riot of 1849.[20] Although this competition was the ostensible cause of the disorders, the riot drew much of its energy from partisans of a broadly based nativist movement and from prevailing class antagonisms that were energized by the notorious exclusivity of the Astor Place Opera House.

According to Richard Moody, leaders and members of the "American Committee" or "Order of United Americans (forerunner of the Know-Nothing Party)" served as the vanguard of the approximately ten thousand people who filled the streets outside the Astor Place Opera House on 10 May 1849 while another 1,800 people attended Macready's performance of *Macbeth* inside (see Levine 1988: 63–9; Moody 1958: 3–4).[21] Although he had contributed, nine days earlier, a performance of *Jack Cade* "before a large audience which…'greeted the expressions of liberal sentiment which he uttered from time to time with approbation'" (Moody 1958: 95–6), Forrest was neither a member of the Order, nor a direct party to the riot itself. The riot—which left between twenty-two and thirty-one rioters and standers-by dead (Levine 1988: 65)—appears to have been brought to a head by the leader of the American Committee, one E.Z.C. Judson, "an adventurer and rabble-rouser who was better known as 'Ned Buntline'" and would become "best known for his series of novels dealing with the adventures of 'Buffalo Bill'" (Moody 1958: 3–4, 130).

As Moody writes, "It was natural enough that considerable support for the anti-Macready forces should have been drawn from the many 'nativist' societies that were flourishing in the first half of the century" (1958: 131) and more natural yet that "For a man like Judson…the feud between Forrest and Macready [would present] a glorious opportunity to advance the doctrine of 'America for Americans'" (1958: 132). The extent of the nativists' appropriation of what was, presumably, little more than a sustained bout of professional jealousy on the part of two notoriously egotistical actors, is evidenced in the text of "A Typical Astor Place Riot Placard" that was posted a day or two after the riot:

AMERICANS!
AROUSE! THE GREAT CRISIS
HAS COME!!
Decide now whether English
ARISTOCRATS!!!
AND
FOREIGN RULE!
shall triumph in this,
AMERICA'S METROPOLIS,
or whether her own
SONS,
whose fathers once compelled the base-born miscreants to succumb, shall meanly lick the hand that strikes, and allow themselves to be deprived of the liberty of opinion—so dear to every true American heart.

AMERICANS!!
Come out! and dare to own yourselves sons of the iron hearts of '76!!

AMERICA.

(Moses 1929: 260)[22]

That the expression of nativist sentiment also informed Forrest's performances in this period is indicated by an incident the contemporary actor, Lester Wallack, recorded in his diary: "Forrest, in the engagement during which the riots occurred, played *Macbeth*, and when the lines came, 'What rhubarb, senna or what purgative drug will scour these English hence?' the whole house rose and cheered for many minutes" (quoted in Moses 1929: 257–8). Lacking evidence that audience identification with the regicidal Macbeth was a contemporary commonplace, I would conclude that the audience's remarkably animated response to Forrest's rhetorical question was prompted by the line's anticipated capacity to inflame the highly charged atmosphere preparatory to the riot.[23]

The opportunistic or incidental exploitation of nativism was not, however, the *sole* cause of the Astor Place Riot. The arousal of class hatred, already incipient in the very construction of the Astor Place Opera House, in its housing of the presumptuously aristocratic Macready, and in the contrast it made with Forrest's well-advertised preference for more plebeian theaters, played as pivotal a role in the riot itself as in focusing the public's subsequent reaction on the fact that it was the rioters themselves who suffered the brunt of the deaths and injuries, largely at the hands of the National Guards. Indeed, many contemporaries fiercely alleged that the Guards "were called to support the white-kid-gloved aristocrats against warm-hearted Americans," though Moses's contention that "it was really a test of law and order against rowdyism that night of May 10" is probably more reliable (1929: 259). Whatever it "really was," as close a witness to the proceedings as the editorialist of the New York *Home Journal* of 12 May 1849 argued that "Since the basis of the useless quarrel was social…it would be necessary, in the future,…for the wealth of the Republic to 'be mindful where its luxuries offend'." This same editorialist specifically associated the "aristocratizing of the Pit" in the Opera House with the creation of "a *dangerous consciousness* of class" (see Moses 1929: 264).[24]

This effort to isolate or separate the excesses of nativism from the feelings generated by class conflict implicitly calls attention to their linkage in many of the disorders of the period. It also encourages a broader consideration of all that was involved in the attempts by Whitman, Conrad, Leggett, and Forrest either to correct or supersede what they found in Shakespeare. According to Lawrence Levine:

> The Astor Place Riot, which in essence was a struggle for power and cultural authority within theatrical space, was simultaneously an indication of and a catalyst for the cultural changes that came to characterize the United States at the end of the century. Theatre no longer functioned as an expressive form that embodied all classes within a shared public space, nor did Shakespeare much longer remain the common property of all Americans.
>
> (Levine 1988: 68)

While I find the notion that Shakespeare was *ever* "the common property of all Americans" more a symptom of Levine's democratic nostalgia than an historically defensible position, it seems clear that like the Opera House itself Shakespeare became, in the quarrel between Forrest and Macready, a charged site around which theoretically incompatible elements of democratic militancy and demagogic nativism could be reconciled and expressed.[25] In pushing Macready off the stage, into the lap of his allegedly aristocratic patrons, and back across the Atlantic to England, nativists, nationalists, and self-styled democrats alike mounted a collective charge against contemporary manifestations of "the feudal institutes" that radically enlarged upon the positions taken toward Shakespeare by Whitman, Leggett, Forrest, and Conrad.[26] That they did so at the expense of reinvigorating the critique of democracy as mob rule frequently attributed to Shakespeare, and of rehearsing behavior associated with the risings of 1381 and 1450 by "servile historians," is one of the many ironies attendant upon this event. More troubling still is what this confirmation of Shakespeare's critique of democracy may tell us about how little difference the Declaration of (political) Independence really made in effecting America's cultural independence from England. Viewed from this perspective, the modest repositioning of sympathy from ruling class to underclass recorded in *My Own Private Idaho* may seem about as much of a reconstitution of Shakespeare as aggressively democratic Americans should hope to effect.

2

SHAKESPEARE AT HULL HOUSE: JANE ADDAMS'S "A MODERN LEAR" AND THE 1894 PULLMAN STRIKE

> My father grew with the pale faces. He learnt from them that a
> man is worthy of his hire only after he has served well in his
> station; that he should stick to principles and know his limita-
> tions: the rich man in his castle, the poor man at his gate.
> That's what we learnt: of principle, the love of the underdog
> and Shakespeare.
>
> (Erna Brodber 1988)

1.

The conclusions I have reached in my first chapter emphasize the
extent to which an inflated sense of national mission and identity, and a
residual absorption in aristocratic models of character and behavior,
qualify and disable efforts to contest Shakespeare's influential positioning in the cultural body of nineteenth-century America. I do not,
however, offer these conclusions as a last word either on dissenting
constructions of Shakespeare or on what could be made of
Shakespeare in America by means of revisionist criticism or appropriation. In this respect among others, I am anticipated by Whitman who,
in yet another of his celebrated contradictions, considered the possibility that an *"essentially controlling plan"* informed Shakespeare's tragedies
and histories: a plan that retrospectively supplies a demystifying critique
of the "feudal institutes" and prescient rationale for their revolutionary
transformation. As Whitman writes in "What Lurks Behind
Shakespeare's Historical Plays?" (1888):

> Will it not indeed be strange if the author of "Othello" and
> "Hamlet" is destin'd to live in America, in a generation or two,

46

less as the cunning draughtsman of the passions, and more as putting on record the first full exposé—and by far the most vivid one, immeasurably ahead of doctrinaires and economists—of the political theory and results, or the reason-why and necessity for them which America has come on earth to abnegate and replace?

(Whitman 1907: 391)

Whitman suggests here that under the auspices of the realized triumph of U.S. democracy, of the development of a "genuinely" post-feudal, if not postcolonial, society, the personal tragedies of characters like Hamlet and Othello will seem less momentous than Shakespeare's incisive assessments of the corrupt and corrupting social systems in which he saw them embedded. Whitman adds that a "future age of criticism, diving deeper, mapping the land and lines freer" may see in Shakespeare's "portraitures of the mediaeval world, the feudal personalities, institutes, in their morbid accumulations," a critical intelligence at work—either "unconscious, or (as I think likely) the more or less conscious"—that means (in words Whitman attributes to his friend, William O'Connor) neither to celebrate an atmosphere of "barbarous and tumultuous gloom," nor to "indoctrinate the age with the love of feudalism" which his own drama "certainly and subtly saps and mines" (Whitman 1907: 391–2).

Although Whitman's projective optimism about the legacy of Shakespeare remains tied to a valorization of American political authority, his statement points toward a more generalized stage of cultural development when Shakespeare might function more in the service of critique than in that of mystique, more in the interest of socially progressive values and assumptions than in that of individualist self-assertion. Prescient as he was, Whitman could not anticipate that only six years after his competing impressions of Shakespeare were recorded in *November Boughs*, the Chicago social reformer, Jane Addams, would develop and apply a remarkably responsive reading of *King Lear* to the contentious debate between management and labor that lay at the heart of the recently concluded Pullman Strike of 1894. Whitman would scarcely find more imaginable Addams's deployment of Shakespeare to anatomize the development in America of a "new feudalism" by native-born plutocrats and the struggle against it of masses of largely immigrant laborers caught up in its toils.

In "A Modern Lear," an essay written in the aftermath of the strike but left unpublished until 1912, Addams appropriates *King Lear* as a text of universal application to scrutinize what she elsewhere calls "a clash between individual or aristocratic management, and corporate or democratic management" (Addams 1907a: 139), transposing a product of early modern British culture to fit the contours of a struggle against a neo-feudalist impulse in America's democratic experiment. Addams represents *Lear* as Shakespeare's unequivocally progressive critique of feudal family relations, and positions Shakespeare as a forward-looking authority on, and potential adjudicator of, industrial conflicts that were proving increasingly divisive at the turn of the century and a threat to democracy itself.[1] Departing from conventional assessments of *Lear* as a passionate rendering of "a man more sinned against than sinning," Addams employs the play as an exemplary text on the dangers of paternalistic philanthropy, though she also uses it to call attention to the collateral dangers of a "narrow conception of emancipation" dominated by a "sense of possession" which she associates with Lear's elder daughters and the more uncompromising elements of the contemporary workers movement. Just as *Lear* allegedly argues on behalf of a post-feudal conception of family life, grounded in the vision of interdependence and mutual respect that reconciles Lear with Cordelia, the Pullman Strike demonstrates the need for advances in industrial relations that will allow the "*social* standpoint" to supersede the "*commercial* standpoint," a "community of interests" to prevail over narrow self-interest.

Addams begins by claiming that "those of us who lived in Chicago during the summer of 1894" were confronted by "a drama which epitomized and, at the same time, challenged the code of social ethics under which we live," and calls particular attention to "the barbaric instinct to kill, roused on both sides" by the drama in question (Addams 1965: 107).[2] This "drama" pitted, on one side, the celebrated industrialist and philanthropist, George Pullman, and, on the other, the residents of the "model town" Pullman had built and named after himself, and eventuated in what Alan Trachtenberg has called "an epic insurgence of sympathy in the form of a national boycott in support of the Pullman strikers" (Trachtenberg 1982: 208). This boycott led, in turn, to President Cleveland's deployment of federal troops to restore order and to a clash between soldiers and strikers that "resulted in the most destructive civil violence since the Civil War" (Trachtenberg 1982: 208).

In her essay, Addams moves rapidly from a depiction of these scenes of "anger and bitterness" to the conclusion that "the shocking experiences of that summer…can only be endured if we learn from it all a great ethical lesson," that lesson being "To endure is all we can hope for" (Addams 1965: 107): a statement drawn (presumably) from Edgar's observation that "Men must endure their going hence, even as their

48

coming hither" in *King Lear* (5.1.9–10).[3] However, before Addams establishes a specific connection between *Lear* and the Pullman Strike, she first establishes the partisan divisions that her appropriation of the Shakespearean model will help her to resolve: divisions that preoccupied management and labor and their respective supporters and that precluded any movement toward a settlement. According to Addams, "during the discussions which followed the Pullman Strike, the defenders of the situation were broadly divided between the people pleading for individual benevolence and those insisting upon social righteousness" (Addams 1965: 107). Although Addams's participation in this debate unqualifiedly positioned her in the camp of labor as an advocate of "social righteousness," she states that

> In the midst of these discussions the writer found her mind dwelling upon a comparison which *modified* and *softened* all her judgments...Her attention was caught by the similarity of ingratitude suffered by an indulgent employer and an indulgent parent. King Lear came often to her mind.
> (Addams 1965: 107, my emphases)

The move that Addams makes here is a complicated one. The comparison to *Lear* modifies and softens what we assume to be her own more extreme or sharper judgments, while her employment of terms like "ingratitude" and "indulgent" to describe worker and employer, respectively, seem designed to modify and soften the criticism that management—"the people pleading for individual benevolence"—were likely to lavish on her indictment of their position. Shakespeare thus seems to be enlisted into the debate to expedite a move from the fractious world of labor/management relations to the more pristine world of "culture," where the ethical content of political and social conflicts may, as it were, be considered in its more refined state.

But the use to which Addams initially puts *Lear* effectively takes Shakespeare *off* the shelf, and makes him play a major role in identifying problems and prescribing improvements in the development of family and industrial relations. She starts by contending that "Historically considered, the relation of Lear to his children was archaic and barbaric, holding in it merely the beginnings of a family life, since developed" (108). She then begins to extend her notion of the archaic and barbaric to the conditions that obtained in the relationship between George Pullman and his workers by suggesting that: "We may in later years learn to look back upon the industrial relationships in which we are now placed as quite as incomprehensible and selfish, quite as barbaric and undeveloped, as was the family relationship between Lear and his daughters" (108). The immense gulf that, "historically considered," separates barbaric family life and barbaric industrial relationships is narrowed by the analogy Addams draws between family and industry: an analogy possibly suggested by George Pullman's avowedly paternalistic relationship to his workers and the model town he named after himself.

Prior to the 1894 strike, Pullman was renowned for his application of the principles of enlightened management to modern industrial conditions. One of the earliest experimenters in the model-town concept, Pullman built a town for his workers to inhabit adjacent to the shops and workspaces of his Pullman Palace Car Company. The model town was furnished with parks, hotels, a library, and a fairly lavish shopping arcade. A "large plaster of Paris model of the town" was proudly displayed at the World's Columbian Exposition of 1893, where "a specially prepared illustrated pamphlet telling the story of the sleeping car and the town was distributed free of charge" (Buder 1967: 147).[4]

However, during a turndown in orders for the Pullman Palace cars that very summer, Pullman radically reduced the town's labor force, as well as the wages of those who remained employed, while simultaneously refusing to make any adjustment in the rent charged to the inhabitants of his model town.[5] As his workers moved closer to a strike—which officially began on 12 May 1894—Pullman proved impervious to any and all acts of arbitration, including those undertaken shortly thereafter by Jane Addams herself. Once the strike broadened into a large-scale work stoppage sponsored by the American Railways Union on 26 June, Pullman became more renowned, even among those not normally given to sympathy for workers and the increasingly powerful union movement, for his rigidity and despotism.

The evolution of George Pullman from enlightened industrialist into inflexible despot was not entirely unanticipated. As early as 1885, Richard T. Ely had seen in the structure and organization of the town of Pullman less a progressive model for future industrial development than a retrograde example of neo-feudalism that carried "troublesome paternalistic overtones" (Trachtenberg 1982: 224). After praising the grace and elegance of Pullman's design of the town, Ely notes, for example, that the resident of Pullman "is surrounded by constant restraint and restriction" and that "everything is done *for* him, nothing *by* him" (quoted in Trachtenberg 1982: 224, my emphases). He wonders whether such a state of affairs would not, in fact, foster "new bonds of dependence" of worker to management;

observes that "It is benevolent, well-wishing feudalism, which desires the happiness of the people, but in such a way shall please the authorities"; and concludes that "Everything tends to stamp upon residents, as upon the town, the character expressed in 'machine-made'" (Trachtenberg 1982: 224).[6]

Ely was not alone in discerning the feudalist character of Pullman and his model town. As H. Dalziel Duncan writes:

> Liberal churchmen of the city discovered to their horror that men like Pullman considered themselves to be "stewards of the Lord" and that many churchmen agreed with the Reverend Oggel of the Green Stone Church in Pullman, who delivered a Christian panegyric just three weeks before the strike on "George M. Pullman, his services to his age, his country, and humanity," using as his text: "Thou hast made him a little lower than the angels and hast crowned him with glory and honor."
>
> (Duncan 1989: 182)

Duncan adds that *Watchman*, a Baptist religious paper, expressly "warned its readers against the new feudalism," arguing that "'The doctrine of the divine right of kings was bad enough, but not so intolerable as the doctrine of the divine right of plutocrats to administer things in general with the presumption that what it pleases them to do is the will of God'" (Duncan 1989: 183).

Many of the same concerns are expressed by Jane Addams in "Industrial Amelioration," a chapter of her book, *Democracy and Social Ethics* (1907a), which was published thirteen years after she first drafted "A Modern Lear" and includes considerable material from that essay. In this chapter, half of which is devoted to a discussion of the Pullman Strike, Addams significantly avoids making any specific reference to Shakespeare or George Pullman and concentrates much more intensively on an analysis of what might as much be termed the neo-colonialist as the neo-feudalist model of industrial organization. According to Addams, the unnamed

> president of the company under discussion...socialized not only the factory, but the form in which his workmen were living. He built, and in great measure regulated, an entire town, without calling upon the workmen either for self-expression or self-government.
>
> (Addams 1907a: 143–4)

Writing in full sympathy with "the men [who] resented the extension of industrial control to domestic and social arrangements," she observes that the residents of Pullman "felt the lack of democracy in the assumption that they should be taken care of in these matters, in which even the humblest workman has won his independence" (Addams 1907a: 144–5).

Although she maintains her sympathy for the striking workers throughout "A Modern Lear," it is primarily on the basis of *Pullman's* resentment at the perceived ingratitude of his employees—whom he regarded as his "children" (Buder 1967: 156)—that Addams forges the connection with Lear and his daughters that animates the original essay. As Addams writes:

> The relation of the British King to his family is very like the relation of the president of the Pullman company to his town; the denouement of a daughter's break with her father suggests the break of the employees with their benefactor.
>
> (Addams 1965: 109)

Buoyed by the remarkably suggestive fit of the analogy between Lear and Pullman and by Shakespeare's arguably critical assessment of Lear's overbearing paternalism, Addams sharpens her indictment of Pullman in the following manner:

> If we may take the dictatorial relation of Lear to Cordelia as a typical and most dramatic example of the distinctively family tragedy, one will asserting its authority through all the entanglement of wounded affection, and insisting upon its selfish ends at all costs, may we not consider the absolute authority of this employer over his town as a typical and dramatic example of the industrial tragedy? One will directing the energies of many others, without regard to their desires, and having in view in the last analysis only commercial results?
>
> (Addams 1965: 111)

Implicit in this statement is Addams's delegation to Shakespeare of an assessment of the dangers of paternalism that anticipates and informs her own. The figure who, in Emerson's words, drew "the father of the man in America," ironically supplies Addams with an authoritative argument she may apply to Pullman's effort to impose an historically regressive model of filial relations on the American workingman.

2.

Given the unlikely source of this argument, it is worth asking how Addams derived her notion of Shakespeare's sponsorship of enlightened relations between fathers and daughters. Were they primarily rooted in her own experience of family life? Did they first take shape in her direct engagement with Shakespeare? Or were they grounded in an independently arrived-at theory of social development which she retrospectively applied to Shakespeare for underwriting and support?

The extent of Addams's acquaintance with Shakespeare is difficult to determine, but judging from a "A Modern Lear" and a rather brilliant little essay on *Macbeth* she published at the age of 19 in the *Rockford Seminary Magazine*, the approach she took to Shakespeare was considerably more inventive and wide-ranging than that of most professional Shakespeareans of the period. Though her name has become synonymous with a life devoted to high-minded social reform, Addams demonstrates in the *Macbeth* essay a responsiveness to the transgressive pleasures of the play—she particularly fastens on the "thrilling effect" of "the idea of a man murdering sleep" (Linn 1935: 59)—that might well be said to exceed the bounds of late Victorian propriety. Much the same kind of responsiveness is recorded in Addams's account of her "brutal endurance" of a bullfight in Madrid in April, 1888. As Christopher Lasch describes it, Addams "sat transfixed" by the spectacle long after her "disgusted" companions deserted her (Lasch 1967: 26), and only later "felt herself tried and condemned...by the entire moral situation which it revealed" (Addams 1910: 85–7). While such experiences tell us little about how Addams came to develop her view of enlightened relations between fathers and daughters, they tell us much about her identification with Cordelia which, in my view, underwrites it.

In an essay entitled "Jane Addams: *The College Woman and the Family Claim*" (which takes its title from one of Addams's own papers), Lasch suggestively complicates the received wisdom about Addams's reformist motivations advanced in hagiographic biographies like Allen F. Davis's *American Heroine* (1973) and another written by her nephew, James Weber Linn (1935). Most of these works accept, with some qualification, Addams's own declaration that the most positive and "dominant influence" on her life "was that of her father" (Linn 1935: 1), whom Linn accounts "the great man of his day and place," a man known for "his integrity, his incorruptibility, his grave courtesy to the least as to the ablest" and a host of corresponding virtues (Linn 1935: 21). Lasch, by contrast, writes of Jane Addams as raised "under the authority of a somewhat stern, remote, and even forbidding man"

(Lasch 1967: 6–7), a view that clashes with that of Addams and her biographers, but directly resonates with her conceptualization of George Pullman's relations with his workers in terms of the father/daughter relationship. Should we add to Lasch's characterization of Addams's father the fact that, in addition to being a man of integrity, he was also an enterprising businessman, banker, and state legislator, and that he stood in the way of Jane Addams's pronounced desire to attend Smith College rather than the more parochial Rockford Seminary, we might well conclude that Addams's experience as the daughter of a well-meaning but decidedly authoritarian father profoundly informed her reading of *Lear* and application of that reading to the Pullman Strike.

Lasch goes on to situate Addams's vocational decision and the peculiar turns her social vision took in the context of the severe emotional crises Addams suffered in the wake of her father's death in 1882; of "her tendency...to see life through literature" (Lasch 1967: 34); of her sporadic bouts of religious belief and unbelief; but mainly of "her mounting frustration with the life [of social uselessness] her [step-]mother was trying to get her to lead" (35) which led, in turn, to a nervous breakdown. He also productively situates Addams's personal difficulties in the context of a broader "cultural crisis" of the period that focused on "the gap between the generations" and that was felt both within the confines of native-born middle-class families and in "the conflict of first- and second-generation immigrants" (36–7).

Although Addams "came rather late to the [women's] suffrage movement" (Davis 1973: 186), the personal frustration she felt at this "gap between the generations" was decidedly gender-specific and spoke directly to other educated women of her class and background who, upon graduation from college, found themselves forced back into a life of "pleasure and freedom from care...besotted with innocent little ambitions" that effectively rendered them "miserable" (Addams 1910: 118–20). As Shannon Jackson observes:

> Concomitant with the Progressive Era's urban tumult and emergent spirit of social change was another social trend involving a new generation of late-nineteenth-century women. White, middle and upper-class, and usually of Protestant descent, a group of hereditary American women emerged as the first of an identifiable generation of college-educated females...only to find themselves expected to return to the life of heterosexual marriage, motherhood, and leisured domes-

ticity that was both the burden and privilege of well-to-do young women.

(Jackson 1996: 341)

According to Addams herself, "any attempt" made by such women

> to subordinate or renounce the family claim was inevitably construed to mean that she was setting up her own will against that of her family's for selfish ends…that she could have no motive larger than a desire to serve her family, and her attempt to break away must therefore be wilful and self-indulgent.

(Addams 1907a: 74)

Clearly finding her own experience implicated in this "social trend," Addams concludes, in *Twenty Years at Hull House*, that "we have all the elements of a tragedy" in the "strenuous assertion" of "the family claim" against the college girl's "disposition to fulfill" what she feels to be "her social claim to the 'submerged tenth'" (1910: 118–20): a conclusion that resonates deeply with Cordelia's alleged yearning for "a fuller life" which Addams depicts with unusual energy in "A Modern Lear" and directly links to the drive for emancipation of George Pullman's workers.

In "A Modern Lear," Addams sympathetically (and revealingly) portrays Cordelia's resistance to Lear as "the awkward attempt of an untrained soul to be honest, to be scrupulous in the expressions of its feelings." As is the case with Addams's college girl (and, possibly, with Addams herself), these feelings involve for Cordelia "the notion of an existence so vast that her relationship as a daughter was but part of it." Grounding her assertions on hints of "a fuller life beyond the seas" that she attributes to the suits of France and Burgundy—and which seem more in keeping with women of her own class and generation than with Shakespeare's Cordelia—Addams claims that Cordelia "found herself in the sweep of a notion of justice so large that the immediate loss of a kingdom seemed of little consequence to her," that she was, in short, caught up in the process of "becoming a citizen of the world" (Addams 1965: 113–14): a transaction that again finds Addams recontextualizing Shakespeare in terms of her own identity formation. Cordelia's drive for independence clashes directly with Lear's drive to maintain control, a clash that Addams portrays as a "test which comes sooner or later to many parents…to maintain the tenderness of the relation between father and child, after that relation had become one between adults" (114). In a formulation that possibly embraces the generational crises

55

Lasch and Jackson describe, Addams succinctly concludes: "The mind of Lear was not big enough for this test. He failed to see anything but the personal slight involved; the ingratitude alone reached him" (114).

As for Lear, so for George Pullman who, after years of self-congratulation for his unprecedented largesse, "suddenly found his town in the sweep of a world-wide moral impulse" (114–15). And, as for Cordelia, so for Pullman's workers who "had at last become swept into this larger movement, so that the giving up of comfortable homes, of beautiful surroundings, seemed as naught" (115). Addams's staging of this correspondence notably identifies the drive for emancipation as a moral, not a material, phenomenon; as marking moments in time that meet on a continuum of ethical, not necessarily historical, development, and that require a considerable amount of discomfort and self-sacrifice on the part of those committed to advances in the family and industrial relationship. It is for such reasons that Addams's essay turns, after a stirring indictment of Pullman's feudal inflexibility and defense of the brotherhood of workers, to an assessment of what Cordelia and the contemporary workingman need to contribute to an "inclusive" settlement of the competing claims of fathers and children, capital, and labor.

Prefacing this turn with a remark on "the fatal lack of generosity in the attitude of workmen toward the company under whose exactions they feel themselves wronged," Addams writes that "in reading the tragedy of King Lear, Cordelia does not escape our censure": "Her first words are cold, and we are shocked by her lack of tenderness. Why should she ignore her father's need for indulgence, and be so unwilling to give him what he so obviously craved?" (119). Possibly motivated by the guilt she, herself, was made to feel for her "willfulness" and "self-indulgence" in refusing to fulfill the "family claim," Addams concludes that it is "a narrow conception that would break thus abruptly with the past, and would assume that her father had no part in her new life," adding that "we do not admire the Cordelia 'who loves according to her bond' as we later admire the self same Cordelia who comes back from France that she may include in her happiness and freer life the father whom she had deserted through her self-absorption" (119–20).

These remarks evince the imaginative range and emotional intensity of Addams's engagement with Shakespeare at the same time as they anticipate the breakdown of the analogy between family and industrial relations she is so keen to draw. Lasch is no doubt right to note of Addams's response to the domestic tragedy of first- and second-generation immigrants that "her sympathy both with the rebellion of youth" and "with the plight of the parents…enabled Jane Addams to see their conflicting points of view with equal clarity" (Lasch 1967: 37). But in this instance Addams's identification with Cordelia, and with the conservative turn her rebellion takes, exerts a disproportionate and arguably colonizing influence on her assessment of the very differently ordered industrial relation. She uses her socially specific experience as a privileged "college woman" both to mediate her reading of Shakespeare and to judge the behavior of the contemporary worker.

Addams leans heavily here on a notion of the reciprocal obligations of the family relation that she extends, without further mediation, to a critical appraisal of correspondingly "narrow conceptions" that beset the contemporary workers movement. Just as "the vision of the life of Europe [allegedly] caught the sight and quickened the impulses of Cordelia," so, she claims, "a vision of the wider life has caught the sight of workingmen" (Addams 1965: 120). Addams now makes the crucial move of positioning the workingman's "vision of the wider life" in the context of Cordelia's initial "self-absorption" and subsequently more inclusive reconciliation with Lear. She concludes that

> the emancipation of working people will have to be [similarly] inclusive of the employer from the first or it will encounter many failures, cruelties and reactions. It will result not in the position of the repentant Cordelia but in that of King Lear's two older daughters.
>
> (Addams 1965: 120)

Addams next launches into what she no doubt considered an even-handed critique of the risks of preaching a "doctrine of emancipation" to "wage-workers" that will be accepted "for the sake of fleshpots, rather than for the human affection and social justice which it involves":

> If the workingmen's narrow conception of emancipation was fully acted upon, they would hold much the same relationship to their expropriated employer that the two older daughters held to their abdicated father. When the kingdom was given to them they received it as altogether their own, and were domi-nated by a sense of possession; "it is ours not yours" was never absent from their consciousness. They did not wish to be reminded by the state and retinue of the old King that he had been the former possessor. Finally, his mere presence alone reminded them too much of that and they banished him from the palace. That a newly acquired sense of possession should result in the barbaric, the incredible scenes of bitterness and

murder, which were King Lear's portion, is not without a reminder of the barbaric scenes in our political and industrial relationships when the sense of possession, to obtain and to hold, is aroused on both sides.

(Addams 1965: 120–1)

What is "barbaric" to Addams here is less the "feudal" relationship that allegedly obtains between Pullman and his workers (whose reciprocity she appears to wish to retain) than it is the mutual thrusting after "flesh-pots" that the emancipated drive to possess presumably inspires. Lear's elder daughters embody for Addams the materialist excesses of the contemporary workers movement, as well as its self-destructiveness, which is evinced in its failure to take pragmatic—and moral—account of the competing drive to possess of "those who think they lose" by making any concession to labor.

Moving from an identification with the incipiently revolutionary resistance of Cordelia to the "family claim" in Act 1 of *King Lear* to an endorsement of the magnanimous self-sacrifice Cordelia performs in the closing movement of the play when she re-establishes relations with her father, Addams requires a corresponding shift in the position of workers who, like members of the contemporary family, "together must recognize and acknowledge the validity of the social obligation."[7] Failure to manifest such recognition effectively casts labor in the unflattering role of Lear's elder daughters, whose transgressions are repeatedly represented as monstrous or "unnatural" in Shakespeare's play. Allowing the plot of *King Lear* to dictate the terms of settlement to the conflicts of management and labor, Addams thus permits the humanistic authority of the Shakespearean analogy, which she deployed to highlight the neo-feudalist paternalism of George Pullman, to work its charms on the alleged "barbarity" of the striking workers.

3.

Addams moves here well beyond the parameters of the Pullman Strike which, before it was subsumed into the more widespread and sporadically violent work stoppage engineered by Eugene Debs's American Railways Union, pitted a remarkably civil and restrained group of workers against an unyielding George Pullman who refused any and all efforts at arbitration. In so doing, she pointedly resists the conclusion that an enduring resolution of industrial tragedies like the one precipitated by Pullman's intransigence would require profounder structural changes in American social and economic life than her call for mutually mindful arbitration would allow. In this respect and others, Addams stakes out an impressively articulated, but carefully modulated, ameliorist position toward class conflict, one focused on motivations and effects but reluctant to invoke the specter of wholesale structural transformation. As Daniel Levine observes:

> Jane Addams was far from being a militant trade unionist, far from devoted to the bread-and-butter issues of hours, wages, and working conditions. On the contrary, in her first grappling with the labor question she was a Christian humanitarian. Later the specifically Christian terminology dropped out, but the attitude remained...Miss Addams did not understand, or if she understood she did not approve of, what the union movement was about.
>
> (Levine 1971: 163–4)[8]

For Addams, we are all potential antagonists in a social tragedy when we fail to take into account our "community of interests." Employees as well as employers are responsible to this community; the claims of each competing party must be taken into account. The real social specter is greed and resentment. No social party has a monopoly on either virtue or vice.

Addams's construction of *Lear* as a social text of universal application is the glue that holds these positions together, that anatomizes the problem, that points toward the solution. But, insofar as the solution to which *Lear* points remains dependent on far-reaching social transformations, Addams's essay prompts one to ask to what use Shakespeare might be put with respect to "enduring" the social problem while it persists. In a section of *Twenty Years at Hull House*, Addams describes some of the functions of the settlement's Shakespeare club, which "has lived a continuous existence at Hull House for sixteen years [placing its origin in 1894, the year of the Pullman Strike], during which time its members have heard the leading interpreters of Shakespeare, both among scholars and players." She then offers the following anecdote and conclusion drawn from it:

> I recall that one of its earliest members said that her mind was peopled with Shakespeare characters during her long hours of sewing in a shop, that she couldn't remember what she thought about before she joined the club, and concluded that she hadn't thought about anything at all. To feed the mind of the worker, to lift it above the monotony of his task, and to

connect it with the larger world outside of his immediate surroundings, has always been the object of art, perhaps never more nobly fulfilled than by the great English bard.

(Addams 1910: 299)

In this example, Shakespeare does for the seamstress what Europe does for Cordelia, what the brotherhood of labor does for the individual workingman: he serves as a source of new and emancipating thoughts, as a medium of self-expansion and connection to a wider world outside the self. But, insofar as Addams's seamstress remains rooted to her shop, fastened to her task, with only her mind free to roam the spaces the plays open up to her, Shakespeare may also be said to operate as a source of mystification, offering imaginary resolutions to the immediate problems of labor.[9]

I make this point not to denigrate the power and potential usefulness of Addams's otherwise inspired appropriation of Shakespeare and integration of his plays into the educational programs of Hull House. Indeed, as Shannon Jackson observes regarding the work of the Hull House Players, the Marionette Club, and dance classes conducted by Edith de Nancrede:

> Rather than assuming the traits of absolute power, modernizing control, or hierarchized condescension that circulated in other Progressive Era reform projects, such settlement theatre matched the ethic of neighborliness, subtlety, proximity, continuity, and quiet side-by-sidedness articulated as the method of settlement practice.
>
> (Jackson 1996: 358)[10]

But, as Addams inadvertently indicates in her gloss on the story of "the London showman who used to exhibit two skulls of Shakespeare—one when he was a youth and went poaching, another when he was a man and wrote plays" (Addams 1907b: 9), the wide world that the imagination opens up for the few has a way of closing its door on the many who are materially constrained to lag behind. As Addams writes of the showman's exhibition:

> There was such a striking difference between the roystering boy indulging in illicit sport and the mature man who peopled the London stage with all the world, that the showman grew confused and considered two separate acts of creation less improbable than that such an amazing change should have

taken place. We can easily imagine the gifted youth in the little group of rustics at Stratford-upon-Avon finding no adequate outlet for his powers save in a series of break-neck adventures. His only alternative was to sit by the fire with the village cronies, drinking ale so long as his shillings held out. But if we follow him up to London,…if we can imagine his delight as he gradually gained the freedom, not only of that big town, but of the human city as well, we can easily see that illicit sport could no longer attract him. To have told the great dramatist the night Hamlet first stepped upon the boards that it was a wicked thing to poach, to have cautioned him that he must consider the cost of preserving the forest and of raising deer, or to have made an appeal to his pity on behalf of wounded creatures, would have been the height of folly, because totally unnecessary. All desire, almost all memory of those days, had dropped from him, through his absorption in the great and exciting drama of life. His effort to understand it, to portray it, had utilized and drained his every power.

(1907b: 9–10)

Committed as she was to a developmental model of social education, here Addams champions the completeness of Shakespeare's alleged break with his past, placing him beyond the bounds of sympathy for the "illicit sports" of his "village cronies," who are left to fend for themselves. In so doing, Addams establishes the *dis*continuity of Shakespeare's movement from the village to the city, making his forgetfulness serve as a bridge to the showman's two skulls. The London Shakespeare she imagines as having evolved beyond the memory of his youthful life in Stratford might just as well have been, as the showman insists, another person entirely.

The "two skulls" model of Shakespeare has further application to Addams herself, whose selfless commitment to social reform was often neutralized by an abiding resistance to wholesale social transformation abetted by her own lifelong membership in an established community of wealth and privilege.[11] Indeed, in "A Modern Lear," Addams demonstrates some of the same forgetfulness she attributes to her London Shakespeare by denying full sympathy to immigrant workers still caught in the toils of attempting to break "the tribal bond" in order to embrace a "cosmopolitan affection" they were not yet in the position to afford (1907b: 11–12).

The Shakespeare that emerges in Addams is thus at once the product of prevailing class divisions, of Addams's own gender and family-related identity themes, and, I would argue, of Hull House's function as an internal colonizing venture, a missionary station in the wilds of darkest Chicago, one of whose incidental goals is the assimilation of the "underdog" immigrant worker to the established social formations of U.S. society: "the rich man in his castle, the poor man at his gate" (Brodber 1988: 30).[12]

While Addams's effort to enlist Shakespeare's collaboration in the amelioration of oppressive social conditions both contests Whitman's characterization of Shakespeare as an apologist for the "feudal institutes" and confirms Whitman's more sanguine view of Shakespeare's demystifying potential, "A Modern Lear" ultimately conforms to more politically quiescent U.S. constructions of the bard, particularly the neo-colonial rendering of Shakespeare as "the horizon beyond which, at present, we do not see" advanced by Emerson in *Representative Men* (Emerson 1903: 204). Like Hull House itself—a philanthropic outpost jointly underwritten by a commitment to social enrichment and reform and a dependence on patrician largesse—Shakespeare's pre-emptively radical analysis of self-serving paternalism is balanced, in Addams's account, by his equally prescient representation of the consequences of self-serving emancipation.[13] Drawing from *Lear* an ethic of endurance that transcends narrow self-interest, Addams effectively recuperates a Shakespeare who occupies a principled space beyond the fractious toils of strikes and class hatred where the lion and the lamb can negotiate as one. It is for such reasons among others that Eugene Debs considered Addams's otherwise inspired intervention "just another attempt to put out a fire with rosewater" (Linn 1935: 167).[14]

3

SHAKESPEARE, 1916:
CALIBAN BY THE YELLOW SANDS AND THE NEW DRAMAS OF DEMOCRACY

1.

The effort made by Jane Addams to resolve the fractious struggle of management and labor through the medium of Shakespeare, and her earnest attempts to raise the sights of immigrant workers and their families beyond the level of factory and neighborhood, were echoed some twenty years later in a more allegorical manner and on a considerably grander scale by Percy MacKaye in his Shakespeare tercentenary masque, *Caliban by the Yellow Sands*. Performed by a cast of some thirty professional actors supported by hundreds of mainly "mute figurants" (Franck 1964: 159) representing several of the dominant ethnic groups and immigrant "colonies" of the city of New York, *Caliban* was staged over a ten-day period in the late spring of 1916 in Lewisohn Stadium of the City College of New York. More of a visual pageant or spectacle than a play whose words and dramatic interactions could be easily seen and heard, much less reliably interpreted, by the 135,000 people who packed the stands, the masque was nonetheless accounted "an admirable accomplishment in the way of organization and, in large measure, of beauty—a big thing done, on the whole, in a big way" (quoted by Green 1989: 69).[1]

MacKaye's purported aim was to celebrate the potential of community-based drama as much as it was to commemorate the living heritage of Shakespeare. MacKaye's themes, however, as they emerge from the published text of the masque, are considerably more ambitious and articulate his responsiveness to the anxieties of others of his class and caste regarding how best to "Americanize" the newly arrived masses of immigrants and introduce them to the standards and obligations of Anglo-Saxon culture. For such reasons, *Caliban* may be said to stage the closing of one frontier in America's arguably postcolonial relationship with Shakespeare, evinced in the effort to resist the paternalistic embrace of "feudal" British values and assumptions, and the opening of another, marked by the forging of a neo-colonial accord negotiated in resistance to the threat to Anglo-American culture embodied by the alien and foreign-born.

In the Preface to his printed text, MacKaye identifies a related source of anxiety that shadowed the Shakespeare tercentenary celebrations, namely, the Great War then raging in Europe:

> Three hundred years alive on the 23rd of April, 1916, the memory of Shakespeare calls creatively upon a self-destroying world to do him honor by honoring that world-constructive art of which he is a master architect.
>
> Over seas, the choral hymns of cannon acclaim his death; in battle-trenches artists are turned subtly ingenious to inter his art; War, Lust, and Death are risen in power to restore the primeval reign of Setebos.
>
> (MacKaye 1916: xiii)

MacKaye invokes here a binary of creation and destruction whose sponsors are, respectively, Shakespeare and Setebos, and goes on to isolate the New World of America—at this time still militarily, if not politically, neutral—as a still-point apart from the turning world of the Great War and, consequently, as the only remaining haven for "world-constructive" artistry and the culture that gave birth to it:

> Here in America, where the neighboring waters of [Shakespeare's] "vexed Bermoothes" lie more calm than those about his own native isle, here only is given some practical opportunity for his uninterable spirit to create new splendid symbols for peace through harmonious international expression.
>
> (MacKaye 1916: xiii)

The language MacKaye employs here closely echoes themes he had struck some years earlier in his call for a "*new* drama" of democracy whose main roots "will strike for nutriment deep into English tradition and language" but whose "trunk and branch shall spread themselves over the nation as indigenous and beneficent as our American elms" (MacKaye 1909: 114). The relation envisioned in both passages involves a kind of organic transmission from Old World roots to a New World flowering mediated by the "uninterable spirit" and "nutriment" of Shakespeare. For MacKaye, the native tree of American drama will be sustained and supported by the great works and models of the English literary tradition, a transaction whose product or result will *seem* as American as native-grown trees, but whose formative source or power will be the "uninterable spirit" of father Shakespeare that speaks through it.

In MacKaye's hands, this New World flowering will lead to the development of a "new dramatic art-form...called by the name Community Masque" which he claims to be "a technique of the theatre adapted to democratic expression and dedicated to public service" (MacKaye 1916: xxii), but which in practice will work within a more authoritarian Old World framework. In his Preface, MacKaye quotes from Prospero's speech to Ariel in *The Tempest* 1.2 to isolate the role played by Prospero's "art" in freeing Ariel from the grip of Sycorax which MacKaye likens to "that many-visioned art of the theatre which, age after age, has come to liberate the imprisoned imagination of mankind from the fetters of brute force and ignorance" (MacKaye 1916: xv). The associations travel here from the "art of Prospero" to the "art of Shakespeare" to the "many-visioned art of the theatre" and successively take as the embodiment of that art's usurpation the figures of Sycorax, Setebos, and, finally, Caliban himself. It is here that MacKaye articulates his primary theme and begins to complicate, and to localize in ways that I intend to develop, his initial identification of the Great War as the manifestation of the "primeval reign of Setebos."

According to MacKaye, "The theme of the Masque—Caliban seeking to learn the art of Prospero—is...the slow education of mankind through the influences of cooperative art, that is, of the art of the theatre in its full social scope" (MacKaye 1916: xvii). For MacKaye

> Caliban...in this Masque, is that passionate child-curious part
> of us all [whether as individuals or as races], groveling close to
> his aboriginal origins, yet groping up and staggering—with
> almost rhythmic falls and back-slidings—toward the serener
> plane of pity and love, reason and disciplined will, where
> Miranda and Prospero commune with Ariel and his Spirits.
>
> (MacKaye 1916: xv)

Although he presumably means to identify the races currently embat- tled in the cruel wars of Setebos as occupying the same space of "aboriginal origins" he delegates to Caliban, the model he draws, of "rhythmic falls and back-slidings" contrasted with "the serener plane of pity and love, reason and *disciplined* will" (my emphasis) where Prospero, Miranda, and Ariel "commune," schematizes a more categorical relation of mind over matter, father over child, will over desire, that both reproduces the social organization of Shakespeare's play and extends its applications to an urban population for whom, as a contemporary reviewer noted, "a sense of solidarity and common responsibility" had been "heretofore wanting" (quoted in Franck 1964: 167). Indeed, this hierarchical model of social relations, its heavenly roof studded with the rarefied figures of Prospero and Miranda "communing" with "Ariel and his Spirits," is reproduced as well in the painstakingly detailed organization of the masque itself, with its center and speaking parts delegated to generally well-known professional actors, while its margins and interludes are delegated to "mute figurants" representing still unintegrated latecomers to the feast of Anglo-American civility.

It is, on this account, not insignificant that so elaborate an undertaking solicited, and gained, the backing of some of the wealthiest citizens of New York, among them Daniel Guggenheim, J.P. Morgan, Jacob Schiff, and William Vanderbilt. Nor is it inconsequential that the American ancestry of MacKaye himself "dated back to William Bradford of Plymouth Colony, Roger Williams of Rhode Island Colony, and John Steel, founder of the Connecticut Colony at Hartford in 1635" (Franck 1964: 154). This wedding of New England pedigree and New York commercial energy underwrites the grand scale, ambition, and confidence of MacKaye's project, which very consciously aimed to make Shakespeare the centerpiece of an undertaking reflective of Anglo-American exceptionality and magnificence. MacKaye's devotion and commitment to community theater on the grand scale may be traced directly to the efforts in kind of his father, Steele MacKaye, whose "last work, the so-called *Spectatorium*" was expressly designed to be "the highlight of the Chicago World's Fair in celebration of the four hundredth anniversary of America's discovery by Columbus" (Franck 1964: 156).[2] The elder MacKaye also "enlisted the best men of wealth and art to assist him" in this ultimately unrealized project, "among them George Pullman," whose model town was put on display at the Chicago Fair to demonstrate the marriage of commercial and community aspirations (Franck 1964: 156), but which soon after became the site of their breakdown and fractious divorce.[3] The link between the wealth of men like Pullman and Morgan and the lavish designs of the MacKayes is more than a little suggestive and informs their shared commitment to the development of ostentatious public spectacles that would effectively dwarf the stature of the very men and women whose imaginations and lives they set out to magnify and dignify.[4]

2.

A direct connection may, in fact, be drawn between MacKaye's staging of Caliban as a consistently misinterpreting audience of the seven "inner scenes" MacKaye's Prospero stages for his benefit and the thousands of auditors drawn from all classes of New York society who arguably found MacKaye's playlets too remote for comprehension. Although some commentators waxed eloquent on MacKaye's successful merger of theory and practice, and on his Hamlet-like satisfaction of his father's frustrated desires:

> Out there in the starlight of the Stadium, under the open sky, in the amphitheatre black with people, the great arc lights flashing on the three stages of the masque, as community group after community group passed in review—the Pan Hellenic League, the East Side Settlements, the Greenwich Villagers, the Bronx District, the schools, the representatives of all races, classes, conditions in the great city—I saw the benignant ghost of Steele MacKaye looking down on his dream come true through his son.
>
> (quoted in MacKaye 1927: 2:482)

Others "found in the Masque a great deal of democracy, if not much Shakespeare," Jane Franck's summary assessment that the masque "was an ambitious attempt to weld New York into a community; but [that] the allegory was too remote from everyday life [and] Shakespeare remained aloof" (Franck 1964: 167), probably provides a more reliable index of its effect on its audiences.

Attracted as he was to the technical wizardry and outsized scale of his father's *Spectatorium*, some of which was evinced in the *Civic Masque* he produced in 1914 "with the participation of 7,500 St. Louis citizens" to dramatize "the legendary and historical past" of that city (Franck 1964: 158), Percy MacKaye maintained a more "poetic" or literary orientation in his own career as a maker of public pageants and entertainments, and was particularly drawn to the cultivation of allegorical masques on public themes.[5] In *Caliban*, MacKaye puts this interest to work by reconfiguring the plot of *The Tempest* to fasten on an allegorized contention for the soul of Caliban engaged in by the forces of darkness on the one hand—constituted by Setebos and Sycorax and their surviving surrogates, Lust, Death, and War—and by the forces of light on the other—constituted by the holy triad of Prospero, Ariel, and Miranda. In the process, MacKaye suppresses Prospero's prehistory in

Milan and all that follows from it—his attraction of his enemies to his island and exercise of "rough magic" upon them, his supervision of the mutual wooing of Miranda and Ferdinand, and, most significantly, his acknowledgment of the problematic nature of his power and consequent abjuration of his "art"—choosing to make the education of Caliban his primary objective and the "harrowing" of the realm of Setebos the reason for his arrival onstage.[6]

At the start of the masque, we find Ariel "held fettered" in "the tiger jaws of the idol" Setebos in a scene suggestive of a world caught in the grip of pagan depravity. Like a veritable John the Baptist, Ariel proclaims to Caliban that he is "waiting for one who will come.../One from the heart of the world; [who] shall rise/On tempest of music and in thunder of song" to set free "all my air-born spirits/Whom Setebos holds prisoned in this earth" (MacKaye 1916: 8–9). Prospero's grand entrance onstage, in a style that doubly echoes Christ's harrowing of hell and Moses's destruction of the idols at the base of Mt. Sinai, is preceded by that of Miranda, who advances as an overdetermined embodiment of grace, innocence, and beauty. Caliban's attempted rape of Miranda in *The Tempest* is reprised here in his advance against Miranda with a "hissing growl" and in Sycorax's command to Setebos that they be "mated" at "thine altar" (MacKaye 1916: 21–2). At this point Prospero enters amid "tempestuous song, darkness, and thunder," seated on a "glowing, winged throne...in one hand, a scroll; in the other a miraculous staff" (MacKaye 1916: 23–4), in the aftermath of which Ariel and his spirits emerge out of the "toad-mouth" of Setebos, while Sycorax is discovered "heaped and still by the altar" (MacKaye 1916: 25).[7]

This sequence indicates the extent to which MacKaye envisioned *The Tempest* less as a play set in a specific time and space than as a master narrative concerned with the central role art and the artist play in the eternal struggle of mind and matter, spirit and body, civility and savagism. MacKaye thus translates Prospero's frustrating struggle against Caliban's intractability in *The Tempest* into the more general, and ongoing, struggle of the "power" of art against the "will of Setebos," which is permanently allied to the forces of Lust, Death, and War that will attempt to seduce Caliban in the three Acts of the masque-proper. By positioning Prospero as the unquestioned source and force of goodness and creativity, MacKaye shifts both the focus and burden of responsibility for determining the world's fate to the considerably more unpredictable, though characteristically backsliding, Caliban. MacKaye's logic requires the "immortal Caliban" in man to "rise" to a state of "lordly reason" before his true goal—that is, "Miranda's freedom"—can be realized. For her part, Miranda can never "hold/Her maiden gladness undismayed" until Caliban is rendered permanently tractable and capable of mastering his uncivil urges. The ultimate aim of Prospero's art is thus to "teach" Caliban to help "transform this cave of Setebos/To be a temple to Miranda" (MacKaye 1916: 29).

In all this, MacKaye also imposes a considerable burden on the freestanding "inner scenes" he drew from eleven additional plays of Shakespeare, seven of which MacKaye's Prospero stages for the presumed benefit of Caliban. Although we are apparently meant to assume that Caliban's frequently misguided responses to these scenes document the difficulty Caliban and the Caliban in man experience in their effort to "grow/To reverence Miranda, and forswear/Setebos" (MacKaye 1916: 35), the scenes themselves generally fail to deliver the lessons in civility Caliban is presumably meant to master. What they do deliver, like the overarching masque itself, are "rare visions" to which Caliban is drawn "in childlike fascination" and to which he responds with child-like excitement. In response to *Antony and Cleopatra*, 3.11, for example, Caliban exclaims, "O dazzle-blue, gold-shine, hot lotus smell!/Blood-root in bloom, and scarlet water-weed!/...Float, still float,/You purpling sails! Blaze, thou flame-woman" (MacKaye 1916: 47). And as he watches *Troilus and Cressida*, 1.2, the stage directions call for Caliban to crawl "slowly forward on his stomach to the centre [of the stage], where he lies prone, with head lifted...kicking at times his lower legs...in the air" (MacKaye 1916: 51); to leap up "in loud excited laughter" and "[clap] his hands in the air" at its ending; and to exclaim: "Aha! Troy, Troy! Lips of Troyland and Egypt! Lovers in links of gold! Ho, wine of woman/Bubbling in vats of war!" (MacKaye 1916: 58). Although these scenes succeed in arousing Caliban's imagination and delight, MacKaye clearly expects his audience to construe Caliban's overstimulated imagination as primitive and pornographic. What other moral could it draw as Caliban takes command of Prospero's staff; invokes "a scene of mingled riot and orgy" in the spirit of Caligula; "dances on the throne of Prospero" with "his huge limbs rioting grotesque from his silken garments"; and is ultimately dashed to the ground upon the appearance of "a colossal CROSS, burning with white fire" (MacKaye 1916: 68–71)?

The allegorical triumph of the Christian dispensation—made manifest in the identifying symbol of the Church Militant which MacKaye superimposes on Shakespeare's heterodox Renaissance magus—literally makes "mud" of Caliban, returning him to a state of inchoate matter awaiting Prospero's identifying "imprint" or "seal": "Stir, thou thick clot/Of clay and god-spittle! Let thine atoms thaw/To Mud, where Prosper may imprint once more His blurred seal" (MacKaye 1916: 74). As the chastened Caliban accepts and elaborates on Prospero's estimate of his character—"Mud: yea, methought to be/His Artist, and make dream-things of mine own/Like Ariel his spirits, yet now—am mud"— and Miranda "pitifully" and more optimistically avers "Nay, star-dust!" (MacKaye 1916: 74), it becomes evident that MacKaye has repositioned Shakespeare's "devil, on whose nature/Nurture can never stick," on an evolutionary time-line that will chart Prospero's repeated attempts to imprint his "seal" of civility on the "mud" of Caliban in the hope that it *will*, at some undesignated future moment, finally hold.

As the masque proceeds, Caliban is hurried through a pageant of Western history as both witness and participant, sometimes won over by the visions and tableaux from Shakespeare that Prospero paints in MacKaye's "inner scenes," sometimes in a state of active revolt against their mockery of his character and aspirations.[8] Consistent with the Shakespeare-centered compass of the masque, "history" is rendered in (and on) three stages, representing classical, medieval, and Elizabethan culture and civilization, its culminating point reached in the tenth and last inner scene, which dramatizes Henry V's "Once more unto the breach" speech and concludes with the shout "Ho, God for Harry, England, and Saint George" (MacKaye 1916: 137–8). MacKaye's decision to place this scene in so climactic a position is problematic enough, given his masque's frequent references to the Great War and its identification of warlike behavior with the forces of Setebos. It becomes doubly problematic in the context of the scenes that precede it. The first of these, drawn from *As You Like It*, 2.7, appears to exert a calming influence on Caliban. However, in the interim between this and the ninth inner scene, drawn from the Herne the Hunter sequence (5.5) of *The Merry Wives of Windsor*, the backsliding Caliban is again caught up in the fires of lust and possessiveness for Miranda which it is apparently the purpose of this scene to "douse" by assuming Caliban's capacity to recognize the impropriety of his own desire in the "lustful fire/Of old John Falstaff" and "to laugh at apings of it" (MacKaye 1916: 126–7).

What Caliban does instead is to interpret the scene as mocking his amorous aspirations by identifying him as "A man with horns/And heart of monster" (MacKaye 1916: 133). As the "voice of War calls deeply from below" (stage directions), "Miranda shall be thine!," Caliban, instead of renouncing his desire, resolves to go to war for it:

> Mine!—Yea, now I am mocked to know myself
> What rutting stag I am! And her, the doe

I mate, my horns shall battle for, and be
Mine own—mine, mine! Miranda!

(MacKaye 1916: 135)

It is in such a mood that Caliban receives the final "imprint" of the scene from *Henry V* and adapts its concluding salvo, "Ho, God for Harry, England, and Saint George," to one of his own: "Ho, God for Caliban and Setebos!/War, War for Prosper's throne! Miranda's shrine!" (MacKaye 1916: 139).[9] A conflict is "detonated" at this concluding moment of the masque-proper between the "Powers of Setebos" and the "Spirits of Ariel" that leads to the defeat of the latter, the taking captive of Prospero, Miranda, and Ariel, and to an oddly anticlimactic confrontation between Prospero and Caliban. This exchange is entirely dominated by Prospero, who admits his temporary defeat, but points "yonder" to the "Yellow Sands" where "deathless artists of the plastic mind" are at work building "the beauty of the world" under the sponsorship of "The Spirit of Time" (MacKaye 1916: 141).

A grand concluding pageant is staged under Time's sponsorship in the form of an epilogue that embraces "a Pageant of the great Theatres of the world...in symbolic groups, with their distinctive banners and insignia" and a procession of "the creators of the art of the theatre from antiquity to the verge of the living present: the world-famed actors, dramatists, producers, musicians, directors, and inventors of its art" assembled in "national pageant groups" (MacKaye 1916: 143–4). This group significantly includes the two notorious combatants of Astor Place, Edwin Forrest and William Macready, still divided by their national affiliations, but drawn together by their filial relationship to the true "author" of these revels, "the modest figure of Shakespeare," who enters with his own "national group" before approaching, and changing places with, Prospero. As this transfer of identities is completed and "Prospero moves silently off with the group of Dramatists" (stage directions), "the only light remains on the figure of Shakespeare—and the two with him: Ariel tiptoe behind him, peering over his shoulder; Miranda beside him, leaning forward, with lips parted to speak" (MacKaye 1916: 144). Before the masque predictably concludes with Shakespeare "as Prospero" reciting the Revels speech, Caliban emerges "out of the dimness" to address the trinitarian tableau:

Lady of the Yellow Sands! O Life! O Time!
Thy tempest blindeth me: Thy beauty baffleth.—
A little have I crawled, a little only

Out of mine ancient cave. All that I build
I botch; all that I do destroyeth my dream.
Yet—yet I yearn to build, to be thine Artist
And stablish this thine Earth among the stars—
Beautiful!

(MacKaye 1916: 145)

In the end, Caliban himself becomes part of the tableau of "bright Beings," as "with gesture of longing, he crouches at Shakespeare's feet, gazing up in his face, which looks on him with tenderness" (MacKaye 1916: 145).[10]

Caliban's dog-like fawning at the feet of Shakespeare, and the "tenderness" of Shakespeare's regard for his recidivist "servant-Monster," paints a very complacent picture of master/slave relations that retrospectively redefines the terms of Caliban's apparent triumph at the end of the masque-proper. As the Epilogue presents it, the triumph of Caliban and the "Powers of Setebos" over Prospero and the "Spirits of Ariel" is an event that takes place from time to time in the annals of history, but which, viewed as a moral phenomenon, registers man's failure or incapacity to achieve the kind of happiness or satisfaction he really craves. Rather than being identified as a permanent acolyte of Setebos, Caliban is portrayed as always and ever yearning to gain the fellowship of the "bright Beings" headed by Prospero/Shakespeare. His backsliding into the camp of Setebos is symptomatic of his insufficiently evolved capacity to gain mastery over himself and of his impatience with the fact that before such mastery can be gained he must serve an indefinite term of apprenticeship. Only in the prospect of a time not yet measured by history can such self-mastery be realized. Until that time, Caliban must continue to exist in a dependency relationship with Prospero.

3.

Since MacKaye's masque eschews specific social and political references, apart from those made to the Great War in the preface which are reprised in the triumph of Setebos at the end of Act 3, the dependency relationship of patience, trust, and forbearance established between Caliban and Prospero unsurprisingly offers only the most imaginary resolution to the social contradictions of the urban community of New York circa 1916. In fact, during the two-week period in which the masque was rehearsed and performed, the pages of the *New York Times* were littered with a host of reports testifying to a different kind of war being waged on a daily basis between the entrenched institutions of New York and a variety of ethnic groups attempting to gain entrance to them. On the same day in May that students of the elite Riverdale School staged the first American production of *Coriolanus* since 1886 under the direction of their headmaster, a near riot took place at Columbia University over the protest of Jewish students who had been elected to positions on the Law School's student council but whose election had been voided by claims of "irregularities" lodged by Christian students (*New York Times*, 20 May 1916). A week later, the *Times* records the passage of a resolution to establish a segregated Negro regiment of the New York National Guard on the same day that a suit was filed by Jews who were barred from enlisting in the Guard on any terms (*New York Times*, 26 May 1916). On the same page in which the first production of MacKaye's masque was reviewed, a brief article announcing the imminent production of "a drama of Negro life" written by one Lawrence Eyre is careful to add that "the play tells a genial story and makes no attempt to solve the race problem" (*New York Times*, 25 May 1916).

One might well attribute the same geniality to MacKaye's masque were it not for the fact that it does attempt, in howsoever coded a manner, to solve what had become known in some quarters as the problem of "the Caliban type" in U.S. society, which was, for all rights and purposes, the problem of the immigrant and immigration.[11] MacKaye was, of course, acutely conscious of what we today would call the "multicultural" cast of his intended auditory, and, true to his commitment to community drama, aimed "to reverse the traditional order of theatrical procedure and—so far as possible—to take the public, as participants, into the confidence of 'behind the scenes' beforehand" (MacKaye 1916: 151). As he goes on to observe, "An interesting American phase of the New York production is the problem of carrying its community meaning to the still polyglot population, so that steps have been taken for the immediate translation of the Masque into Italian, German, and Yiddish" (MacKaye 1916: 152). Since such steps would little profit members of the Italian, German, and Jewish immigrant communities who had neither the skill, nor the money, to read or purchase such translations, MacKaye's efforts to enlist members of "the Greek Colony" for the Greek interludes, of "the Italian colony, for the Roman," of "the German University League, for the German," and "members of the Alliance Française, for the French" (MacKaye 1916: 153), would appear to constitute a more effective means of community engagement. But as the names of these comparatively well-established "colonies" and organizations indicate, MacKaye took few steps to enlist the participation of the masses of semiliterate Irish, Italian, and Jewish immigrants, much less representatives of New York's African-American communities, who inhabited the city's already notoriously teeming and disease-ridden slums.[12] A reviewer from the *New York Times* could confidently write that "It was a real—not a typical—New York audience that saw the first performance of the Masque last night," that "in it were representatives of all the elements that make up the city, from the lower east side to Riverside drive," and could conclude with some justice that "in that sense it was perhaps more nearly a community affair than any dramatic performance that has been ever held here" (*New York Times*, 25 May 1916). But it seems clear from the elitist content of the masque itself, its list of wealthy sponsors, and the comparatively privileged cast of its "ethnic" participants that the masque fell short of attaining the proportions of a genuinely democratic, much less populist, event.

I am, however, less interested in retrospectively criticizing MacKaye for being insufficiently multicultural than in highlighting the contradictions between the democratic claims advanced on behalf of the masque and the largely anti-democratic bias of its themes and organization. These contradictions are given revealing expression in an otherwise unobjectionable speech presented on behalf of the masque by Otto H. Kahn, the Chair of the Mayor's Honorary Committee for the New York Shakespeare Celebration, that was later published under the title *Art and the People* (1916) by the Shakespeare Tercentenary Celebration Committee. In his speech, Kahn asserts that:

> This Tercentenary Celebration…is not a "high-brow" affair, it is not a benevolent uplift movement backed by a few men and women of wealth. It stands upon a deep and popular base; it enlists and has significance for Avenue A no less than to Fifth Avenue; it has the enthusiastic support and active cooperation of two thousand different organizations directly representing 800,000 constituents. It is the most democratic, most comprehensive and most promising response which has ever been given in this community to the appeal of art.
>
> (Kahn 1916: 18)

To substantiate his claim, Kahn recounts making a motion at a meeting of the Celebration Committee committing all parties concerned to continued efforts on behalf of community drama: a motion that was moved by "a corporation lawyer and a stalwart Republican" and seconded by "a tribune of the people and a leading exponent of Socialistic doctrine" (Kahn 1916: 29). From the perspective of present-day U.S. political culture in which it has become anathema to claim publicly any kind of relation to "Socialistic doctrine," Kahn's depiction of this harmonic reconciling of mighty opposites around the occasion of Shakespeare seems positively refreshing. Yet, as in the earlier section of the speech where Kahn rhetorically bridges the practically unbridgeable distance between Avenue A and Fifth Avenue, the described communion of "stalwart Republican" and fervent Socialist has about it a strained and coercive quality, as if the motion and its seconding were choreographed to accomplish what mere rhetoric could not. Kahn's designation of this unnamed Socialist as "a tribune of the people" is even more suggestive, since, like the term's possible inspiration, *Coriolanus*, it positions both tribune and people in an emulative and secondary role in relation to the "motions" of the patrician class, while reminding anyone familiar with that play of its protagonist's relentlessly anti-democratic bias.

Apparent both in Kahn's and MacKaye's efforts to bridge the distance between Fifth Avenue and Avenue A, Republican and Socialist, economic aristocrat and indigent immigrant, is the desire to sustain the myth of America's democratic sufficiency and a corresponding anxiety about how that myth might be sustained given the distance America had traveled from colony to postcolony to burgeoning imperial power with more huddled masses on its doorstep than it knew how to accommodate. In each instance, Shakespeare is appropriated in the interests of an internal or domestic colonizing venture that seeks to enlist the consent and participation of the masses in their enforced acculturation. MacKaye's masque ostensibly stages an experiment or test in participatory democracy which its subject, Caliban, is doomed to fail, but which he is allowed to repeat so long as he is willing to accept the role of eternal subordinate and submit himself to the wise governance of Prospero. As the surrogate of New York's great unwashed, many of whom were regularly depicted in literature of the period as similarly self-destructive, impatient, impetuous, and undisciplined denizens of Setebos, Caliban is constructed as a figure who needs to make decisions for himself but always makes the wrong ones and, hence, needs to entrust himself to more highly evolved individuals who inhabit "that serener plane of pity and love, reason and disciplined will" which MacKaye describes in his Preface. Shakespeare is thus made the occasion to celebrate both the willingness and the necessity of the American masses to be led by larger-than-life individuals whose energy, power, wealth, and creativity can make all things possible, even the promised transformation of the cave of Setebos into "a temple to Miranda."

The projected triumph over Setebos that MacKaye transacts in his

Epilogue is revealingly staged in a space conspicuously free of history that freezes the principal actors of *The Tempest* in postures decidedly unlike those which characterized the contentious relations between the living referents of Prospero and Caliban in 1916 New York. By choosing to translate the contention between Prospero and Caliban to a space "above and *beyond* sordid actuality" (MacKaye 1927: 2:483), MacKaye avoids having to contend with the complications introduced by the tumultuous decades of social, political, and economic strife that filled the space between the 1894 Pullman Strike and the onset of the Great War, and by events that put particular pressure on the paternalistic settlement or reckoning imposed on Caliban in the masque's Epilogue.[13] Labor unrest, the rise of Socialism as a social and political force, the continued flocking to America of masses of unassimilated immigrants, and the often violent reactions against them sponsored by the lords of capital and nativist organizations like the Ku Klux Klan, are reductively displaced in *Caliban* to a Manichaean struggle between forces of darkness and light. And the "light" that MacKaye supplies is selectively drawn from the spaces of Shakespeare's art that are the least closely linked to matters of social and political concern, largely from the most unproblematic scenes of the "romantic" tragedies, "festive" comedies, and late romances.[14]

This selective separation of the light from the dark of Shakespeare is underwritten and enabled by MacKaye's appropriation of *The Tempest* as both a master and metanarrative of Shakespeare's art, as a play that most uniformly highlights the idealist perspectives that MacKaye attempts to put to work. From the magisterial, Prospero-like vantage point MacKaye commands as "Masque-Director," the patrician playwright displays an understanding of the Shakespeare canon that consigns the materiality of history to the domain of Setebos. Setebos, in turn, serves as a displaced representation of the rush of ambition and desire, of the noise and clamor of the war in Europe, of the daily war for space and sustenance of New York's immigrant neighborhoods, in short, as an extended embodiment of Jane Addams's "fleshpots": a false god to whom it is too easy for unevolved man to turn.

4.

In contrast to its demonization of Setebos, there is, in MacKaye's masque, a concomitant valorization of English Renaissance culture which, given its status as the setting in which the stone of Shakespeare's genius is set, is made to function both as a "peak experience" of Western civilization and as the originary source of America's own exceptionalism. This simultaneous demonization of the body of history and celebration of the idealized productions of "father" Shakespeare "suggests the extent to which MacKaye's work affirms both a politics of social control and the genteel evasions whereby such control masks its own force and effect" (Bloom 1992: 54). In this sense and others, *Caliban* may well be read as an ambitious effort to reassert America's status as a bastion of Anglo-Saxon culture at a moment in time when that status was being threatened both from within and without by events ranging from the Great War to what Henry James termed "the Hebrew conquest of New York" (James 1907: 132). This double threat to Anglo-Saxondom was countered in America by efforts to strengthen the historic bonds between Great Britain and America that were rooted in the "conviction that the British and American people were bolder, braver, truer, nobler, brighter, and certainly better than anyone else in the world" (Lord 1960: 7). This conviction is given graphic expression in Senator Albert Beveridge's turn-of-the-century pronouncement that:

> God has not been preparing the English speaking and Teutonic peoples for a thousand years for nothing but vain and idle self-contemplation. No! He has made us the master orga-nizers of the world to establish system where chaos reigned...He has made us adepts in government that we may administer government among savages and senile peoples.
>
> (quoted in Lord 1960: 8)

Beveridge's conscious echoing of the British imperial mandate helps bring into focus the social and political implications of MacKaye's staging of Prospero's unqualified right to maintain mastery over Caliban as well as his assigned status as the establisher of "system" over the chaotic realm of Setebos.[15] Insofar as it defers to the purported literary and cultural ideals of Shakespeare's England, and attempts to universalize British culture's evolving feudal, paternalist, and imperial bias, *Caliban* as both text and event may thus be relatedly construed as either an aggressively neo-colonial or regressively postcolonial phenomenon: one that in either event operates within the circuit of a colonial model of human relations and attempts to impose that model on a radically altered array of social and political conditions.

Although MacKaye invites the agents and products of these altered conditions to participate in his new "drama of democracy," his project casts them more as objectives than as collaborators in the performance he would have them help transact. And while he is careful in his Preface to identify his own imperfections with those of Caliban, who is said to represent "that passionate child-curious part of us all," by casting himself as masque-director and as privileged transmitter of an unproblematized Anglo-American cultural accord, MacKaye assumes a role that is more analogous to the one delegated to Prospero in his masque and to "English speaking and Teutonic peoples" in Senator Beveridge's pronouncement. Similarly, by attempting to turn the celebratory occasion of the masque into an exercise in community-building, and by making the education of a clearly differentiated Caliban the objective of the transformative claims of dramatic art, MacKaye endows his masque with many recognizable trappings of the Americanization movement that was moving into high gear in 1916 and to which MacKaye had himself contributed a "civic ritual" entitled *The New Citizenship* the previous year.[16] Indeed, by promoting throughout the masque the universal viability of Anglo-Saxon literary and cultural ideals, MacKaye stakes out a position in the increasingly contentious debate about the formation of an American national identity that he had disclaimed in his Preface to *The New Citizenship*.[17] As John Dewey argued in an address "delivered in 1916, in the context of the loyalty debates triggered by the war in Europe" (Sollors 1986: 88):

> No matter how loudly any one proclaims his Americanism if he assumes that any one racial strain, any one component culture, no matter how early settled it was in our territory, or how effective it has proven in its own land, is to furnish a pattern to which all other strains and cultures are to conform, he is a traitor to an American nationalism.
>
> (quoted in Sollors 1986: 88)

Set in the context of Dewey's assertion, even MacKaye's intention of "carrying [his masque's] community meaning to [New York's] still polyglot population" seems a symptomatically neo-colonial impulse at odds with the implicitly more multicultural model of American nationalism Dewey appears to promote. But what even better reveals the neo-colonialist bias in MacKaye's efforts at community-building is their similarity to what Werner Sollors calls the "most famous solution" to the problem of "the making of new Americans" which "was offered by the Ford Motor Company English School Melting Pot rituals of 1916."

In these rituals, "the baptismal blessings of the melting pot were conveyed to foreign-born employees who underwent a ritualistic rebirth especially designed for them by their employers" (Sollors 1986: 89). To supplement his discussion of these events, Sollors quotes from accounts of two of these exercises published in "the company-owned *Ford Times*" in April and November of 1916. The first of these ran under the heading, "A Motto Wrought into Education" (Sollors 1986: 89):

> Across the back of the stage was shown the hull and deck of an ocean steamship docked at Ellis Island. In the center of the stage and taking up about half of the entire area was an immense caldron across which was painted the sign "Ford English School Melting Pot." From the deck of the steamship the gangway led down into the "Melting Pot." First came the preliminaries of docking the ship and then suddenly a picturesque figure appeared at the top of the gangway. Dressed in a foreign costume and carrying his cherished possessions wrapped in a bundle suspended from a cane, he gazed about with a look of bewilderment and then slowly descended the ladder into the "Melting Pot," holding aloft a sign indicating the country from which he had come.
>   Another figure followed, and then another...From it they emerged dressed in American clothes, faces eager with the stimulus of the new opportunities and responsibilities opening out before them. Every man carried a small American flag in his hand.
>
> (*Ford Times* 1916: 409; Sollors 1986: 89–90)

It may well be objected that the Ford Company rituals were coercively designed to commemorate, and effect, the conversion of immigrants into uniformly flag-waving Americans, whereas MacKaye's masque has as its primary aim merely the demonstration of dramatic art's capacity to raise the sights of men and women to the apprehension of a "serener plane of pity and love, reason and disciplined will." But in his identification of that "serener plane" with a space "where Miranda and Prospero commune with Ariel and his Spirits" (MacKaye 1916: xv), and of Caliban as both "the protagonist of aspiring humanity" (MacKaye 1916: xvi) and embodiment of "the mob-yearnings of Demos after a soul" (MacKaye 1927: 2:483), MacKaye establishes a social typology that is easily translated into the framework of the Ford Company rituals. Like the "six instructors of the Ford school" who, "with long ladles, started stirring" the melting pot at the superintendent's urging in the more elaborate Ford outdoor rituals of November 1916, it is the purpose of MacKaye's masquers to dip the unregenerate souls of their immigrant auditors into the melting pot of Shakespeare to bring them closer to that "serener plane" of "reason and disciplined will" made available by the rituals of Shakespeare's England, which, throughout his masque, "furnish a pattern to which all other strains and cultures are to conform."

It is, then, less specifically Americanism into which MacKaye seeks to integrate his audience than it is the presumptive originary grounds of Americanism which he makes available not only in the many scenes from Shakespeare he dramatizes but also in the eight "successive episodes" that celebrate the communal rituals of "merry England" in the third, last, and longest of the masque's Interludes. English Renaissance culture is put on display in these sections of the masque as a civilizing medium whose effects on its audience are neither as immediate nor as definitive as those of Ford's melting pot which turns out men dressed in "neat suits" and "American in looks" as opposed "to the shabby rags they wore when they were unloaded from the ship" (Sollors 1986: 91). It will take MacKaye's Caliban and the mass of immigrants he represents considerably longer to accommodate themselves to the protocols of respectability and the obligations of citizenship. Indeed, as Jacob Riis contended in his books on the urban poor written around the turn of the century, it is the very childlike quality of the Negro—who "is at least as easily moulded for good as for evil" (Riis 1890: 155)—the Italian—who is "gay, light-hearted and, if his fur is not stroked the wrong way, inoffensive as a child" (Riis 1890: 53)—and the Jew—"I, for one, am a firm believer in this Jew, and in his boy. Ignorant they are, but with a thirst for knowledge that surmounts any barrier" (Riis 1902: 193)—that gives most promise of their capacity for growth and maturation, hence, of their susceptibility to the "imprint" of Prospero's "blurred seal."[18]

Some of the same paternalistic condescension to the "unformed" state of the laboring masses colors MacKaye's more candid comments on Caliban's relationship to Prospero in the pages of *Epoch* (1927), his encyclopedic encomium to his father:

> The only immortal hope of *Caliban* is his arch-enemy and saviour, *Prospero*. If groping Aspiration ask for vision, it must ask it of Genius. If there be any utility in the mob-yearnings of Demos after a soul, it will be in his "Great Discovery" of a faith in the Aristocrat potential in his own passional being— the austere *Artist* of democracy. And if there were ever an artist of our own potential democracy, tested in the austere fires of courage and validated by the vision of genius, this record has surely revealed him as the protagonist of its central theme: an ideal Theatre of democracy above and *beyond* our sordid actuality.
>
> (MacKaye 1927: 2:483)

Identifying the aspirations of Caliban with "the mob-yearnings of Demos after a soul," MacKaye patronizingly equates the ambitions of common people with the inchoate murmurings of a mob. According to MacKaye, the only thing that can qualify "Demos" for membership in "our own potential democracy" of the future is, paradoxically, faith "in the *Aristocrat* potential in his own passional being" (my emphasis) and in the achieved potential of such master-spirits as Prospero and Percy MacKaye's father, Steele MacKaye. Positioning the "ideal Theatre of democracy" both "above and *beyond*" the "sordid actuality" of the present, in a future in which we will all become aristocrats under the skin, MacKaye effectively models the future of the Republic itself on Caliban's surrender to the guiding hand of men like himself and his father who, as leading members of "a family which preaches democracy," made, in the words of Walter Lippman, "the best argument I ever saw for an aristocracy of birth" (MacKaye 1927: 2:470).[19]

The surprising slippage of democracy into aristocracy in both these formulations—the first developed by MacKaye himself, the second rehearsed with his approval—is significantly positioned in the Epilogue of his two-volume biography of his father which celebrates "the mystic pilgrimage of a genius 'prince' along the torrent of a biologic stream" (MacKaye 1927: 2:484) that pointedly spawns and embraces the accomplishments of the entire MacKaye clan. The slippage reveals even more clearly than the Epilogue to MacKaye's masque the extent to which a sense of aristocratic entitlement underwrites his claims about the transformative, civilizing function of art. Art and the artist are situated in a rarefied domain of austerity, courage, vision, and genius that bespeaks an aristocracy of the spirit and marks their clear-cut separation from the "sordid actuality" of Caliban and the "mob-yearnings" of the immigrant hordes. And it is within this same space of artistic and aristocratic transcendence, accessible only to those who swim the same "biologic stream," that MacKaye also situates Prospero and Shakespeare.[20]

5.

In *Highbrow/Lowbrow*, Lawrence Levine concludes his survey of Shakespeare's increasing separation from the world of popular culture with the observation that

> by the [end] of the [nineteenth] century Shakespeare had been converted from a popular playwright whose dramas were the property of those who flocked to see them, into a sacred

author who had to be protected from ignorant audiences and overbearing actors threatening the integrity of his creations.

(Levine 1988: 72)

More recently, James Bloom has contended that "MacKaye's mugwumpish defeat of Caliban, his denaturing and demeaning appropriation, clearly affirms prevailing hierarchies just as the masque's popularity establishes resoundingly who—still—owns Shakespeare" (Bloom 1992: 55). While there can be little doubt of the masque's affirmation of prevailing hierarchies, or of MacKaye's treatment of Shakespeare as a "sacred author" most reliably mediated by fellow initiates in the mysteries of art, forces were at work in U.S. culture during and after the period in question that would dispute the patrician claim to ownership of Shakespeare and that would soon consign MacKaye and his anachronistic masque to obscurity. In the pioneering work of New York's Yiddish theater—which by 1901 could already boast differently gendered appropriations of *King Lear* (the *Jewish King Lear* and *Jewish Queen Lear*, respectively), as well as a version of *The Merchant of Venice* in which Shylock spoke Yiddish while the other actors spoke English (see Howe 1976: 466–75)—of the drama clubs spawned by institutions like Hull House, of Orson Welles and his "voodoo" *Macbeth*, of Paul Robeson in his taboo-breaking "appropriation" of the role of Othello, it would become clear that it was finally less a question of *who* owned Shakespeare as *which* constructions of Shakespeare would be preferred by the different parties laying claim to him.[21]

By appropriating *The Tempest* to serve as the master narrative of his tercentenary masque, and by deploying Prospero as the unquestioned agent of Shakespeare's godlike approach to dramatic art, MacKaye was selectively attempting to privilege and promote a construction of Shakespeare that was consistent with the paternalist ideology of his own social caste. Though the claims he advanced on behalf of Shakespeare were universally oriented, his own aims were, in this respect, decidedly more parochial. That turn-of-the-century Jews should choose to translate *King Lear* and *The Merchant of Venice* into Yiddish and make the plays reflect Jewish preoccupations is, by comparison, as much a sign of Shakespeare's availability for other kinds of applications as it is a demonstration of shared ownership of property in the public domain. What the Yiddish theater could not do was to conduct the kind of high-profile commerce with Shakespeare that MacKaye's alliance with the lords of capital enabled. Yet, rather than establish any kind of patrician *ownership* of Shakespeare, MacKaye's mannered and overrefined appropriation of Shakespeare might better be said to have established the tenuousness of the hold over Shakespeare maintained by the increasingly embattled members of his particular "biologic stream."[22] Now that the "Hebrew conquest of New York" has been succeeded by that of African-Americans, Italian-Americans, Latinos, and Asian-Americans, an equally viable claim to ownership of Shakespeare has passed down to descendents of what was once unflatteringly called the Caliban-type. Indeed, in the New York Shakespeare Festival's recent production of its "New World" *Tempest*, a black-skinned Caliban's *refusal* to kneel and "seek for grace" at the play's end may well have marked a new development in a "backsliding" America's efforts to renegotiate a relationship with Shakespeare as democratic in practice as it has been in theory.[23]

Part II

PROSPERO'S BOOKS

4

PROSPERO IN AFRICA: *THE TEMPEST* AS COLONIALIST TEXT AND PRETEXT

> No part of the house was stamped more clearly with his individual taste than was his library.
>
> > (Lockhart and Woodhouse 1963 on Cecil Rhodes)

> *The Tempest* was created by Shakespeare to harm no one.
>
> > (Ruby Cohn 1976)

Most students of Shakespeare and the Cold War will understand what former U.S. Secretary of State George Shultz meant when he asserted, during the policy debate over Nicaragua in the 1980s, that America would not become "the Hamlet of nations," since most presumably share his assessment of Hamlet as a character who (with fatal consequences) cannot make up his mind. The image of ruined bodies draped across the stage at play's end and familiarity with the Reagan Administration's position on the fatal consequences of U.S. indecision in Vietnam combine to suggest that if decisive action is required to enforce yet another Cold War intervention, the United States is well prepared to play the role of late imperial Fortinbras. However objectionable one may find both the logic in question and Shultz's resolve, Shakespeare functions in such transactions as an unassailable source of wisdom and common sense, as a touchstone not only of what is right and just but also of what is necessary and practical. His name lends both wisdom and probity to the positions his appropriator wishes to advance.[1]

Although I will in the following chapters be concerned with a different array of repositionings of Shakespeare and the consequences of such practices, I want to use this occasion to consider the ideological ramifications of producing readings and misreadings of Shakespearean texts. I borrow my working definition of ideology from Louis

Althusser's well-known contention that "it is not their real conditions of existence, their real world, that men 'represent to themselves' in ideology, but above all it is their relation to those conditions of existence which is represented to them there" (Althusser 1971: 164). Viewed from such a perspective, Shultz's statement about *Hamlet* can be construed as an objectified representation of what he has brought to his understanding of the play: as the product of what he associates (or thinks Shakespeare associates) with its title character, viz., cowardice, indecisiveness, a general moral squeamishness. The political success of his reading depends upon its consonance with prevailing estimates of *Hamlet*, which, in turn, can be traced to the way in which the play has been taught or transmitted to its American readers and audiences. And it depends as well on the compatibility of this "common understanding" of Shakespeare with a carefully orchestrated insistence on the viability of U.S. interventions in the internal affairs of Third World countries. His reading is not, in short, exclusively identifiable with the text of *Hamlet* itself, much less with Shakespeare's own disputable intentions regarding his play. It is, instead, symptomatic of the ideological assumptions which produce it.[2]

Clearly, a Hamlet who is construed as chronically indecisive is very different from a Hamlet who, for good reasons, has decided not to do what his ghostly father urges him to do, and what, presumably, the less introspective Fortinbras would do were he in Hamlet's position. Approached from *this* direction, *Hamlet* may be said to involve an understandably alienated individual's attempt at self-determination in the face of a paternal imposition that presents revenge as a "natural" response to his dilemma and delay as an "unnatural" deviation from an obligation that has taken on the force of a moral imperative. This alternative Hamlet swims against an ideological tide that appears not to have changed greatly in the nearly 400 years since his play's making. Were this Hamlet the character authoritatively transmitted to a younger George Shultz and his far-flung interpretive community, it is at least imaginable that the former Secretary of State might have chosen to affirm America's ties to a Hamlet who chooses *not* to play the protagonist in a bloody vendetta, in the name of an America that chooses *not* to intervene in the internal affairs of another nation.

The scenario I have concocted clearly overstates the effect of art on those in high places. But it is not fanciful to contend that the reading and transmission of culturally privileged texts (and there are no texts in the West that are as privileged as Shakespeare's) play influential roles in the development of those imaginary representations of the world Althusser identifies as ideologies. This is not to suggest that texts like

Hamlet are themselves free of ideology and, hence, bear no responsibility for the uses to which they are put. Indeed, Hamlet protests far too much against his own indecisiveness for one to deny its dramatic, cultural, or political significance. In a similar vein, I shall argue in the following that *The Tempest* is a responsible party to its successive readings and rewritings insofar as it has made seminal contributions to the development of the colonialist ideology through which it is read.

1.

There are, of course, many who would quarrel with the idea that *The Tempest* speaks the predatory language of colonialism on behalf of the governing structures of Western power and ideals (see, e.g., McDonald 1991 and MacKaye 1916). But for members of the non-Western interpretive community, *The Tempest* has long served as an unmistakable embodiment of colonialist presumption. The development of "new literatures," both critical and creative, in the newly emergent nations of Africa and the West Indies has witnessed the repeated use of *The Tempest* as a site around which the age-old conflicts between colonizer and colonized continue to be played out and rehearsed. Sustained encounters with *The Tempest* are recorded in a host of imaginative and theoretical texts of the postwar decades of national emergence, beginning with Octave Mannoni's *Psychology of Colonization* (1950) and Frantz Fanon's *Black Skin, White Masks* (1952), and notably including George Lamming's *The Pleasures of Exile* (1960) and *Water with Berries* (1971), Aimé Césaire's *A Tempest* (1969), Roberto Fernández Retamar's *Caliban* (1971), and *A Grain of Wheat* (1968), among other works, by the Kenyan Ngũgĩ wa Thiong'o. In most of these works, contemporaneous British and American attempts to problematize the traditionally stereotyped critical estimate of the relationship of Prospero and Caliban are resisted in favor of recuperating the starkness of the master/slave configuration, thus making it appear to function as a foundational paradigm in the history of European colonialism. In this process, writers like Ngũgĩ, Lamming, and Césaire regenerate out of their own firsthand experience of colonization a conception of Shakespeare as a formative producer and purveyor of a paternalistic ideology that is basic to the material aims of Western imperialism.

In *A Grain of Wheat*, a novel that focuses on the negotiation of reprisals and reconciliations within a group of former Gikuyu freedom fighters and "loyalists" on the eve of Kenyan independence, Ngũgĩ has an idealistic and (in his own eyes) "well-meaning" British colonial functionary plan to write a book on his experiences in Kenya entitled

"Prospero in Africa" prior to becoming a brutally vindictive agent in Britain's suppression of the Mau Mau association in the "Emergency" of the early 1950s. The character's movement towards this resolve is worth following in detail:

> After the war he returned to his interrupted studies in Oxford. It was there…that he found himself interested in the development of the British Empire. At first this was a historian's interest without personal involvement. But, drifting into the poems of Rudyard Kipling, he experienced a swift flicker, a flame awakened. He saw himself as a man with destiny, a man poised for great things in the future. He studied the work and life of Lord Lugard. And then a casual meeting with two African students crystallized his longings into a concrete conviction. They talked literature, history, and the war; they were all enthusiastic about the British Mission in the World. The two Africans, they came from a family of Chiefs in what was then Gold Coast, showed a real grasp of history and literature. This filled Thompson with wonder and admiration… Here were two Africans who in dress, in speech and in intellectual power were no different from the British. Where was the irrationality, inconsistency and superstition so characteristic of the African and Oriental races? They had been replaced by the three principles basic to the Western mind: i.e. the principle of Reason, of Order and of Measure.
>
> (Ngũgĩ 1968: 47)

What may first strike a contemporary reader of this passage is the seemingly caricatured nature of Ngũgĩ's portrayal of John Thompson. Thompson's movement from professional detachment to "personal involvement" through the medium of Kipling seems anachronistic, as does his equally bookish adoption of a more practical estimate of the white man's burden as taught by Lugard, under whom the British first secured Nigeria. This reader's credulity may be stretched further when Thompson's refresher-course approach to British imperialism culminates in the "wonder and admiration" with which he responds to its success at transforming Africans into veritable Englishmen. Thompson's virtually classic adjustment of his initial view of Africans as different and therefore unequal to the more "enlightened" position that transforms equality into identity—hence denying Africans the integrity of an Otherness that balances the English claim to selfhood—reads like a textbook case of inverse racial stereotyping.[3] But Ngũgĩ opposes here what may be termed aesthetic realism with an historical realism that he deftly employs both to raise and resolve the charge of caricature. What the "informed" reader might consider a naiveté stretched beyond the bounds of belief proves to be strongly grounded in postwar British colonial policy and practice. Indeed, Thompson's attitudes are symptomatic of beliefs and positions that have characterized Western encounters with the "Other" throughout the course of colonial history.

Thompson's initial conception of Africans as both different and unequal expressly echoes Prospero's insistence on Caliban's incapacity to master civil behavior in *The Tempest*. It has a more immediate source in the stories of African intractability brought home by such Victorian explorers as Richard F. Burton, according to whom:

> [The East African] is inferior to the active-minded and objective, the analytic and perceptive European, and to the...subjective, the synthetic and reflective Asiatic. He partakes largely of the worst characteristics of the lower Oriental types—stagnation of mind, indolence of body, moral deficiency, superstition, and childish passion.
>
> (Burton 1876: 326)

As for more modern examples of a "Victorian" attitude toward racial difference, one need look no further than depictions of the Gikuyu produced in Britain *after* Kenyan independence. A representative example presents them as "excessively susceptible to superstition, witchcraft, animism, and magic" but so committed to believing themselves "inherently superior to every other kind of East African" that "they are prone to become infected with that type of mass neurosis which, masquerading as patriotism or nationalism, can temporarily drive a people mad" (Majdalany 1962: 29–30). In short, Thompson's naiveté is as much a culturally conditioned and historically reinforced habit of mind as is the two Africans' notion that to be civilized is to be British. That it seems so caricatured testifies to the absurd persistence of the colonialist stereotypes from which it derives. And there is more than a little irony in this being brought home to us by a latter-day descendent of "the Caliban type" who possesses a far better "grasp of history and literature" than John Thompson can claim. Ngũgĩ continues:

> Thompson was excited, conscious of walking on the precipice of a great discovery: what, precisely, was the nature of that heritage?...

"My heart was filled with joy," he wrote later. "In a flash I was convinced that the growth of the British Empire was the development of a great moral idea: it means, it must surely lead to the creation of one British nation, embracing people of all colours and creeds, based on the just proposition that all men were created equal..."

Transform the British Empire into one nation: didn't this explain so many things, why, for instance, so many Africans had offered themselves up to die in the war against Hitler?

From the first, as soon as he set his hands on a pen to write down his thoughts, the title of the manuscript floated before him. He would call it: PROSPERO IN AFRICA.

(Ngũgĩ 1968: 47–8)

As Ngũgĩ reconstructs Thompson's enthusiastic development of his "great moral idea" of fraternity and equality, he again appears to court the charge of caricature. In this instance, however, it is colonialist idealism, not racism, that is the object of his critical scrutiny. What makes Thompson's idealism censorious is that it is just as Eurocentric as his racism. While the latter is premised on a belief in African difference and inequality consistent with an assumed sense of European superiority, the former starts from an "improved" notion of African equality only to become "corrupted" by an assimilationist ethic that operates in concert with ethnic chauvinism (see Todorov 1984: 42–3, 146). Caricature thus again yields to an incisive statement of the truth behind colonialist apppearance, or, more correctly, of truth as the colonized Other perceives it, independent of whatever unresolved mix of intentions may preoccupy the colonizer.

Although it may be objected that Thompson's association of *The Tempest* with the "great moral idea" that is the British Empire is critically mistaken and historically inaccurate, what makes his apparent misappropriation of Shakespeare's text both possible and plausible is his identification of it with a series of other texts and events that it variously resembles, rehearses, and anticipates. In the complicated interplay of texts and observations that goes into the forging of Thompson's project, Britain's alleged success in the voluntary enlistment of Africans into military service recuperates Prospero's failed attempt to civilize Caliban (that is, to have Caliban *willingly* do his bidding) in the form of a moral idea. Success on this front promotes the possibility of a second chance for Prospero in Africa. It promotes as well a second chance for more recognizable literary proponents of the great moral idea Thompson mistakenly (or presciently?) associates with Prospero. For it is

Marlow and, to a greater extent, Kurtz from Conrad's *Heart of Darkness*—possibly the most influential colonial text in postcolonial African literary circles (see Hamner 1984; Brantlinger 1985)—who fill in the outline first sketched by Prospero's treatment of Caliban in *The Tempest*. However, Thompson never explicitly refers to Conrad, much less Kurtz who, if we allow literary history to supply chronology, had already tried and failed to apply his moral idea to Africa, and had revealed his own moral and cultural impoverishment in the process. Nor does he exhibit any awareness that the Africans who "had offered themselves up to die in the war against Hitler" had, in fact, like modern Calibans, been involuntarily conscripted. By means of such lapses in the logic of fact and fiction, Ngũgĩ challenges the informed Western reader to bring his or her "superior" grasp of history and literature to bear on the gaps in Thompson's argument, but complicates the challenge by revealing related gaps in the reader's own interpretive strategies, not to mention gaps in knowledge about Africa. We know, for example, that it is Kurtz, not Prospero, Conrad, not Shakespeare, who employs the language of missionary idealism that occupies so prominent a position in nineteenth-century colonialist discourse. Such knowledge compels us to "correct" Thompson's obvious misreading of Shakespeare by dissociating Prospero from his implied connection with Kurtz. But Ngũgĩ insists on the validity of the connection "we" attempt to resist. He opposes our intervention by again making strictly literary history blend with colonial fact, rehearsing both on the level of plot by having John Thompson re-enact Prospero's failure to make a willing slave of Caliban in the colonial present, and by linking that failure to Thompson's subsequently brutal treatment of intractable Africans in the manner of Kurtz.

A full appreciation of the intertextual complexity of *A Grain of Wheat* requires deeper probing of a novel that is, in the end, less interested in the misbegotten idealism of John Thompson than it is in the efforts of its Gikuyu protagonists to recover from the effects of punitive detention and personal betrayal.[4] But it should be sufficient to note that as a result of the Mau Mau rebellion, Thompson experiences a profound disillusionment with Africa and Africans. His disillusionment leads ultimately not to a book, but to an official investigation of his role in the deaths of eleven prisoners in the concentration camp over which he comes to preside. One of his notebook entries, made prior to his taking command of this camp, reveals the gradual emergence of the Kurtz latent from the start in Thompson's conception of Prospero:

Colonel Robson, a Senior District Officer in Rung'ei, Kiambu, was savagely murdered. I am replacing him at Rung'ei. One must use a stick. No government can tolerate anarchy, no civilization can be built on this violence and savagery. Mau Mau is evil; a movement which if not checked will mean complete destruction of all the values on which our civilization has thriven.

(Ngũgĩ 1968: 49)[5]

And a last echo of Kurtz before the eleven prisoners are killed should clarify Ngũgĩ's point of view: "Thompson was on the edge of madness. Eliminate the vermin, he would grind his teeth at night. He set the white officers and warders on the men. Yes—eliminate the vermin" (Ngũgĩ 1968: 117). It is clear from Ngũgĩ's close paraphrase of Kurtz's desperately scrawled message, "Exterminate all the brutes," that he may not be able to avoid the charge of caricature in this instance. But I am committed less to evaluating his style on this occasion than to determining the validity of his placement of Shakespeare at the center of this intertextual transaction. Can we simply say that Thompson's identification with Prospero is the product of misreading, and that his ultimate reproduction of Kurtz's rhetoric and violence is symptomatic of Ngũgĩ's ill-considered attempt to reveal the arbitrariness of colonialist distinctions? Or should we ask to what extent Kurtz can be considered a latent, potential, or actualized version of Prospero? Might Ngũgĩ be telling us something about the ideological function of *The Tempest* we did not know, something that could contribute to a fuller understanding of Prospero's contribution to the development of colonialist discourse and behavior?

As Ngũgĩ presents it, Thompson's identification with Prospero is motivated by an ideological single-mindedness that is not and cannot be careful about distinctions. Thompson's inability to discern a break or juncture between the "moral idea" he associates with "Prospero in Africa" and his actions in Rung'ei is meant to serve as a representative example of his culture's limitations. "Civilization" is the privileged commodity in each instance, and what stands in civilization's way is simply an obstacle to be surmounted or destroyed. It is in direct opposition to Thompson's designation of European civilization as "the centre of the universe and man's history" that Ngũgĩ's own ideological position takes shape: a position that reads into Prospero's dispossession of Caliban the entire history of the destruction of African cultures (Ngũgĩ 1983: 14, 7–11). That he advances, through Thompson, a reading of Shakespeare in which Prospero—the character who is critically identified with his playwright-creator more often than any other Shakespearean figure—is associated with Kurtz suggests an aggressive attempt to bring European assumptions of cultural superiority into unflattering contact with the history those assumptions have imposed on the culturally dispossessed. And, in choosing Shakespeare to represent those assumptions, Ngũgĩ takes strategic aim at the one aspect of colonialism that continues to resist unconditional censure, namely, its purportedly high-minded intentions. In this respect, it may be said that if Thompson and Ngũgĩ misread Shakespeare at all, they do so in consistency with the way colonial history has inscribed itself on colonizer and colonized alike.

One may attempt to free Shakespeare from these competing ideological appropriations by employing a developmental model to explain Thompson's implicit association of Prospero with Kurtz. From this perspective, it may appear that Thompson's initial identification with Prospero actually represents his identification with an early, idealist phase in Western imperialism, and that his subsequent embrace of Kurtz's "unsound methods" is representative of what becomes of such idealism in the course of colonial history. Working through this model would allow us to recuperate *The Tempest* as an historically "innocent" text that is corrupted by later historical developments. It would also allow us to construct an innocent moment in colonial history to which we could refer with the same nostalgia some historians continue to bring to bear on their representations of early European explorations of Africa and the New World (see, e.g., Hibbert 1984). But colonial history is no longer exclusively written by and for Western eyes in a manner that privileges the glory of discovery at the expense of the people discovered, or celebrates the advantages of progress at the expense of those who fail to advance.[6] Nor does Ngũgĩ present Thompson's development in evolutionary terms; Kurtz is latent in this would-be Prospero from the start. For Ngũgĩ, a Kurtz whose crimes are premised on an unquestioned claim to superiority is culturally and psychologically coextensive with a Prospero whose "high-minded" treatment of Caliban is premised on the same. And, by extension, a Prospero who can meditate "rarer actions" but actually executes rougher justice against his designated inferiors is coextensive with a Kurtz who would suppress savage customs in the name of his own definitions of what is human or humane.

What Prospero contributes to the possibilities of a Kurtz (or a Thompson, or a Rhodes or Stanley, for that matter) is a culturally privileged rationale for objectifying what are really always subjective representations of the Other, for presenting as facts what are really only fictions. Although no precise equation can be drawn between Kurtz's unsound methods and Thompson's murder of his prisoners, on the one hand, and Prospero's "stying" of Caliban "in this hard rock," on the other, each character's actions derive from and focus on a construction of the colonized Other as "A devil, a born devil, on whose nature/Nurture can never stick" (*The Tempest*, 4.1.188–9).[7] Roughly schematized, a psychological profile of the three characters reveals a movement from an ethnocentric idealism that founders on difference and defiance to an equally ethnocentric pragmatism that rationalizes violence as a suitable response to frustration. Each, moreover, rehearses a movement that may be considered characteristic of the European response to the colonial encounter. As Ngũgĩ writes elsewhere, "In the story of Prospero and Caliban, Shakespeare had dramatized the practice and psychology of colonization years before it became a global phenomenon" (Ngũgĩ 1983: 7–11).

2.

The Tempest, then, would appear to operate in concert with enduring colonialist assumptions from both Thompson's and Ngũgĩ's respective points of view. For character and author alike, *The Tempest* supplies a pedigreed precedent for a politics of imperial domination premised on the objectified intractability of the native element. It provides a pretext for a paternalistic approach to colonial administration that sanctions a variety of enlightened procedures, ranging from the soft word to the closed fist. The play's ability to fix the shared parameters of two otherwise opposed ideological positions should not, of course, obscure the extent to which *The Tempest* resists oversimplification and subordination to the ideological functions it has been made to serve. To clarify a point I have made above, in considering himself a Prospero in Africa, Thompson may be accurately reading his own colonialist condescension into a character but also *mis*reading Shakespeare's attitudes toward that character. The position which *The Tempest* occupied at its moment of production may not, for example, have been as decidedly colonialist as Thompson and Ngũgĩ consider it to be at its point of reception. Paul Brown, in his demonstration that *The Tempest* "is not simply a reflection of colonialist practices but an intervention in an ambivalent and even contradictory discourse" (Brown 1985: 48), provides a comprehensive re-examination of the play's position in its historic moment that is especially persuasive given the oft-noted lengths to which Shakespeare goes in endowing the play's colonized voices (both Ariel's and Caliban's) with an undeniable grace and authority. And Francis Barker and Peter

Hulme's equally cogent observation that "Prospero's play and *The Tempest* are not necessarily the same thing," and hence that Prospero is himself often the object of Shakespeare's critical scrutiny, would appear to offer a crucial corrective to those who "identify Prospero's voice as direct and reliable authorial statement" (Barker and Hulme 1985: 199).[8]

For his part, Ngũgĩ presents Thompson's identification with Prospero as a predictable choice, given the available possibilities in a colonialist canon within which *The Tempest* maintains a prominent position, along with other seminal texts like *Heart of Darkness*. Shakespeare's attitude toward Prospero is no more to his point than is Conrad's similarly complex attitude towards Kurtz. Given Ngũgĩ's political commitments, *The Tempest*'s historical distance from *Heart of Darkness* is insignificant, Prospero's difference from Kurtz negligible, insofar as each participates in a colonialist enterprise that has seldom been known to make distinctions between its colonized subjects.[9] Ngũgĩ thus creates a character whose apparent contradictions are presented as symptomatic traits of a colonialist temperament that habitually represents its own inhumanity in the form of virtuous activity.[10] Since contradiction is, for Ngũgĩ, the characteristic state of Prospero in Africa, he sees nothing contradictory in the ensemble of texts to which John Thompson alludes and from which he derives. With respect to the problem of Shakespeare's attitude toward Prospero, Ngũgĩ would no doubt endorse Tony Bennett's observation that "The position which a text occupies...at its originating moment of production is...no necessary indicator of the positions which it may subsequently come to occupy in different historical and political contexts"; and that it is "not a question of what texts mean but of what they might be *made* to mean politically" (Bennett 1982: 229). For Ngũgĩ, an historically or critically "correct" reading of *The Tempest* that isolates the play "at its originating moment of production" would serve merely an antiquarian's interest, documenting an alleged "intervention" in colonialist discourse that made no discernibly positive impact on the subsequent development of colonial practices. His own variety of historicity would, alternatively, focus on all that has intervened between the text's originating moment and the present moment of reception; it would thus focus less on the text's status as an historically determined literary artifact, now open to a variety of interpretations, than on its subordination to what history has made of it.

Since history, as he perceives it, has made *The Tempest* a celebrated early example of white paternalism exercising its prerogatives on and against its colonial subjects, Ngũgĩ employs Prospero as a figure who would "naturally" appeal to an idealistic Englishman seeking a high-minded rationale for his own and his nation's imperial designs in the repository of his cultural heritage. In so doing, he offers an implied commentary on a seldom-acknowledged contributor to history's productions, that is, a scholarly tradition which has long prided itself on its professed objectivity and disdain for ideologies and ideologues alike, but which is responsible for the dissemination of the ideologically charged reading of Shakespeare that makes Thompson's identification with Prospero inevitable. It is only reasonable to assume that Prospero's appeal would be felt most strongly by someone whose estimate of his dramatic status in *The Tempest* was uncomplicated by critical considerations of the kind we have reviewed above: considerations which are, for the most part, products of the past twenty years of Shakespeare criticism, during which time Shakespeare's assigned status as "national poet" and as spokesman for British political and social ideals has been in the process of radical revision. Were we to review slightly earlier examples of the critical literature on the play—not necessarily drawn from Britain's high imperial past—we would find that Prospero's dramatic status has, for the most part, been unclouded.

The admittedly extreme example of G. Wilson Knight's identification of Prospero with "Plato's philosopher-king" and of *The Tempest* as "a myth of the national soul" (Wilson Knight 1966: 254–5) cannot be considered entirely representative. But Knight's ability to celebrate within the same pages of a book originally published in the year of Indian independence by Oxford University Press (and reprinted at least six times thereafter) *The Tempest*'s "alignment with Shakespeare's massed statements elsewhere in definition of true sovereignty and...of British destiny" and, in respect to that destiny, British colonization—"especially [Britain's] will to raise savage peoples from superstition and blood-sacrifice, taboos and witchcraft and the attendant fears and slaveries, to a more enlightened existence"—strongly suggests the availability and staying power of such ideas. Were we to look further afield, into the domain of U.S. Shakespeare criticism, we would find equally conspicuous examples of the ways in which Prospero's dramatic burdens—vis-à-vis his usurping brother, Antonio; the "foul conspiracy" of Caliban and friends; etc.—have been traditionally privileged at the expense of the burdens actually carried in the play by Ariel, Caliban, and Ferdinand.[11] We observe here, as in the previous example, that an ethnocentric scholarly community has generally discerned in an ethnocentric Prospero the mirror image of its own self-involvement and obliviousness to the claims of an Other who does not really seem to inhabit the same dimension of existence as itself.

Academic scholarship is not, of course, the primary mediator between *The Tempest*'s moment of production and the modern moment of its reception. As should be obvious from the example of Wilson Knight, the ideological position of the scholarly community itself, with respect to works like *The Tempest*, has largely been shaped by its understandably one-sided acquaintance with colonial history. For many members of that community, colonial history has presented itself (as it did to the young Joseph Conrad) in the form of a succession of romantic exploration narratives that celebrate the courage and daring of adventurers in the wilds of Africa and the South Pacific, while only superficially portraying the lives of indigenous peoples (which are frequently presented with less scrupulous regard than the authors lavish on the local landscapes; see, e.g., Pratt 1985). That such a mode of transmission should eventuate in the racial chauvinism of a Thompson or the nationalism of Wilson Knight is not surprising. But it is one of the many ironies of colonial history that the reading of *The Tempest* I have attributed to Ngũgĩ also appears to draw heavily from the same literary and historical matrix that impels Thompson to effect the imaginative transfer of Prospero from Shakespeare's fictionally cross-referenced island to Africa.[12]

The Tempest's capacity to make a significant intervention in the formation of colonialist discourse and in the development of colonialist practices was inhibited from the start by the play's generic resemblances to, and rehearsals of, contemporary reports of colonial encounters.[13] Indeed, the play's very participation in this formative moment through the medium of Prospero's appropriation of Caliban's island, and his act's perceived consistency with the colonial ventures of a Raleigh and the partisan writings of the Hakluyts, may be said to have condemned the play to participate also in that discourse's evolution and eventual rigidification in the imperial moment of Britain's colonization of Africa. It is, of course, in the nature of colonial encounters that stereotypes are privileged at the expense of distinctions. Prospero's unqualified assertion that Caliban is a devil "on whose nature/Nurture can never stick" resonates more strongly in a mind bent on self-justification and an escape from uncertainty than does his ambiguous and, finally, puzzling acknowledgment of Caliban as his own. But this is also the case because the assertion finds so many echoes in the literature and history of colonization, and the acknowledgment so few that are problematic. In a similar vein, it will ultimately be the "unsound methods" of a Stanley that will prove more influential than the efforts of a milder-mannered Livingstone among practical colonialist considerations. An example of the kind of intervention such a figure could make in Ngũgĩ's reading of

Prospero into Africa is provided in the following excerpt from Stanley's exploration diaries:

> We tried to make a camp at Kiunyu...As we spoke they mocked us. When we asked them if they would sell some grain, they asked us if they were our slaves that they should till their land and sow grain for us. Meanwhile, canoes were launched and criers sent ahead to proclaim we were coming. The beach was crowded by infuriates and mockers. Perceiving that a camp was hopeless in this vicinity, we pulled off, but [quickly] perceived we were followed by several canoes in some of which we saw spears shaken at us. We halted and made ready, and as they approached still in this fashion I opened on them with the Winchester Repeating Rifle. Six shots and four deaths were sufficient to quiet the mocking...and to establish a different character for ourselves—somewhat more respectable, if not more desirable. We captured three canoes, some fish and nets etc. as spoil.
>
> (Stanley and Neame 1961: 125)

From its reminder that magic in *The Tempest* occupies "the space inhab-ited in colonial history by gunpowder" (Hulme 1981: 74), to the comparison it suggests between Stanley's "respectable" transformation of stolen goods into "spoils" and Prospero's self-righteous transforma-tion of Caliban's bid for freedom into a "foul conspiracy," there is much here that could negatively color any latter-day Caliban's reading of Prospero into Africa.[14] Yet Stanley can also evoke the idealist strain of colonialist discourse, and does so in a disturbingly apposite manner in concluding the preceding anecdote:

> I had an opportunity also to prove that although able to resent affronts and meet hostility we were not inhuman nor revengeful, for a wounded man struggling to escape from dread decapitation—the common fate of the wounded in battle—cried out for mercy and the rifle was lowered and he was permitted to go.
>
> (Stanley and Neame 1961: 125–6)

In its own context, Stanley's choice of the "rarer action" is clearly six shots too late for those who have just been taught a different lesson; it is a largely gratuitous gesture that hardly offers proof of the humanity he claims to anyone apart from himself and his companions. But, placed within the broader framework of colonial history, Stanley's lesson of mercy exemplifies that curious convergence of a mind convinced of the virtuousness of its intentions with a will focused on demonstrating its mastery through force, which characterizes the colonialist temperament from Prospero on down to John Thompson. This convergence of assumed high-mindedness with brutality is exactly what dissolves the differences between Prospero and Stanley from the perspective of the colonized Other, whose claim to self-determination ("they asked us if they were our slaves") is summarily denied in each instance and made the basis for his exclusion from humane consideration. In *The Tempest*, what appears to disturb Prospero even more than Caliban's foiled attempt to violate Miranda's honor is Caliban's insistence on recalling his former sovereignty, his repeated effort to lay claim to a history and inheritance which imply a state of equality at odds with his assigned status as slave. It is in the face of Caliban's assertion that "I am all the subjects that you have,/Which first was my own King" (and not to any denial of his attempt to rape Miranda) that Prospero responds, "Thou most lying slave,/Whom stripes may move, not kindness" (1.2.343–4, 346–7). And, similarly, in Stanley's anecdote it is more the mockery of the African "infuriates" than their show of hostility that incites him to a show of the same.

It will, perhaps, be objected that, in comparison to Stanley's methods, Prospero's punishment of Caliban is negligible in intensity and consequence, and eventuates in a pardon that is prelude to Caliban's liberation. But, in terms of *The Tempest*'s status as a privileged text in the history of colonialist discourse, it is difficult to recuperate this apparent exercise in enlightened paternalism as an historically insignificant action. Because Prospero's brutality—like Stanley's—operates out of an assumption of high-mindedness that differentiates itself from the brutality of an Other who does not make the same assumption or cannot claim the same relationship to "civil behavior," it will remain privileged in the eyes of actor and civil beholder alike.[15] Caliban's unregenerate response to Prospero's accusation regarding his attemped rape of Miranda—"O ho, O ho! would't had been done" (1.2.351)—and Stanley's unqualified remark about the "common fate" of "dread decapitation" both serve to disqualify the Other from the consideration he would otherwise be granted were he to subscribe to Western standards of civil behavior. They both confirm the Other's ineradicable difference from "us" and sanction the measures taken to assure his containment (recall Wilson Knight's remarks about blood-sacrifice). We should, moreover, notice that an ultimately chastened Caliban's acceptance of the pardon that succeeds punishment—"I'll be wise hereafter,/And seek for grace" (5.1.294–5)—actually serves to validate Prospero's procedures from the victim's perspective, thus making the duly conditioned slave a willing accomplice in a system of domination that has come to seem natural.[16] Wisdom, for Caliban, has now become synonymous with complete acquiescence to Prospero's initial claim to cultural superiority (cf. Cohen 1985: 400). In this respect, Shakespeare's staged fantasy establishes the parameters of a colonialist procedure Stanley will rehearse with a rougher magic in Africa; and it produces exactly that effect on the Other Stanley aims at in his lesson.[17]

3.

I do not suggest here that Stanley needed *The Tempest* as a pretext either for his brutality or for the lesson in moral superiority that succeeds it, anymore than I suggest in my epigraph that Cecil Rhodes's attachment to his library was modeled on Prospero's attachment to his books. My point is that the well-advertised colonialist methods of men like Stanley and Rhodes—to the extent that they resemble and rehearse the actions and rhetoric of Prospero—have the effect of valorizing what they resemble and rehearse, and of dissolving distinction into identification. And these effects will be felt more strongly in those readings of *The Tempest* that are motivated and informed by the culturally divisive history of colonization than in those that maintain a critical distance from ideological polarization. As the West Indian George Lamming writes:

> I cannot read *The Tempest* without recalling the adventure of those voyages reported by Hakluyt; and when I remember the voyages and the particular period in African history, I see *The Tempest* against the background of England's experiment in colonisation...*The Tempest* was also prophetic of a political future which is our present. Moreover, the circumstances of my life, both as a colonial and exiled descendant of Caliban in the twentieth century, is an example of that prophecy.
>
> (Lamming 1984: 13)

In a more incisive vein, Derek Walcott has a character in his play, *Pantomime*, demonstrate that the specific form colonialism takes in different places makes no real difference from the perspective of the colonized Other. Prospero is always master, Caliban is always slave:

For three hundred years I served you. Three hundred years I served you breakfast...in my white jacket on a white veranda, boss, bwana, effendi, bacra, sahib...in that sun that never set on your empire I was your shadow, I did what you did, boss, bwana, effendi, bacra, sahib...that was my pantomime.

(Walcott 1980: 112)

What plays no role in Ngũgĩ's depiction of Thompson—and emerges only at the end of Walcott's play as a result of his Caliban's overpowering insistence—is the possibility of Prospero's acknowledgment of responsibility for making a "thing of darkness" out of someone who never really was his own in the first place.[18] This is, of course, no more than a possibility in the text of *The Tempest* itself, one that has, moreover, occasioned all manner of critical dispute regarding its precise implications.[19] On this account, we would do well to recall that the work *The Tempest* does in service to the competing ideologies of colonizer and colonized has, finally, as little to do with ambiguity as it does with whatever intervention in the formation of colonialist discourse Shakespeare may have attempted to contribute. It is also worth recalling that similarly promising examples of Shakespeare's possible departures from the colonialist rule are seldom acknowledged as such by contemporary postcolonial scholars and writers who have, in different circumstances, been willing to accept dissenting colonial voices as welcome disturbances in a characteristically one-sided conversation.[20] As Aimé Césaire observes of Prospero:

To me Prospero is the complete totalitarian. I am always surprised when others consider him the wise man who "forgives." What is most obvious, even in Shakespeare's version, is the man's absolute will to power. Prospero is the man of cold reason, the man of methodical conquest—in other words, a portrait of the "enlightened" European.

(quoted in Baxandall 1972: 172)

In attempting to extricate Shakespeare from the politically divisive functions he has been made to serve, we should not, then, be blind to the possibility that the apparent marginality of Shakespeare's interventions may also be predicated on their actual marginality in Shakespeare's text, where departures from the colonialist rule—"You taught me language, and my profit on't/Is, I know how to curse" (1.2.365–6)—always lead back to the same colonialist destination: "I'll be wise hereafter."

It is no doubt true that *The Tempest* has long functioned in the service of ideologies that repress what they cannot accommodate and exploit what they can. One consequence of this subordination of text to ideological transaction is that it is still a generally uneducable, bestial Caliban who survives the adjustments that have been made in Western racial prejudices; mainly a blindly self-righteous, authoritarian Prospero who presides in Third World inversions of the same.[21] Yet the text of *The Tempest* continues to allow Prospero the privilege of the grand closing gesture; continues to privilege that gesture's ambiguity at the expense of Caliban's dispossession; continues, in short, to support and substantiate the very reading of itself transacted by the ideologies in question. It is in this respect, among others, that *The Tempest* is not only complicit in the history of its successive misreadings, but responsible in some measure for the development of the ways in which it is read.

5

AFTER *THE TEMPEST*:
SHAKESPEARE,
POSTCOLONIALITY, AND
MICHELLE CLIFF'S NEW,
NEW WORLD MIRANDA

1.

The Merchant-Ivory film *Shakespeare Wallah* (1965) records the demise of an aging, out-of-date troupe of primarily English Shakespearean actors in post-independence India. Written by Ruth Prawer Jhabvala, herself a citizen of two worlds, the film functions both as an affectionate elegy for a time when the troupe played for "the most wonderful audiences in the world" and as testimony to the failure of British culture to sustain its hold on the increasingly decolonized imaginations of those audiences. In a particularly telling moment, the leader of the company, named Mr. Buckingham no less, ventures a piece of clever small talk with the headmaster of a school that is no longer interested in commissioning performances. When the headmaster refers to a recent speech given by India's Minister of Mining and Fuel, Buckingham archly adds, "full of misquotations from Shakespeare no doubt," only to be corrected, "No, from our ancient Sanskrit authors."

The moment is a small one in the film, but it is symptomatic of a transitional stage in some postcolonial cultures when an enforced identification with the colonizing power becomes displaced by the espousal of indigenous cultural icons that underwrite emerging nationalist aspirations. In the film, Shakespeare still functions as a source of prestige and proverbial wisdom for the nabob who quotes self-dramatizing passages from his plays, but the plays themselves no longer serve as a dependable, or commercially viable, item of cross-cultural exchange. The Shakespeare wallah can no longer market plays whose ideological supports have been pulled out from under him; first, by the withdrawal of British political control over India, and, second, by the erosion of cultural authority which that withdrawal has encouraged. Like the British Raj whose power and authority it has been made to serve, Shakespearean drama seems a worn, outdated thing, incapable of rising to the occasion of a newly independent India, intent on divorcing itself from England's overextended hold on its past.[1]

Shakespeare Wallah's approach to this transitional stage of postcoloniality is a good deal more conclusive than that of most literary works produced in the wake of the empire's dissolution, both in India and elsewhere in the Third World. Instead of dismissing Shakespeare as a residual irrelevance of the colonial period, many of these works employ Shakespeare as a politically charged site around which the counter-discursive work of independence needs to be conducted. The practice of postcolonial writers to "write back" to the center has by now been exhaustively documented, especially with respect to *The Tempest* whose appropriators made a common practice of responding to, and repositioning, the Prospero–Caliban configuration during the first stage of Third World postcoloniality, a period Anthony Appiah associates with nationalistic African novels of the 1950s and 1960s (like *A Grain of Wheat*) but that also embraces other examples of postcolonial writing (Appiah 1991: 348–9).[2] A secondary industry, rooted in the institutionalization of Commonwealth studies in the 1970s and 1980s, has derived from such works critical paradigms that it liberally applies to other texts that either repeat the appropriative gesture or make only passing reference to Shakespeare or *The Tempest*. The names Prospero, Caliban, Ariel, and Miranda now operate as interpretive touchstones for critics who search out their permutations in writing as far afield as the poetry of Ireland's Seamus Heaney and the novels of the Canadian Margaret Atwood, the Australian David Malouf, and the South African, Nadine Gordimer.[3] In the process, Caliban has become the aggressively defiant muse of both West Indian espousers of a militant "nation language" and French-language writers of Québec; the paternalistically silenced Miranda has become the oft-cited surrogate of Canadian writers still responsive to Britain's imperial influence; and Ariel has been reconstituted as the name of an influential journal of postcolonial writing.

However questionable the critical practice of applying *Tempest* paradigms to postcolonial literature may be, writing back to the center has clearly been constructive for some postcolonial writers. As Chantal Zabus writes:

> The adaptation and re-interpretation of the earlier Old World literature of colonization, i.e., *The Tempest*, as literature of

decolonisation is, at its worst, sheer parasitism but, at its best, superior in effectiveness to an anti-colonial polemic. As an articulate literary riposte, it constitutes one of the most cogent strategies of decolonisation in literature.

(Zabus 1985: 49)[4]

Produced at comparatively early moments in the evolving European imperial enterprise, works like *The Tempest* render the relationship of colonizer and colonized in fixed, oppositional terms which remain influential long after the interpretive gulfs between cultures have narrowed. Caught up in a situation in which a polarizing discourse operates at an evolutionary remove from prevailing political conditions, but maintains its affective and institutional hold on both sides of the colonial encounter, the contemporary postcolonial writer often must fight his or her first battle at the level of discourse, and consequently must attempt to appropriate, alter, or redirect the master- or seed-texts in which the writer has already been inscribed.

This is a particularly formidable task when the writer operates within the language, style, and favored formats of the receding colonial power, and proceeds as if he or she—Caliban-like—had no prior language at all in which a markedly different literature could be written. One means of coping with this dilemma has been to reject the European language, if not the format, in which what has heretofore counted as literature has been inscribed.[5] Left with only residual contact with a precolonial language they might claim as their own, some West Indian writers have espoused writing in the dialect or "nation language" of their officially English-speaking homelands.[6] Even as committed an English-language writer as Salman Rushdie—whose earlier work parodically refers to Kipling, Forster, and Edward Fitzgerald, among others—has lately deferred to his non-Western religious and cultural background in choosing to employ the Koran as the primary seed-text of *The Satanic Verses* (1988). In this context of cultivated difference and indifference we may imagine Shakespeare being replaced by stories, myths, and other literary practices that have both an older pedigree and exist in a more strategic relationship to contemporary social and political imperatives.

Although Shakespeare and other influential canonical figures of the English literary tradition have clearly lost much of their relevance to the present generation of Third World postcolonial writers—whose immediate predecessors regularly mined the pages of Yeats, Eliot, Conrad, and Forster for titles, epigraphs, and general grist for their counter-discursive mills—they have not been entirely superseded.[7] Nor can they avoid being addressed, contested, or otherwise remarked as long as writers and their critics continue to speak of, or out of, a state of mind or being defined by the condition of postcoloniality.[8] As the Jamaican writer, John Hearne, notes in a review of Jean Rhys's *Wide Sargasso Sea*, a classic example of a novel that "depends on a *book* from elsewhere, not on a basic, assumed life":

> is this not a superb and audacious metaphor of so much of West Indian life? Are we not still, in so many of our responses, creatures of books and inventions fashioned by others who used us as mere producers, as figments of their imagination; and who regarded the territory as a ground over which the inadmissible or forgotten forces of the psyche could run free for a while before being written off or suppressed?
>
> (Hearne 1990: 188, quoted in Slemon 1987: 10)

Hearne's remark implies, that for West Indians at least, there is no significant distinction between lived experience and textuality. In their efforts to represent West Indian experience, West Indian writers inevitably reinscribe themselves in the textual constructions of colonialism.[9] Access to precolonial habits of mind and feeling, stories, and beliefs is either mediated or blocked by a history that has been thoroughly colonized and that leaves in its wake only a residue of African words and rituals that survived the Middle Passage. And since expressive access to a clearly demarcated *post*-colonial experience is, as Stephen Slemon writes, "overshadowed by a discourse of Empire,…a measure of determinism continues to mark the literary productions" (Slemon 1987: 13) of writers otherwise committed to the work of decolonization.

Houston Baker contends that an analogous determinism marks the efforts of revisionist critics engaged, like the writers themselves, in what Baker terms a "hermeneutics of overthrow." As Baker writes, these critics "attempt—by bringing to bear all the canny presentational dynamics of the [established, First World] overseers—to prove that 'A' is *as good as* 'B' and to induce shame in defenders of 'B' who have made other axiological choices." Employing the specific example of Gayatri Spivak's (1986) contention (in a discussion of *Jane Eyre* and *Wide Sargasso Sea*) that "the suppressed 'native' woman [Bertha] is as important as…Jane Eyre," Baker concludes that "as long as [Spivak] preserves the middle ground of 'as good as,' the primary text of 'B' (*Jane Eyre*) will be timelessly taken up" (Baker 1986: 388). By re-enacting on the level of criticism what writers like Rhys and Césaire allegedly enact in fiction, Spivak and other well-intentioned revisionists relegitimate master-narratives that were presumably in the process of being subverted or demystified. And, as Lemuel Johnson observes, "readings which (merely) re-invent sub/versions of master plots can only work out a dangerously 'true', because indeed quite circular hermeneutic" (Johnson 1990: 118).

Although each of these arguments is persuasive, I don't finally think that they can, or should, be applied indiscriminately to all postcolonial literatures, to all forms of contemporary West Indian writing, or, for that matter, to revisionist criticism of the same. Like Arun Mukherjee, I find particularly troubling: "The collapsing of separate histories [of postcolonial cultures] in the name of a 'shared...post-colonial experience'" (Mukherjee 1990: 5). Mukherjee specifically takes issue with the "binary framework" of prevailing postcolonial theory which rather imperially reduces all postcolonial experience to a center vs. margin paradigm. As Mukherjee observes:

> the theory insists that the subjectivity of the post-colonial cultures is inextricably tied to their erstwhile occupiers...It claims that "the empire writes back to the centre"...implying that we do not write out of our own needs but rather out of our obsession with an absent other.
>
> (Mukherjee 1990: 6)

Mukherjee possibly sounds naive in insisting on the freedom of her own subjectivity in the context of Hearne's and Slemon's certainties. I would, however, submit that the points she makes are not only applicable to much contemporary Indian writing (particularly to works written in the indigenous languages of the subcontinent), but also to other examples of "second-stage" postcolonial writing that self-consciously attempt to construct alternatives to political and cultural dependency by resisting the authority of colonialist paradigms, by appropriating for their own purposes the traces of colonialist discourse, and by establishing the authority of their own discursive constructions.

Such writing has, to a certain extent, been relieved of the liability of mimicry by the efforts of transitional figures like Rhys, Césaire, Lamming and others whose reworking of colonialist texts has superimposed new meanings and applications on those texts and whose own work has often superseded them, contributing to the establishment of a postcolonial literary canon that operates as an alternative to the established canon of English-language literature, not as its disposable supplement or appendage. Having laid the counter-discursive groundwork for a second generation's more sweeping "space-clearing gestures"

(Appiah's term), and having been seconded in their efforts by critics like Spivak, "first-stage" postcolonial writers have set into motion a process of decentering that often makes avowedly central texts like *The Tempest*, *Heart of Darkness*, and *Robinson Crusoe* seem marginal, or merely historically prior, in the context of their successive rewritings. Although Baker is probably correct in noting that these procedures produce the unintended effect that such texts will be "timelessly taken up," they also indicate that works like *The Tempest* will seldom any longer be taken up in isolation from what postcolonial writers and critics have made of them in their efforts at appropriation and transformation.[10]

2.

No Telephone to Heaven (1989), a novel by the Jamaican-American writer, Michelle Cliff, represents perhaps the most ambitious recent attempt by a contemporary West Indian to work through and master the impulse to write back to the center. Rather than choose to ignore the circumstances of interdependency and belatedness that condition West Indian textuality, Cliff turns them to the advantage of an emergent creolized sensibility, counter-colonizing the established plots of a still dominant, but imaginatively exhausted, imperial master narrative. Cliff's novel speaks in many voices—literary English, colloquial "American," Jamaican patois—and positions them in a manner that requires its "centered" Western readers to assemble a mental glossary of names and definitions that the printed glossary at the back of the book only partially satisfies.[11] By speaking casually and knowingly of familiar Jamaican places, people, and events, Cliff challenges the Western reader's confidence in his or her ability to map West Indian experience, placing that reader in the position of a disoriented tourist reliant on a guidebook that speaks too inwardly and elliptically to be easily apprehended, much less mastered. Cliff's novel is also one of the few postcolonial works to claim an epigraphical authority for other postcolonial writers and for the traces of precolonial cultures. Her chapter headings are studded with quotations from fellow West Indians like Derek Walcott and Aimé Césaire, from Yoruba hymns, and Jamaican proverbs. And her text often alludes to the work of Jean Rhys, C.L.R. James, and the black British dub poet, Linton Kwesi Johnson, among others.

Canonical Western writing, however, maintains a hold on the novel from beginning to end, most obviously in its protagonist's pivotal encounter with Jane Eyre. Cliff's protagonist, Clare Savage, encounters Jane at a moment of weakness when the temptation to merge her subjectivity with Jane's is strong. Alone in London where she "passes" as white in a deeply polarized society, Clare finds that "The fiction had tricked her. Drawn her in so that she became Jane" (Cliff 1989: 116). This at least is her first response. Her second response is more complex:

> Comforted for a time, she came to. Then, with a sharpness, reprimanded herself. No, she told herself. No, she could not be Jane. Small and pale. English...No, my girl, try Bertha. Wild-maned Bertha...Yes, Bertha was closer the mark. Captive. Ragout. Mixture. Confused. Jamaican. Caliban. Carib. Cannibal. Cimarron. All Bertha. All Clare.
>
> (Cliff 1989: 116)

What Clare "comes to" here is a more densely textualized and histori-cized identification with Jane Eyre's West Indian Other. Clare's identification with Bertha is clearly negotiated by Cliff's own reading of Jean Rhys's *Wide Sargasso Sea*, a book that both encourages and enables the West Indian reader to appropriate as central what is arguably marginal to the novel *Jane Eyre*. But it is also negotiated, at least within the confines of the novel itself, by Clare's readiness to accept what has been rendered marginal by others as central to her own experience. What Cliff seems to be after, both here and elsewhere in her novel, is to have Clare act out, in the life of her fiction, what Rhys has previously enacted on the level of textuality. Cliff effectively attempts to take charge of the process that has made West Indians "creatures of books and inventions fashioned by others" by demonstrating how a newly emergent postcolonial textuality may help to engender new subject positions for West Indians to inhabit.[12]

Much the same effort appears to motivate Clare's associative identifi-cation with Caliban. This is the first and only time that the novel makes the characteristic postcolonial move of explicitly identifying Caliban with past and present inhabitants of the West Indies. But it provides a key that opens up the novel's less explicit, but more sustained, appropri-ation and rewriting of *The Tempest*. Cliff herself has elsewhere remarked that Caliban's famous response to Prospero—"You taught me language, and my profit on't/Is, I know how to curse"—"immediately brings to my mind the character of Bertha Rochester, wild and raving ragout, as Charlotte Brontë describes her, cursing and railing, more beast than human" (Cliff 1990: 264). Both Bertha and Caliban are, according to Cliff, "washed in the notion that life before discovery in the forest, Middle Passage, civilization, represents only brutishness and therefore he or she must forget, deny, be silent about that part" (Cliff 1990: 264). By extension, Cliff claims that it has been:

> part of my purpose as a writer of Afro-Caribbean (Indian, African, and white) experience and heritage and Western experience and education (indoctrination)...to reject speech-lessness by inventing my own peculiar speech, one that attempts to draw together everything I am and have been, both Caliban and Ariel and a liberated and synthesized version of each.
>
> (Cliff 1990: 264)[13]

In a later version of this essay, Cliff suggestively drops the closing phrase, "a liberated and synthesized version of each," replacing it with "At times, Miranda too" (Cliff 1991: 67). In so doing, she indicates that although her investment in Caliban and Ariel makes its presence felt in the course of her novel, it is Miranda—like Cliff herself, "the colonized child...who is chosen...to represent the colonizer's world, peddle the colonizer's values, ideas, notions of what is real, alien, other, normal, supreme. To apotheosize his success as civilizer" (Cliff 1991: 67)—who plays a more prominent role in underwriting Clare Savage's subjective development and evolution into an agent of social and political change.

Unlike the majority of those of her silent or silenced postcolonial sisters who have been identified as socially or politically updated versions of *The Tempest*'s Miranda, Clare Savage is presented as the self-determining agent of her own education who, in the end, refuses to use the advantages of pale skin and privileged class-standing either to "pass" or to deny the Caliban within. Abandoned by her defiantly Jamaican mother, raised in exile in New York by her Americanized father (who is perhaps too coyly named Boy Savage and functions, both here and in Cliff's earlier novel, *Abeng* [1984], as a deeply flawed Prospero figure), tutored in Renaissance studies at a university in London, this New World Miranda rejects father and London alike in order to return to Jamaica, where she attempts to redeem her grand-mother's homestead and, with it, a sense of "basic, assumed life."[14] In the process of her transit between New York, Europe, and Jamaica, she has casual sex with Paul H., a spoiled prince of the Jamaican economic aristocracy; enters into a consciously restorative relationship with a physically and psychically maimed Caliban, a black American veteran of Vietnam who has had his childhood dreams of "catching shrimp with [his] mother...gathering okra, and dodging the snakes" (Cliff

1989: 158) permanently invaded by nightmares of dismemberment; and allies herself in "sisterhood" with an androgynous Ariel who doubles as a Jamaican nationalist. Her New World consciousness raised by a chance discovery of the grave of Pocahontas in England, Clare/Miranda eventually turns her inherited land over to the cause of nationalist rebels and dies with them, victim of an airborne tempest conjured up by the new, New World magic of American money.[15]

As formulaic as my synopsis makes it sound, the novel seamlessly incorporates and, more to the point, extends the New World typologies of earlier rewritings of *The Tempest*. It does so most distinctly with respect to Clare's sexually and politically collaborative contact with its American Caliban and Jamaican Ariel figures; rejection of her father and the Euro-American structures of respectability to which he would have her aspire; and decisive return to her native land. The novel also extends its *Tempest* applications to an early scene of mass murder perpetrated by Christopher, a native-born Caliban, against the family of Paul H.—which rather degradingly fulfills the potential of Caliban's foiled attempt to despoil Prospero and Miranda in *The Tempest*—and a description by Harry/Harriet, the androgyne Ariel, of his sodomy-rape at the hands of a white colonial policeman. Deformed by a malnourished childhood lived in the heart of the "dungle," Kingston's slum of cardboard shacks, Christopher is presented without glamor or approval (though with considerable sympathetic understanding) as the denatured product of independent Jamaica's reproduction of colonial inequity. Like *Jane Eyre's* Bertha, Christopher roars and bellows, haunted, Caliban-like, by "duppies," and seeks to bury his demons in the bellies and genitals of people with lighter skin who live in houses where he is set to work.[16]

A homosexual who can "pass" as man or woman, Harry/Harriet initially frames his boyhood violation in the broader context of the colonialist violation of Jamaica. But, as the novel's most insistent advocate of social and political change, he notably resists clothing himself in a language of colonial signifiers that has kept Jamaica in unacknowledged bondage to the past. As he states:

> ...we *are* of the past here. So much of the past that we punish people by flogging them with cat-o'-nine-tails. We expect people to live on cornmeal and dried fish, which was the diet of the slaves. We name hotels Plantation Inn and Sans Souci...A peculiar past. For we have taken the master's past as our own. That is the danger.
>
> (Cliff 1989: 127)

Cliff arguably courts the same danger in allowing her narrative to be overrun by a promiscuous intertextuality that threatens to re-establish her writing's dependence on the master narrative of colonialism. But, like Harry/Harriet, Cliff also resists the impulse to represent Jamaican experience in a strictly deterministic manner. She does so, in this instance, through her character's insistence on both the singularity and collectivity of his personal history:

> I have been tempted in my life to think *symbol*—that what he did to me is but a symbol for what they did to all of us, always bearing in mind that some of us, many of us, also do it to each other. But that's not right. I only suffered what my mother suffered—no more, no less. Not symbol, not allegory, not something in a story or a dialogue by Plato. No, man, I am merely a person who felt the overgrown cock of a big whiteman pierce the asshole of a lickle Black bwai—there it is. That is all there is to it.
>
> (Cliff 1989: 129–30)

The claim for singularity is made in the brutally specific words Cliff chooses to isolate the act suffered by her character from a more rhetorically (and politically) expansive interpretation. The claim for collectivity is made in Harry/Harriet's association of the material circumstances of his rape with his mother's sufferance of economic violations that Jamaica's postcolonial status has done nothing to diminish. Of course, the phallic language and Jamaican diminutives—"lickle Black bwai"—also enhance our sense of the uncontestable power of the "big whiteman" who continues to tower, literally and symbolically, over the narrative, and both sponsors and stages the destructive conflagration with which the novel—and the fictional lives of its *Tempest* surrogates—ends.[17]

Each of these sequences indicates the restrictive hold that the neo-colonial present maintains over what may be ventured even on the level of postcolonial narrative. In this respect, among others, Cliff's attempt to master the impulse to write back to the center should, perhaps, only be considered a qualified success. But, in extending the range and resonance of her appropriations of *The Tempest* into the province of contemporary social history, especially with respect to such concerns as underclass deracination, dissident sexualities, and feminist self-assertion, Cliff's rewritings of the roles of Caliban, Ariel, and Miranda move beyond the meanings of both Shakespeare's *Tempest* and the often predictable, and arguably circular, rewritings and inversions of Fernández Retamar, Lamming, and Césaire.

One of the obvious ironies of the contemporary postcolonial fascination with *The Tempest* has been its acceptance of the play's limited cast of characters as representative of enduring colonial(ist) configurations, as if Shakespeare had immutably fixed the only available attitudes of master, servant, and rebel at a comparatively early and ill-defined moment in the imperial enterprise. Even in the act of critique and appropriation, writers like Fernández Retamar and Césaire accept positional stereotypes whose only real claim to legitimacy is their continued circulation. By having his Caliban persona greet Prospero with the salutation, "Uhuru," and refuse the name Caliban in favor of the sobriquet "X," Césaire conflates the language and ethos of African nationalisms and U.S. black militancy of the 1960s at the expense of developing a more culturally specific response to the "condition" that is Caliban in the contemporaneous West Indies (see Lamming 1984: 111). In this respect and others, Césaire is more successful at evoking a pan-Africanist perspective on the colonial phenomenon broadly considered than he is at evoking an endemically West Indian, much less Martinican, point of view. And, while Fernández Retamar makes a seemingly uncontestable case by proclaiming on behalf of Latin America, "what is our history, what is our culture, if not the history and culture of Caliban?" (1989: 14), he does so at the expense of proposing as "our symbol" what he, himself, classifies as an "alien elaboration" (Fernández Retamar 1989: 16).

There are, of course, moments in each writer's work that move beyond the host plot of *The Tempest*, that introduce variations on, and complications of, the originary configurations. The dialogue between Ariel and Caliban in 2.1 of Césaire's *A Tempest*, for example, stages at least the possibility of a future alliance between opportunistic and defiant participants in the colonialist configuration: one that is literally "colored" by later stages of political development and, hence, may be said to historicize the relationship of differently unequal parties to colonialist exploitation. This scene, however, remains locked in a parasitic relationship to Shakespeare's play, which itself can claim only the most formulaic application to the widely variegated nature of colonial and postcolonial experience in the Caribbean.

A considerably more resonant intervention is effected by E.K. Brathwaite in his essay, "Caliban, Ariel, and Unprospero in the Conflict of Creolization" (1977). Brathwaite pointedly appropriates *The Tempest*'s cast of characters in order to enrich his account of a process of *"negative or regressive creolization"* particular to a slave revolt in Jamaica 1831–32, but that continues to underwrite black insurgency in the Caribbean down to the present day.[18] While Brathwaite's historicized Caliban figure, Samuel Sharpe, "repeats" the movement back to something like an originary African identity rehearsed by Césaire's Caliban, he does so in the context of a more richly detailed social and historical setting: one in which the planter-figure associated with Prospero is so incidental to "a growing crisis of identity and orientation" among the slaves themselves, "the unresolution of which was causing tension and conflict—as it still does today," as to be rendered "*Un*prospero" (Brathwaite 1977: 47). This "slave Ariel/Caliban crisis" alludes to the debate/dialogue Césaire stages in his *Tempest* and correspondingly devolves upon the assumption of Africanist positions by those situated in the "condition" of Caliban. But, as reproduced by Brathwaite, it supersedes both what is made imaginable in Shakespeare and reimagined in Césaire by discounting "the omnipotence of Prospero's magic" and by giving voice, power, and presence to a series of heretofore anonymous actors on the stage of West Indian history (Brathwaite 1977: 46).

By way of extension, what is needed to break the spell of *The Tempest* on contemporary West Indian writing that chooses to confront it is a narrative that disenchants *The Tempest*'s monopoly on the available forms of postcolonial identity by reconfiguring and superseding the fixed subject positions established both by the play itself and its appropriators. The fact that *The Tempest* operates less as a plot than as a residual presence in *No Telephone to Heaven* allows both new plots and new subject positions to emerge in the novel. Cliff is particularly successful at moving her work a stage beyond that of her West Indian predecessors, whose "subject," as George Lamming writes, was "the migration of the West Indian writer, as colonial and exile, from his native kingdom, once inhabited by Caliban, to the tempestuous island of Prospero and his language" (Lamming 1984: 13).

3.

For Lamming, the absence of an "extraordinary departure which explodes all of Prospero's premises" implicitly cedes possession of "Caliban and his future" to Prospero (Lamming 1984: 109). Although no revolutionary change is imminent even in her novel's construction of history, Cliff's decision to have her potentially mobile protagonists reject migration and exile in an effort to regenerate a sense of "basic, assumed life" in Jamaica leaves them largely unsubjugated both to Prospero's symbolic authority and to the need to contest that authority which is usually associated with Caliban. In effecting the release of her characters and the language she constructs for them from "the prison of Prospero's gift" (Lamming 1984: 109), Cliff engages in exactly the kind of "revisionist metaphoric activity" Gay Wilenz considers necessary to heal the "isolating and subjugating" rupture "in the correlation of language and accepted reality" that Hearne describes and that characterizes Caliban's dispossession (Wilenz 1992: 266).[19]

Nor is this the only "extraordinary departure" from "Prospero's premises" recorded in the novel. The patriarchal authority exercised by Prospero both in Shakespeare and Césaire yields, in *No Telephone to Heaven*, to the attempt by the children of postcoloniality to negotiate an authority of their own, grounded in the recovery of what has survived the sustained tempest of colonialism and colonial self-hatred. The parables of escape, denial, and determinacy that the novel's native-born Prosperos tell these children are countered not only by the predictable rage of a servant-monster who inscribes his frustration on the bodies of his neo-colonial masters, but by Clare's mother-centered recovery of her cultural and racial identity, and by Harry/Harriet's rejection of the authority of symbols in the process of his regendering. Indeed, what most distinguishes the novel from both its colonial and postcolonial forebears is its wholesale rejection and denial of the very notion of patriarchal authority embodied either in Prospero or in a successfully mated and politically redeemed Caliban figure.

In this novel, patriarchal power and authority effectively operate only in a violently displaced, corporate manner as an army bought and paid for by an American film company ultimately has its way with Clare and her confederates, summarily erasing the latest attempted intervention in Jamaica's ongoing (neo-)colonization. In the end, the magical power of American money even has its way with language—as articulate speech dissolves under the joint onslaught of artillery and animal sounds—but not before an alternative history of rebellion and resistance has been reconstructed and re-evoked in the fictional present by characters who have either been exiled from, or have exiled, their fathers.

The weakness, recessiveness, or dispersion of paternal authority into corporate engines of power in *No Telephone to Heaven* is countered by the strength, persistence, and clearly defined commitments of the novel's female characters, most notably Clare and her mother. Yet neither of these women qualifies, or consents, to play the role that constitutes, in Sylvia Wynter's terms, "the most significant absence of all" in Shakespeare's play, namely, that of "Caliban's Woman" (Wynter 1990: 360). Wynter conspicuously rejects the possibility of a West Indian appropriation of Miranda as one of its own, identifying her solely in terms of her relationship to Prospero, with whom she forms a racially based and morally valorized "population-group" (Wynter 1990: 361–3). According to Wynter, Miranda serves as:

> both a co-participant, if to a lesser *derived* extent, in the power and privileges generated by the empirical supremacy of her own population; and as well, the beneficiary of a mode of privilege unique to her, that of being the metaphysically invested and "idealized" object of desire of all classes (Stephano and Trinculo) and all population-groups (Caliban).
>
> (Wynter 1990: 363)

As such, Miranda shuts off the possibility of Caliban's mate appearing "as an alternative sexual-erotic model of desire; as an alternative source of an alternative system of meanings" (Wynter 1990: 360).

Wynter's intervention in what could be called the demography of *Tempest* appropriations would appear to require a critical re-examination of my reading of Miranda into and out of *No Telephone to Heaven*, in addition to indicating why *The Tempest*'s Miranda cannot, without substantial transformation of the play itself, sustain the interpretive effort to mate her with Caliban. In *The Tempest*, of course, Miranda is already (happily) bethrothed to Ferdinand—her "brave new world" has only people like him in it—and operates within the same cultural field that frames Peter Greenaway's unrelievedly Eurocentric construction of the play in his film, *Prospero's Books* (1991).[20] In order to divorce Miranda from Ferdinand and satisfactorily re-mate her with Caliban, one would have to dispense with *The Tempest* entirely or, as in the case of Césaire's *A Tempest*, enlist a vigorously revised version of the play in the cause of a racialized West Indian nationalism. To satisfy Wynter's objections, a revised *Tempest* might also require the continued consignment of Miranda to a subordinate position in a postcolonial power complex dominated by Caliban and an ethic of male sexual possessiveness signaled by the phrase "Caliban's Woman."

Cliff, however, is committed to a reconfiguring of both power and gender relations in the social economy of her novel. She also appears to recognize, as Laura Donaldson has argued, that "Miranda—the Anglo-European other—offers us a feminine trope of colonialism, for her textual and psychological selflessness in *The Tempest* exposes the particular oppression of women under the rule of their biological and cultural Father" (Donaldson 1988: 68). Cliff is, moreover, also committed to a process of "negative or regressive creolization" in the culturally and racially mixed construction of her Miranda figure, analogous to that described by Brathwaite in his essay.[21] As if in answer to

Wynter's objections, Cliff has her Miranda consciously reject her capacity to "pass" as the "metaphysically invested and 'idealized' object of desire of all classes" in favor of serving "as an alternative source of an alternative system of meanings." Cliff specifically has Clare reject her role as a co-participant in a Prospero/Miranda racial complex by having her choose to "become" black in the wake of her father's earlier choice to "become" white. Clare's consciously crafted divorce from her father is effected so that she might establish a similarly deliberative (if clearly belated) relationship with another figure who is conspicuously absent in Shakespeare's *Tempest*, namely, Miranda's mother, Prospero's wife.[22] And, although Cliff in her own words, as in the words she delegates to Clare, rhetorically affiliates herself with Caliban, she also adds a significantly feminist twist to the transaction by reconfiguring a *Tempest* in which Miranda chooses not to mate at all.[23]

In his 1987 essay on appropriations of *The Tempest*, Rob Nixon describes the alleged fading out of "*The Tempest*'s value for African and Caribbean intellectuals" in the 1970s and attributes it to the play's lack of a sixth act, "which might have been enlisted for representing relations among Caliban, Ariel, and Prospero once they entered a postcolonial era" (1987: 576). He adds that "The play's declining pertinence to contemporary Africa and the Caribbean has been exacerbated by the difficulty of wresting from it any role for female defiance or leadership in a period when protest is coming increasingly from that quarter" (Nixon 1987: 577). But it is precisely the awakened defiance of the dramatically silenced Miranda that Cliff wrests from *The Tempest* at an even later moment in the "play's declining pertinence" to postcolonial writers. Instead of writing a sixth act for a postcolonial *Tempest* that will, once and for all, separate the boys from the men, she writes a thoroughly womanized novel in which the new, New World Miranda effectively replaces both Prospero *and* Caliban as an agent of defiance, self-determination, and cultural change. In the process, Cliff may be said to have inadvertently engendered a second life for *The Tempest* at a stage of postcoloniality when, as *Shakespeare Wallah* suggests, "every third thought" is Prospero's grave.

Part III

THE OTHELLO COMPLEX

6

ENSLAVING THE MOOR: *OTHELLO, OROONOKO,* AND THE RECUPERATION OF INTRACTABILITY

1.

The Nigerian writer Ben Okri begins the first installment of his two-part "Meditations on Othello" by registering the reaction of surrounding playgoers when, as "practically the only black person in the audience" at an RSC production of *Othello,* he had the temerity to tell a group of giggling white girls to be quiet: "Faces turned, eyes lit up in recognition. My skin glowed. I felt myself illuminated, unable to hide" (Okri 1987: 562). He begins his second installment by observing that "Two centuries of Othello committing murder and suicide on the stage has produced no significant change in attitude towards black people" (1987: 618). Although Okri does not identify the specific "change in attitude" he has in mind, his first installment makes plain that it is the long-standing regime of white racism that *Othello* has done nothing to alter and that *Othello* is, in fact, "a negative myth for black people in the West" (1987: 564).

The socially divisive references to *Othello* generated by more recent events like the O.J. Simpson trial indicate that *Othello* has not only failed to unsettle or dislodge established racial stereotypes, but has played a formative role in shaping them into what may well be termed the "Othello complex."[1] Understood in the starkest terms, this complex functions as an "anthropologized" racial construction in which the "assimiliated savage" predictably "relapses into primitivism under stress" (Neill 1989: 393). From within the terms of this construction, Othello's murder and suicide conform to a horizon of expectation whites maintain about blacks that underwrites Okri's "doubt that Othello as a play really disturbs as many people as it should" (Okri 1987: 618). The prevailing "complacency" of white responses to the play that

Okri notes, and that the play's reception history confirms, testifies to the staying power of this complex or construction. By way of contrast, the "black person's response to Othello" is, according to Okri, considerably "more secret, and much more anguished, than can be imagined" (1987: 618).

This racial divide of complacency and anguish generated by *Othello* seems, at least among the ranks of scholars, to have recently arrived at a point of re-examination and renegotiation. As the proliferating number of contemporary critical responses to it indicates, *Othello* is well on the way to replacing *The Tempest* as a favored field of debate and contention both for scholars and critics of Shakespeare, and for the increasingly numerous workers in the field of postcolonial studies.[2] This is the case for many reasons, not least because, as Third World cultures emerge from the shadow of colonialism, as self-styled Calibans and Mirandas begin to counter-colonize the plots laid by the receding figure of Prospero, and as "First World" societies find themselves compelled to address the inequities of internal colonization and the imperatives of multiculturalism, race—and the difference it makes—seems to matter more than ever.

Unlike Caliban, locked into his island kingdom where he must sink or swim, Othello has functioned from his moment of production as the exotic outsider, licensed, from the early modern period to the present, to move freely about the metropolitan "First World" and to interact, on a privileged basis, with its movers and shakers. Yet, whereas Caliban and Miranda, even Prospero for that matter, are now free to develop sixth and seventh acts for themselves, to construct alternative endings—and beginnings—for the postcolonies in which they are locked, Othello still moves in worlds not of his own making, and not, assuredly, made for him, a striking, but decidedly "minority" presence in a sea of white. For Othello, the fifth act is always the last act. Even if he survives the jury's verdict, he remains condemned, constructed, to fail the test—and text—of civility.

Iago is the name Shakespeare gives to the agent of his protagonist's demise, despiser of the marriage of races, the wedding of difference. And Shakespeare has, from that vexed moment of production to the present, assured that it is always Iago, not we, who wills and sponsors the Moor's fall, who constructs the test/text Othello is always fated to fail. Horn-mad and resentful, Iago is himself (so we are led to feel) more margin than center, exception than rule, however central he may be to the play's designs as the "true" contriver of the villainies Shakespeare puts into play. Yet when Othello enters Desdemona's chamber he enters alone. Alone, he makes a ghost of her, and, islanded in bondage to his transgression, makes a second ghost of himself. Who thinks of Iago when Othello snuffs out her life?

Iago is the agent, the medium, of a transaction that takes place beyond him, that is framed by a paradigm, a complex, it is his function to catalyze, but not to invent. Othello's fate is figured forth in the need (call it cultural) for his exceptionality to be rendered moot, for his privileged centrality to be decentered, pushed back to the margins presumably delegated to Iago, but, in fact, reserved for outsiders who dare to think they can live inside the Big House or tent (see Boose 1994: 38–40). It is Shakespeare's play—not merely Iago's—that stages this transaction, that invents or shapes the complex or paradigm the Moor will inhabit and fulfill.[3] *Othello* stages a fantasy of inclusion, a glamorous bridging of differences, only to restate, in the starkest manner, the terms of exclusion it seems initially to discredit. The play is, in this sense, complicit with Iago in systematically deconstructing the fantasy of interracial and intercultural concord it stages.[4]

For some, Aphra Behn's novel *Oroonoko* would appear to operate in exactly the manner we would like to think *Othello* operates; that is, outside and against the parameters of Iago's racist constructions.[5] Behn's narrator, for example (hereafter designated "Behn" as she, herself, would have it), speaks warmly and admiringly of the "royal slave" she has, in many respects, modeled on the figure of Othello. She positions herself in opposition to, and vilifies, the vulgar and mercenary colonists of Surinam who torture, castrate, and incinerate Oroonoko. But, as I aim to demonstrate in this chapter, Behn's text—which purports to be a recounting of actual events but does little to legitimate that claim—effectively reproduces the degradation of the exoticized protagonist modeled by *Othello*.[6] In so doing, it also recuperates the already-established conception of the intractable savage, sketched out in *The Tempest* but subsequently filled in by succeeding English accounts of encounters with native Americans and Africans and fixed in Samuel Purchas's formulaic anatomy of the leopard that cannot change its spots. Though uniformly identified as an early example of anti-slavery advocacy, *Oroonoko* ultimately dissolves the suspect distinction between the "royal slave" and the ordinary race of enslaved Africans it is initially at pains to cultivate.[7] By the end of the novel, as Oroonoko impassively smokes an Indian tobacco pipe in the face of his progressive dismemberment, yet another distinction Behn cultivates—namely, that between the enslaved Africans and the initially idealized but increasingly more restive Surinam Indians—is elided. As these distinctions collapse, the "royalty" or nobility of Oroonoko is glimpsed only in terms of the courage and patience with which he responds to the brutality of his tormentors. Yet even Oroonoko's courage is coded by markers—the Indian pipe, for example, that is adjunct to his impassivity—that transpose it into an item of ethnographic curiosity. Oroonoko's silence and stolidness objectify him in ways that call out for explication, but are given none beyond the likeness they suggest with the similar inscrutability of the Surinam Indians. The man who initially was made of nothing but soul and spirit is, in the end, recast as lumpish, inanimate, and inarticulate, and "speaks" to the Surinam plantations only in the form of his quartered flesh. He has, in short, been Calibanized, though, given his long fall from royalty to abjection and the claims Behn advances on behalf of his nobility, it would be more accurate to say "Othelloed."

The motive or cue for Oroonoko's passion can be traced back to the long movement in *Othello* that begins with Othello's seduction by Iago and concludes with his ritualized murder of Desdemona and oddly subdued murder of the "turban'd Turk" in himself. As commentators on the play have often noted, we first meet or encounter Othello by indirect representation. His reputation, both as celebrity general and as "black ram" or "thick lips," literally precedes him onstage. And when he does speak he commands our hearing through additional forms of mediation, standing outside himself, as it were, to make the case for himself to an onstage auditory from which we are also physically separated. Indeed, throughout the play, Othello seldom speaks *to* us: he is either "inward" with Iago or inward with himself, yet never really in a way that gives us direct access to his subjectivity.[8] Like Oroonoko, he presents himself to us, or, more accurately, is presented to us as a phenomenon whose eventfulness it is our task to witness and monitor, but seldom really to engage on any inward or familiar basis. As both a represented and self-described exotic, Othello is set at an affective and epistemological distance from his audience that becomes increasingly more remote the more he "lapses" into subject positions that extant discourses of the savage or uncivil or African Other have rendered curious and arresting, but never as reliable indexes of shared assumptions about humanity.

"Haply, for I am black" (3.3.269) is the pivot around which succeeding manifestations of difference and uncontrol are assembled: the superstitious assessment of the weaving of the handkerchief; the enormous passions of insecurity and sexual possessiveness set off by the smallest hint of infidelity; the precipitous descent into an intellectually and emotionally servile relationship with Iago who leads him by the nose; the convulsive seizure, foaming at the mouth, lapses into syntactically disorganized speech; the striking of Desdemona, an action that "would not be believed at Venice"; and, finally, the ritualized murder and similarly ritualized, but self-degrading, suicide. All these, I would submit, are clearly products of Iago's indisputable manipulative genius. But they are just as surely symptoms or markers of an enveloping racial construction that will become even more deeply inscribed in Aphra Behn's delineation of Oroonoko.[9]

2.

Some eighty years stretch between Shakespeare's composition of *Othello* and Behn's *Oroonoko*, a span of time bridged most prominently by the English Civil War and its aftermath, events that play no small role in Behn's construction of her oxymoronic "royal" slave. An even more crucial determinant of Behn's composition, however, is England's burgeoning participation in the slave trade and development of its over-seas empire during this same period. It is this story or history—abetted by England's decision to cede its colony of Surinam to the Dutch—that informs and sponsors Behn's transformation of Shakespeare's self-styled man "of royal siege" into a "royal slave."[10]

Historically speaking, the figure of the exotic/exceptional royal slave occupies the space of romantic or sentimental fantasy at the end of the century filled by the exotic/exceptional mercenary general at its begin-ning. Although John Gillies has recently proclaimed the precipitous "demise of the Elizabethan moor" on the seventeenth-century stage, grounding his conclusion on the "contempt" Thomas Rymer expressed in 1693 "for the heroine who allows herself to be talked into marrying a 'Blackamoor' and for the playwright who expects his audience to sympathise" (Gillies 1994: 33), the Moor continued to figure promi-nently on the Restoration stage, most notably in *Abdelezar, or the Moor's Revenge*, Behn's 1677 adaptation of Dekker's *Lust's Dominion* (1600), as well as in the many contemporary productions of *Othello*.[11] Gillies correctly observes that:

> The gap between [Rymer's and] Coleridge's [conception of Othello as a] "veritable Negro" and Shakespeare's moor is partly explained by the institutionalisation of plantation slavery in the New World in the course of the seventeenth century, a phenomenon which (as Winthrop Jordan has argued) required a sharp distinction between "Negroes" and other types of "savage" (such as the Amerindian), and a hierarchisation of difference defining the "Negro" as the lowest of the low.
>
> (Gillies 1994: 33)

But Gillies makes these statements in the course of insisting on "the discontinuity between the Elizabethan and Restoration constructions of the 'exotic'" (1994: 33); a thesis that leads him astray in several ways that are significant to the argument I am attempting to develop. While differences of many kinds obtain between Elizabethan and post-Elizabethan ideas of the African Other, Gillies's emphasis on discontinuity prevents him from remarking the many signs and symptoms of *continuity* that Behn puts to work in *Oroonoko* and that had already been put to work in the development of plantation slavery throughout the period in question.[12]

Shakespeare no doubt mines rich veins of classical and contemporary reference to generate "the promiscuous or 'pandemic' quality of Othello's exoticism, the way in which his Africanness is constantly being telescoped into other notorious forms of exoticism: Turkish, Egyptian and Indian" (Gillies 1994: 32). But to imply that Shakespeare's representation of Othello is not racially specific would be to ignore the primary distinguishing trait in Othello's imaginative construction. As Winthrop Jordan observes of Iago's overt racist baiting of Brabantio:

> This was not merely the language of (as we say) a "dirty" mind: it was the integrated imagery of blackness and whiteness, of Africa, of the sexuality of beasts and the bestiality of sex...The drama would have seemed odd indeed if [Shakespeare's] audiences had felt no response to this cross-inversion and to the deeply turbulent meaning of black *over* white.
>
> (Jordan 1968: 38)

Jordan highlights here the way Othello's *blackness*, his *Africanness*, overarches "the promiscuous or 'pandemic' quality of [his] exoticism" and directs the play into a racially specific channel of reference that more narrowly subsumes "other notorious forms of exoticism." It is into this same channel that Behn directs her later tale of "a gallant *Moor*" who was no Moor at all, nor complected as "tawny" as Gillies oddly chooses to claim (1994: 33), "but of perfect Ebony, or polish'd Jett" (Behn 1973: 8).[13] Behn effects this translation with as full a sense of the "barbarous," the "transgressive," and the "marvellous" (cf. Gillies 1994: 30) that informs Shakespeare's conception of Othello, however much she may ultimately ground it on her avowed firsthand experience of England's overseas colonies and slave plantations.

We move, at the start of *Oroonoko*, to a site as geographically specific and as culturally cross-referenced as Shakespeare's Venice but which, as Behn represents it, bears a generally uneven resemblance to the site "at

Coromantine in the Gold Coast" where the African Company built "the first permanent English post in Africa…in 1631" (Craton 1974: 56). In developing her Coromantine setting, Behn fills a geographic space Shakespeare left vacant in *Othello*, one that is only evoked in Iago's remark to Roderigo about Othello's plan to go "into Mauritania" with Desdemona. Yet, true to her commitment to novelty, the space Behn fills is an eclectic amalgam of cultural, ethnic, and racial fantasies and influences. Oroonoko's name, for instance, is modeled on the name of the South American river; that of his female consort, Imoinda, also resonates more surely with the opposite shore of the Atlantic than it does with her alleged site of origin.[14] By contrast, the culture of Coromantien, especially its court, is more evocative of North, than West, Africa and is correspondingly Orientalized. Oroonoko's grandfather, for example, enjoys the pleasures of unlimited polygamy and keeps a large, luxurious seraglio for his entertainment. Oroonoko's own pursuits as warrior, slave-maker, and slave-trader readily mark him as a West African, whereas physically and culturally he looks and speaks like a "European aristocrat in blackface" (Laura Brown 1987: 48; see Ferguson 1993: 26 and Newman 1987: 154).

That Behn was modeling her cross-referenced portrayal of Oroonoko on Shakespeare's superficially Europeanized Moor is clear from her earliest remarks about his character where Behn takes her cue from Othello's account of himself and of the stories he used to tell Desdemona:

> Rude am I in my speech,
> And little bless'd with the soft phrase of peace;
> For since these arms of mine had seven years' pith,
> Till now some nine moons wasted, they have us'd
> Their dearest action in the tented field;
> And little of this great world can I speak
> More than pertains to feats of broil and battle.
>
> (1.3.83–9)

Of Oroonoko, Behn writes that:

> as soon as he could bear a Bow in his Hand, and a Quiver at his Back, [he] was sent into the field to be train'd up by one of the oldest Generals to War; where, from his natural inclination to Arms, and the Occasions given him,…he became at the Age of seventeen, one of the most expert Captains, and bravest Soldiers that ever saw the field of *Mars*.
>
> (Behn 1973: 6)

And just as Othello insists that he can speak "little of this great world.../More than pertains to feats of broil and battle" while holding the floor of the Venetian Senate in thrall to his eloquence, so too will Behn claim that prior to encountering Imoinda he "never knew Love, nor was us'd to the Conversation of Women" (10) and note with wonder:

> where 'twas [Oroonoko] got that real Greatness of Soul, those refined Notions of true Honour,...and that Softness that was capable of the highest Passions of Love and Gallantry, whose Objects were almost continually fighting Men, or those mangled or dead, who heard no Sounds but those of War and Groans.
>
> (Behn 1973: 7)

Conceding that "Some part of it we may attribute to the care of a *Frenchman* of Wit and learning" (7), Behn acknowledges that "this young Black" is not quite the African prodigy she otherwise implies he is. Indeed, given his linguistic facility, his dedication to "Wit" and honor, his "Greatness of Soul," his admiration and emulation of European culture, it may well be said that all Europe has gone into the making of Oroonoko. And that I think is the point. Although rooted more deeply than Othello is in a specific African setting, and rooted as well (despite his European interests and training) in the cultural and religious norms and beliefs Behn delegates to that setting, Oroonoko, like Othello, is meant to represent the best of his kind, the furthest possible development of the Europeanized (hence, civil) African. And, as is the case with Othello, Oroonoko's failure to sustain this development, however much this failure may owe to the actions of corrupt Europeans, tends to exemplify the intractability of even the most promising Africans, and thus to justify their continued subjugation and containment.

The agency Shakespeare exclusively delegates to Iago in precipitating his Moor's decline is much more broadly distributed in *Oroonoko*, and embraces the formerly friendly English captain who transports him to Surinam; Byam, the lieutenant governor of the English colony who treacherously misuses him; and Banister, the "wild *Irish* Man" who barbarously dismembers him. Oroonoko is so repeatedly made to play the part of the noble and guileless innocent dishonestly abused by corrupt and depraved Europeans that it is easy to understand why Behn's book has been read as a pioneering document of the anti-slavery movement. Yet, as *Othello* suggests, and the history of European encounters with natives of Africa and the Americas demonstrates, constancy, guilelessness, and a "native" nobility are not, as applied to non-Europeans, reliable markers of civility, maturity, or equality. Such virtues were, on the contrary, often considered reliable indices of the quality of slaves. And it is no coincidence that Behn's identification of Oroonoko as a native of Coromantien corresponds to the fact that English slave-traders considered "Gold Coast blacks, especially those shipped from Coromantine, for whom they paid the highest price of all" (Craton 1974: 74) to make the best slaves. As Michael Craton has observed, for "Kormantees," as for "the Fantin, Akin, and Ashanti Negroes...was reserved that exaggerated praise (granted in India, for example, to the Sikhs) that English colonials gave to those proud people who made the best subjects because they were most difficult to assimilate" (1974: 74).

Alternatively, guilelessness, constancy, and native nobility or integrity can be—and were—read as veneers, thin coatings of other attitudes and behaviors that were not considered desirable in slaves—superstitiousness, unpredictability, irrationality, inflexibility, for example, with a corresponding stress on what happens when the innocence of the innocent is offended or scorned: sudden violence, vengefulness, sexual rapacity, unrestrainable rage. The full range of these positions was, in fact, often attributed to Coromantines in the same period in which Behn is writing:

> "They are not only the best and most faithful of our slaves," rhapsodized Christopher Codrington of Barbados in 1701, "but are really born Heroes...There never was a raskal or coward of the nation, intrepid to the last degree, not a men of them but will stand to be cut to pieces without a sigh or groan, greatful and obedient to a kind master, but implacably revengeful when ill-treated. My Father, who had studied the genius and temper of all kinds of negroes 45 years with a very nice observation, would say, No man deserved a Corramante that would not treat him like a Friend rather than a Slave."
>
> (quoted in Craton 1974: 74)

Observable here is the often contradictory English estimate of African slaves that Behn puts to work in *Oroonoko*, evident in the attribution to Coromantines of the capacity to endure sufferings without a sigh and the tendency to resist hard treatment with a violence that made the name "Coromantine" synonymous with defiance and rebelliousness in later eighteenth-century accounts of the slave trade (see Craton 1974: 94–5 and Laura Brown 1987: 59–60 for related examples).

Behn could have found similar representations of African slaves in two works that are often alleged to have served as sources for *Oroonoko*, namely, George Warren's *An Impartial Description of Surinam* (1667) and Richard Ligon's *A True and Exact History of the Island of Barbados* (1657). Although both are sympathetic to the hard lot of Africans in the New World—"their Lodging is a hard Board, and their black Skins their Covering," writes Warren (1667: 19)—and Ligon is particularly insistent that "there are as honest, faithfull, and conscionable people amongst them, as amongst those of *Europe*, or any other part of the world" (1657: 53). Both are chary of making rules of their exceptions, preferring instead to sustain prevailing constructions of racial and cultural inferiority: "they are a people of a timorous and fearfull disposition, and consequently bloody, when they finde advantage" (Ligon 1657: 50); "the most of them are as neer beasts as maybe, setting their souls aside" (Ligon 1657: 47); "they'l manifest their fortitude, or rather obstinacy in suffering the most exquisite tortures can be inflicted upon them, for a terrour and example to others without shrinking" (Warren 1667: 19); "they are naturally treacherous and bloody, and practice no Religion there" (Warren 1667: 19).

Many of these symptoms of the savage or uncivil temperament are encoded or displayed in *Oroonoko* just as they are in *Othello*: "And yet I fear you; for you're fatal then/When your eyes roll so," as Desdemona says to Othello on her deathbed (5.2.39–40). But what most clearly links the two works is their protagonists' insufficiently large repertoire of subject positions, or improvisational skills, a trait represented as a token of inferiority in Warren's substitution of "obstinacy" for "fortitude" in his assessment of African endurance. While "character" as it is revealed in fixity of purpose, constancy, integrity, etc. looms large in the criteria for nobility in the early modern period, in the plays of Shakespeare improvisers and skeptics like Prince Hal, Prospero, and Hamlet are often more favorably represented than, say, stubbornly single-minded characters like Coriolanus, Caliban, or Timon of Athens.[15] It is, after all, Caliban's incapacity to grow or evolve under the tutelage of Prospero that classifies him as intractable, that qualifies him to function as slave to the will of another (just as Othello's commitment to absolute determinations of right and wrong, guilt and innocence, may be said to "qualify" his enslavement to Iago).

Othello itself operates as a case study of the occupational hazards of fixity of belief and purpose, while provocatively casting Iago, the villain of the piece, in the role of master improviser. In so doing, it vividly documents how easily a man bound by no commitments or illusions may overmaster another given over to a fixed course of thought and action. The play also more insidiously suggests that men like Othello who are so easily mastered may not, after all, be fit for command but only to be commanded. Othello himself internalizes this thought both in the famous "Othello's occupation's gone" speech and at the play's conclusion when he sees himself diminished to the stature of someone who can be disarmed by "every puny whipster" (5.2.253). Once we untie the moral knot that otherwise requires us to condemn Iago for so enslaving (and degrading) the Moor, we may see in the prospect of the calm, deliberative Iago lording it over the deracinated Othello the image of white lording it over black that becomes "naturalized" in the development of plantation slavery. Indeed, we may see in Iago's successful effort "to plume up my will" a "proof" of the white mind's capacity to dominate black "matter," a vindication even of slavery itself.[16]

Works like *Othello* and *Oroonoko* that overtly attempt to complicate or correct false stereotypes often become privileged bearers of the contagion they seek to cure or eradicate. They do so in one way by attributing to their characters virtues that are of no pragmatic account in European society, virtues that have long been compartmentalized as constitutive of only the most pious temperaments, of idealistic young men, virginal women, and children. What's noble about the noble savage is that he is not like *us*, we mature and worldly Europeans. Valuation in this mode does not proceed from the perception of similitude, but from the noting of difference. And, after an initial idealization of what is different, difference is quickly rerouted into inequality, based on normative ways of delegating the effeminate, the infantile or immature, the precipitately violent or irrational. If avowedly mature men can be so honest, innocent, guileless, and trusting in a world that requires cunning and circumspection of those who expect to thrive, then perhaps they are not mature or even men after all. As Okri writes, "When a black man in the West is portrayed as noble it usually means that he is neutralised. When white people speak so highly of a black man's nobility they are usually referring to his impotence" (1987: 564). And, as Iago observes: "The Moor is of a free and open nature,/That thinks men honest that but seem to be so,/And will as tenderly be led by the nose as asses are" (1.3.400–2).

The closing scenes of *Othello* are particularly effective at fixing and enforcing the racial stereotypes that the opening scenes of the play are at pains to deny. As Othello begins to act out in public (in front of formerly supportive Venetian emissaries) behaviors that "would not be believ'd in Venice" (4.1.243), and to do so without the constant baiting and abetting of Iago that inform his actions in the body of the play, he appears to emerge from a shell of decorousness and restraint that had previously encouraged his associates to consider him an exception to prevailing racial constructions. As Lodovico exclaims in response to Othello's striking of Desdemona and on the cue of his exiting line, "Goats and monkeys":

> Is this the noble Moor whom our full Senate
> Call all in all sufficient? Is this the nature
> Whom passion could not shake? Whose solid virtue
> The shot of accident, nor dart of chance,
> Could neither graze nor pierce?

> (4.1.265–9)

Lodovico directly echoes here claims that Othello himself has made in affirming his stature as a *noble* Moor, and thus implicitly confirms the suspicion that Othello harbors a "nature" that *can* be shaken by passion, a "virtue" that *can* be grazed or pierced by "shot of accident" and "dart of chance." Although Lodovico continues to question whether this is "his use" or whether the letters he has delivered have "work[ed] upon his blood" and have "new-create[d] this fault," he reluctantly concludes that "I am sorry that I am deceiv'd in him" (4.1.275–7, 283).

As the play proceeds, the number of onstage characters who confess to having been deceived in Othello steadily mounts to include Desdemona, Emilia, Cassio, and Montano, earlier constructions of Othello's nobility of mind and heart ceding to representations of him as a "devil" (5.2.136, 138), a "gull" or "dolt" who is "as ignorant as dirt" (5.2.170–1), a "dull Moor" (5.2.232), a "murd'rous coxcomb" and "fool" unworthy of "so good a wife" (5.2.240–1). Though all these words are spoken by Emilia who, in the economy of the play, speaks out of her own passion and the heat of the moment, they comprise an opposing, corrective assessment of Othello's promotion of himself as an "an honorable murderer," helping to transform what he considers a sacrifice into what she construes a "monstrous act" (5.2.197). Emilia's judgments of Othello also ironically conform to those of her husband as he stands watch, in the play's fourth act, over the once-commanding figure of Othello now fallen into a trance: "Thus credulous fools are caught;/And many worthy and chaste dames even thus,/All guiltless, meet reproach" (4.1.45–7).

Behn provides similar markers regarding the "dullness" of Oroonoko's judgments and his susceptibility to emotional paralysis even in the comparatively uncomplicated Coromantien scenes, where, "forced to retire to vent his Groans" of lovesickness, Oroonoko "fell down on a Carpet, and lay struggling a long time, and only breathing now and then—Oh *Imoinda*!" (Behn 1973: 17). Although such moments are framed in the period in question as unexceptional ways of representing true expressions of passion or love, Oroonoko's propensity to "lay negligently on the ground" (23) in sustained bouts of passivity, like his failure to anticipate the treachery of the English captain who "betrays" him to slavery, mark him as a figure lacking command of his faculties just as surely as Othello's disintegrative lapse into a trance— "Pish! Noses, ears, and lips.—Is't possible?—Confess—handkerchief! —O devil! (3.4.42–3)—marks his incapacity to operate on the same level of balance, sophistication, and control as Iago. Though scholars continue to see the sympathy evinced for Oroonoko, in the captivity scene in particular, as indicative of Behn's humanitarian motives, we would do better to see it as symptomatic of the condescendingly "primitivist" approach Behn brings throughout to her construction of Oroonoko.[17]

Behn deploys her primitivist approach most tellingly in the scenes that take place in Surinam, beginning at what might be termed the hinge of her novel, the moment when Oroonoko's "sullenness," suspiciousness, and impatience begin to prompt even her to have "a doubt in him" and "a fear of him" (46). As Behn writes:

> I took it ill he shou'd suspect we wou'd break our Words with him, and not permit both him and *Clemene* [Imoinda] to return to his own Kingdom, which was not so long a way, but when he was once on his Voyage he wou'd quickly arrive there. He made me some Answers that shew'd a doubt in him, which made me ask, what advantage it would be to doubt? It would but give us a fear of him and possibly compel us to treat him as I should be be very loath to behold: that is, it might occasion his Confinement.
>
> (Behn 1973: 46)

This moment reveals much about Behn's preferred construction of Oroonoko. What disturbs her here, and generates a rupture in her relationship with Oroonoko, is his refusal to make his thoughts conform to her prescription of what it is allowable for him to think and his irrationality in even harboring thoughts that Behn and her fellow colonists might consider the least bit threatening. The operative assumption is that the royal slave should only think thoughts that would "advantage" him. To do otherwise—to adopt, for instance, a suspicious or hostile attitude toward his patrons—would mark him as "primitive" or unreasonable and require a "confinement" that would be to the royal slave what enforced labor is to the common slave.

Oroonoko responds to this threat with palpable resentment, "with an Air impatient enough to make me know he would not long be in bondage" (47), which leads to the consensus judgment that he should no longer be trusted "much out of our view," that he should be obliged "to remain in such a compass," that "he should be permitted, as seldom as could be, to go up to the Plantations of the *Negroes*," and that, when he did, he should be accompanied by "Spies" in the guise of "Attendants" (48). One might consider such responses minimal in comparison to those that could be applied to even a potentially unruly slave, but they seem disproportionately elaborate given all the energy Behn has heretofore expended in ennobling Oroonoko. No doubt much of the anxiety generated by Oroonoko's impatience and resentment is attributable to the colonists' fear of a "Mutiny," which, as Behn writes, "is very fatal sometimes in those Colonies that abound so with Slaves, that they exceed the Whites in vast numbers" (1973: 46). But the heretofore discounted attribution to Oroonoko of superhuman strength, and the capacity to express it in indiscriminate shows of violence, also underwrites both the continued tolerance for Oroonoko's relative freedom of movement and the preparations taken for his containment. And just as Othello's sudden show of violence to Desdemona begins to unsettle the consensus view of his exceptionality, so too does Oroonoko's sullenness and impatience begin to erode the notion that he "was more civiliz'd, according to the *European* Mode, than any other [of his kind] had been" (32).[18]

The character who at the start of the novel was said to have "nothing of Barbarity in his Nature" (7) now is revealed to harbor "a Spirit all rough and fierce" (47). Marked associations of that spirit with animal life occur throughout this section of the novel, which finds his "large Soul...still panting after more renown'd Actions" than those "this World afforded, as Running, Wrestling, Pitching the Bar, Hunting and Fishing, Chasing and Killing *Tygers* of a monstrous size...and wonderful *Snakes*" (47). Nonetheless, it is into such pursuits that Behn tries to channel his energies, leading him into a confrontation with a tiger, a "monstrous Beast of mighty Size and vast Limbs, who came with open Jaws upon him," which Oroonoko kills in hand-to-hand combat (50–1), as well as with a giant eel (53–4). His subsequent "defeat" of another tiger gives Oroonoko "occasion of many fine Discourses, of Accidents in War, and strange Escapes" (53), phrases drawn directly from Othello's recounting of the stories he used to tell Desdemona.[19]

Behn's decision to superimpose this intertextual connection on the back of Oroonoko's conquest of a tiger has the effect of bringing Othello's otherwise undocumented prehistory into the circuit of Oroonoko's primitivized exploits, rendering them brothers under the skin. Oroonoko's connection to Othello is sustained in the visit Behn and Oroonoko pay to the closest thing to *Anthropophagi* Surinam has to offer, namely, a tribe of Indians, some of whom "wanted their Noses, some their Lips, some both Noses and Lips, some their Ears," whom Behn initially "took...for Hobgoblins, or Fiends, rather than Men" (57). Upon better acquaintance, Behn concludes that "however their Shapes appear'd, their Souls were very humane and noble" (57). Oroonoko also "express'd his Esteem of 'em," though, upon learning that they undertake self-mutilation in competitive shows of valor and endurance, he concludes that theirs is "a sort of Courage too brutal to be applauded" (58).

This sequence is of considerable interest for the light it casts on Oroonoko's subsequent physical deformations which are endured with the same brutal courage Behn's "*Black* Hero" (58) initially eschews. The visit Behn and Oroonoko pay to the "*Indian* Towns" is undertaken at a very unsettled stage of Anglo-Indian relations. While Behn paints an idyllic picture of the Indians at the start of the novel, only incidentally noting that they are too "useful" and numerous for the English to enslave them, by the novel's midpoint "Disputes" have arisen that have issued in wholesale massacres, Behn's own footman having been cut "all in Joints, and [the Joints having been] nail'd...to Trees" (54). Similarly, while the beauty, innocence, and passivity of the Indians are stressed at the start, their aggressiveness and ugliness are emphasized later, concomitant with the references to disputes and massacres, thus further unsettling our sense of who—or what—they are in fact. One could assume that Behn is describing different tribes of Indians, but she never says this and, moreover, refers to "Our *Indian Slaves*" (59) in her later account of them, thus contradicting her earlier statement that Indians are never enslaved.[20] One may only conclude that, as with the ensuing degradation of Oroonoko, a change in Indian behavior has generated a corresponding shift in representational claims and emphases. What provokes this shift in the representation of Oroonoko is his decision to lead an ill-fated slave revolt, whose end finds Oroonoko, a last remaining consort, Tuscan, and Imoinda encircled by the colonists, Imoinda defending herself Amazon-like with "a Bow and a Quiver full of poisoned Arrows" in the manner of the late revolting Indians (64).

When news is first brought to Behn that Oroonoko had "betaken himself to the Woods, and [had] carry'd with him all the Negroes," she and her consorts "were posses'd with extreme Fear, which no

Persuasions could dissipate, that he would secure himself till night and then, that he would come down and cut all our Throats." She adds that "This Apprehension made all the Females of us fly down the River, to be secured" (67–8). The fear that "possesses" Behn here duplicates and intensifies the "many mortal Fears" "we were in…about some disputes the *English* had with the *Indians*" (54) and extends the recently established connection between the barbarity of the Indians and the potential for barbarity of Oroonoko. Yet, at the very moment at which Oroonoko has been more deeply "primitivized" by being identified with a people whose practices earlier seemed "too brutal to be applauded by our *Black* Hero" (58), he is also in the process of being "Othelloed" by means of the fear he awakes in Behn and her consorts.[21] Although I intend to reserve until later a discussion of the racial displacement Behn enacts by supplying Oroonoko with a black lover, something clearly is emerging here that has heretofore been repressed by Behn's overarching commitment to the celebration of her "*Black* Hero." That "something" pits a fear considered to be beyond reason against the freedom of movement of a powerfully endowed black man, formerly considered to be the soul of honor and civility. And the fear itself is narratively expressive and specific; it produces the specter of the black slave moving under cover of night to cut the throats of white women who have heretofore been his admirers, sponsors, and protectors.

The fear also underwrites the punishment of the black man for his (imagined) transgression inscribed in the form of a brutal whipping that leaves "a thousand Wounds all over his Body" (67). Though Behn avers that she "had Authority and Interest enough there, had I suspected any such thing, to have prevented it" (68), and identifies the whipping itself as an act of "Barbarity" (67), the punishment effectively forecloses Oroonoko's freedom of movement and returns his now-disabled body to her sponsorship and protection. From this point forward, the threat against white women and white male paternalist control of the Surinam plantations embodied by Oroonoko becomes redirected against himself and against the one female over whom he is still capable of exercising physical control, namely "the brave, the beautiful, and the constant *Imoinda*" (78). This shift in emphasis is, moreover, entirely sponsored by Behn's controlling hand, under whose supervision Oroonoko grows more stubborn, silent, and intractable.

The slave revolt, or, rather, the distrust and impatience that leads to it, occupies the space in *Oroonoko* delegated to jealousy in *Othello*. It is the pivot around which the momentum of the royal slave's exceptionality is turned back against itself, rendering him unworthy of the privileges that have been claimed on his behalf. Oroonoko's attempt to cultivate a space of freedom for himself and Imoinda is "read" by the author who "writes" him as the sign of a crisis in her own effort at identity-building. It signifies Oroonoko's unbridgeable difference from the plantation society that has stretched its own rules to honor and contain his "sameness," and licenses his subjection to the same standards of treatment that govern the relationship of slaveholders to the common run of slaves. The whipping of Oroonoko effectively dissolves the distinction even he attempts to maintain between himself and other enslaved Africans in his bitterly dismissive description of them as "the vilest of all creeping things" (66). Oroonoko's concluding embrace of practices that Behn has associated with the most primitive tribes of Surinam Indians—his defiant acts of self-mutilation, his smoking of an Indian pipe, his courageous endurance of his own dismemberment—may, in fact, be read as an attempt at another kind of identity formation, one that "out-Others" the differences between Africans and Europeans, and positions him at the farthest verge of alterity.[22]

The concluding movement of the novel, which dramatizes Oroonoko's ritualized murder of Imoinda, his eight-day fast beside her decaying body, and his execution and dismemberment, is significantly prefaced by a brief ethnographic observation that effectively positions Imoinda and Oroonoko alike in a space heretofore reserved for the Surinam Indians. Like the Indians, the two will put to the test "a sort of Courage" presumably "too brutal to be applauded" by their white protectors. Behn assures us, however, that Imoinda's acceptance of the opportunity to "die by so Noble a Hand, and [to] be sent into her own Country (for that's their Notion of the next World) by him she so tenderly loved" (72), was thought "brave and just" (71) by all who were privy to Oroonoko's resolve, including Behn herself.[23]

In practice, Oroonoko's "severing" of Imoinda's "yet smiling Face from that delicate Body, pregnant as it was with the Fruits of tenderest Love," tests the limits of sentimental fantasy and works to quite different effect: an effect that can best be gauged by Oroonoko's response to his action and the response of those who discover it. Formerly the soul of courtesy and civility, Oroonoko "tore, he raved, he roar'd like some Monster of the Wood, calling on the lov'd Name of *Imoinda*" (72), not unlike the way Othello does as he cries "Blow me about in winds! Roast me in sulphur!/ Wash me in steep-down gulfs of liquid fire!/O Desdemon! Dead, Desdemon! Dead! Oh! Oh! (5.2.288–90). Like Othello, Oroonoko is rendered passive and impotent by his act, incapable of compassing his planned revenge against his white tormentor, as he lies for eight days amid the "Stinks" of Imoinda's decaying body (73–4). The discovery of this grotesque scene is, moreover, greeted in much the way in which Othello's "tragic loading" of his bed is hailed: "*Oh, Monster! that hast murder'd thy Wife*" (74).

A crucial difference between the play and the novel is marked, however, by Behn's decision to foreground the monstrousness of Oroonoko's behavior by making him a grotesque spectacle of savagery turned inward. Whereas Shakespeare has Othello recover his poise and rhetorical control in the last moments of his stage life, Behn sends Oronooko plummeting into brutal acts of self-mutilation that exceed those of the Indians she initially took for "Hobgoblins or Fiends":

> *Look ye, ye Faithless Crew*, said he, *'tis not Life I seek, nor am I afraid of dying,* (and at that word, cut a piece of Flesh from his own Throat, and threw it at 'em,)…he rip'd up his own Belly, and took his Bowels and pull'd 'em out, with what strength he could; while some, on their Knees imploring, besought him to hold his Hand.
>
> (Behn 1973: 75)

The manner in which Behn chooses to stage Oroonoko's evisceration is plainly coded in the signs and signifiers of savagery. As in her representational transformation of the "Beauties" of the Indians into the ugliness of hobgoblins, Oroonoko's primitivism now pours out of him, utterly changing his aspect. As Behn writes, "if before we thought him so beautiful a Sight, he was now so alter'd that his Face was like a Death's-Head black'd over, nothing but Teeth and Eye-Holes" (75–6).[24] Reduced to a body of bones and decaying flesh, Oroonoko undergoes the final indignity of having his body systematically dismembered as first his "Members" are "cut off" and thrown into the fire: "after that, with an ill-favour'd Knife, they cut off his Ears and his Nose, and burn'd them; he still smoak'd on, as if nothing had touch'd him" (77). By providing Oroonoko with the appliance of an Indian tobacco pipe, which he patiently puffs as he is being dismembered, and by consigning his execution to "one *Banister*, a wild *Irish Man*" and "Fellow of absolute Barbarity" (76), Behn clearly aims to elicit sympathy and admiration for the suffering and courage of her "mangled King" (77). But the markers she has chosen convey mixed messages, the Indian pipe signaling Oroonoko's identification with the fiendish Indians, while his endurance associates him with his fellow "Kormantees," a tribe as notable in the history of the slave trade for their intractability as for their courage.[25] Indeed, nothing so clearly brands Oroonoko a slave as the brutality with which his life is extinguished (see Jordan 1968: 154–63).[26]

The brutality visited on Oroonoko is no doubt meant to discredit his barbarous tormentors, unsettling further the already unsettled distinction between representatives of civil and uncivil behavior. But Behn's decision to concentrate so much attention on Oroonoko's increasingly grotesque body—and on the body of Imoinda made grotesque by Oroonoko—ultimately brings her work into conformity with conventional forms of racial and cultural stereotyping.[27] The transformation of Oroonoko into an uncivil body takes its place as one curiosity added to and superseding another, particularly the originary, oxymoronic novelty of a "royal slave," in much the way that the initially glamorous marriage of Desdemona to Shakespeare's Moor of Venice becomes an "object" that "poisons sight" (5.2.373). In each instance, the starting intervention is at odds with an established discourse or force that eventually subsumes it. Although we may give a name like Iago, or Byam, or Banister to this force, the primary agent of these transformations is the writer's pen as it moves across the page and inscribes its vision on the world's eye.[28]

3.

But how do we reconcile my construction of *Oroonoko* with evidence that indicates that "Late seventeenth- and early eighteenth-century readers saw [the novel] primarily as a heroic love story, complete with a royal protagonist, who performs deeds of superhuman strength and stoically suffers unbelievable torments for the sake of his honor" and whose "slavery is significant primarily because it illustrates that nobility is inborn and manifests itself even under the most adverse circumstances" (Gallagher 1994: 54–5 n. 12)? We do so in the same way that we isolate and extrapolate the markers of a not-yet formally defined or developed racism from Shakespeare's play of a noble Moor who is degraded by the machinations of a vicious subordinate; that is, by seeing both play and novel as products of a complacently racist and colonialist sensibility that becomes susceptible to interrogation upon the emergence of an anti-racist or anti-colonialist point of view and the deployment of an interpretive grid based on it. Forged as a romance of New World plantation slavery by the self-styled daughter of Surinam's would-be governor, *Oroonoko* brings to light what it seeks to obscure under the pressure of changed circumstance and different interpretive conditions.

As an appropriation of *Othello* that takes its cue from, and elaborates on, the most prominent racial and sexual markers encoded in that play, *Oroonoko* distinguishes itself from most recorded productions of *Othello* in the Restoration period. As Virginia Vaughan has noted, in virtually all

Restoration adaptations of *Othello* "Othello's extremes of passion are carefully modulated to comply with the late seventeenth-century conception of how the noble hero should comport himself—with decorum" (Vaughan 1994: 98). Vaughan concludes that "The slim but suggestive evidence about Restoration performances indicates" that portrayals of Othello enacted by such celebrated actors as Hart and Betterton "privileged the noble Moor and repressed his savagery. Despite his blackness, he was part of the aristocracy, not marginalized from it" (Vaughan 1994: 112). Why "*Othello* was...believed to be a play primarily about jealousy" and not about race is difficult to determine, given the preferences of contemporary Othellos to present themselves as "shockingly black" (Vaughan 1994: 111–12). But I believe it was primarily because Restoration adapters and their audiences, possibly motivated by a resurgent royalist ideology, failed to make the connection Behn made between *Othello* and the moment of plantation slavery.

Interestingly, even Richard Southerne's 1695 stage adaptation of *Oroonoko* appears to have more in common with Restoration adaptations of *Othello* than it does with Behn's novel, and may be said to have done for Behn's graphic rendering of the savage without what Restoration *Othellos* did for Shakespeare's depiction of the savage within. From the changes Southerne makes, we can gain some insight into what were evidently taken to be Behn's novelistic excesses and lapses in decorum, but which we may alternatively construe as her graphic inscriptions of savagism. Although Southerne supplies to *Oroonoko* a provocation that Behn deleted from her "transmutation" of *Othello*—namely, a white wife for the black hero (see Ferguson 1993: 37–40)—his other changes largely conform to the Restoration penchant for moderating extreme passions that is witnessed in contemporary adaptations of *Othello*.[29] Oroonoko does not, for example, cut off his wife's head after cutting her throat in Southerne. In fact, he fails to find the resolve to stab her at all; rather, his knife is guided to its target by the pressure of her own hands after an interminable debate in which he hedges as she encourages. For all rights and purposes, Imoinda kills herself. Instead of languishing by her body and allowing himself to be taken captive, Southerne's Oroonoko lashes out at his enemy, slays him, then kills himself, thus escaping the dismemberment, castration, and incineration Oroonoko suffers in Behn.

Southerne's decision to make Imoinda white impels us to question why Behn, writing in the shadow of *Othello*, chose to make Imoinda black and why she had Imoinda so eagerly court a violent and "barbaric" death at the hands of her beloved. Just as significant as the change of race is the fact that Behn's Imoinda, unlike Desdemona, welcomes, instead of resists, her death and that she dies in so grotesque a manner.[30] Though the white Imoinda continues to court, indeed, to enforce, her death in Southerne's adaptation, the death she dies is far less brutalized and grotesque. What Othello preferred to consider more of a sacrifice than a murder becomes just that in the hands of Southerne, a change that renders Oroonoko virtually guiltless for her death. Behn's choice of black for Imoinda anthropologizes the entire affair, rendering it at once culturally remote and thrillingly attractive to her readers, neither murder nor sacrifice as much as an act marked by excess, desperation, and unreason.

Behn performs here a doubly colonialist maneuver at the expense of her African protagonists by carefully delegating and overseeing the kind of cultural work that her black protagonists do on her literary plantation. She, first of all, exploits the novelty of their intraracial romance and the primitivist form it takes under pressure from the colonial plantation system with which she is deeply complicit. And, as a white woman who, unlike Desdemona, survives the anxious fear engendered by a "relapsed" black man on the loose, she plays a supervisory role in the black man's castration and dismemberment. Ready enough to approve the exceptional black woman's decapitation, hence proving an enemy to her sex if not her race, as the primary "author" of *Oroonoko* she also approves, with however loud a sigh of reluctance, the exceptional black man's dismemberment, hence proving as much an enemy to the race of black slaves as any Byam or Banister. By comparison, Southerne may be said to be recuperating what is most tractable in Othello insofar as he gives Oroonoko a white wife who, for all rights and purposes, kills herself and recreates a black man who, unlike Othello, reserves his violence for the only character onstage who deserves it.

In all this, Southerne paints a picture of what Behn could have done had she wanted to diminish her reader's growing sense of Oroonoko's savagery, had she wanted to remain faithful to the example of black nobility presumably set by Shakespeare, particularly in *Othello*'s Restoration reincarnations. Her failure to do either, possibly enforced by her artistic fidelity to the protocols of plantation slavery in which castration and dismemberment were accounted legal remedies to both slave revolts and sexual transgressions, but just as possibly rooted in a lapsed faith in the civility of Africans, suggests an entirely different range of reference and concerns, one that is clearly linked to prevailing constructions of racial and cultural difference.

It is, on this account, notable that, as anti-slavery advocacy intensified in the eighteenth century, Southerne's rewriting of *Oroonoko* would effectively displace Behn's novel in tributary relation to *Othello*. This much is registered in the anonymously authored *The Royal African or Memoirs of the Young Prince of Annamboe* (1753), a work forgettable for all but its high-minded Introduction and an epigraph which reads:

> *Othello* shews the Muse's utmost Power,
> A brave, an honest, yet a hapless Moor.
> In *Oroonoko* shines the Hero's mind,
> With native Lustre by no Art refin'd.
> Sweet *Juba* strikes us but with milder Charm,
> At once renown'd for Virtue, Love, and Arms.
> Yet here might rise a still more moving Tale,
> But *Shakespears, Addisons*, and *Southerns* fail!
>
> (Anonymous 1753: title page)[31]

This author notably links his fervent abolitionist sympathies with what he takes to be the earlier efforts in kind undertaken by Shakespeare, Southerne, and Addison to paint an ennobling picture of their black protagonists. Reading these works through the filter of the burgeoning anti-slavery movement, the author sees nothing in them degrading to the cause of the embattled African apart from the "haplessness" of Shakespeare's Moor. However, in his spirited Introduction, the author of *The Royal African* ventures into discursive territory that retrospectively indicates just how embedded Behn was in the stereotypical racial constructions enforced by the slave trade.

He stakes out there an expressly anti-racist and anti-colonialist position, claiming that "superior Power or superior Knowledge" does not give "one Race of People a Title to use another Race who are weaker or more ignorant with Haughtiness or Contempt" (1753: ix–x). In this, he makes no distinction premised on the exceptionality of single figures like Oroonoko. Indeed, the author promotes the exceptionality of his protagonist's entire tribe, deconstructing the claim of "*Dutch* Writers" that the "*Fantin*" people "are the haughtiest, proudest, and most insolent *Negroes* on the *Gold Coast*" by translating it into a "plain *English*" that signifies that the Fantins:

> are the Wealthiest and the Freest, upon whom [the] Arts [of the Dutch traders] could never prevail, and with whom whenever they had Occasion to deal, they were obliged to act more upon the Square, than they were ever inclined to.
>
> (Anonymous 1753: 20)

144

Comments like these effect a clear-cut intervention in the contradictory seventeenth-century discourse of slavery, the "insolence" of the Fantin operating as a sign of their freedom and comparative sophistication, not as a symptom of their fierceness or intractability. They also set the stage for *The Prince of Angola* (1788), the last in a line of adaptations of Southerne's stage version of *Oroonoko*, written by John Ferriar, an equally fervent proponent of abolition. Unlike the author of *The Royal African*, who places himself in responsive relationship to Southerne and Shakespeare, Ferriar places his revision of *Oroonoko* in *corrective* relation to Southerne's, as is vividly figured in his play's subtitle: "A Tragedy altered from the PLAY of OROONOKO and Adapted to the Circumstances of the PRESENT TIME." Referring no doubt to the speech of Oroonoko in Southerne's fourth act, in which he regrets having tried "to make those free/Who were by nature slaves—wretches designed/To be their masters' dogs and lick their feet" (4.2.60–2), which closely echoes Oroonoko's representation of his fellow slaves as "the vilest of all creeping things" in Behn (1973: 66), Ferriar claims that Southerne "delivered by the medium of his Hero" no less than "a grovelling apology for slave-holders" (Ferriar 1788: ii). He adds that "an illiberal contempt of the unhappy Negroes is so entwined with the Fabric of the Piece, that it was impossible to separate it, without making large encroachments in the Author's design" (Ferriar 1788: ii). By insisting on the ineradicable centrality of an anti-Negro bias in Southerne's play, Ferriar implicitly draws a similar conclusion about Behn's novel, which he makes explicit when he relates Southerne's contrivance "to degrade [Oroonoko] irretrievably" in a central scene of the play to Behn's primitivist construction of Oroonoko in her tiger-hunt scenes (see Ferriar 1788: iii).

A further pointed variation on Southerne and Behn that Ferriar puts to work involves his hero's refusal to resort to violence in pursuit of revenge; a decision that places the protagonist outside the discursive pale of savagism. Whereas Behn graphically stages Oroonoko's murder and mutilation of Imoinda, and Southerne gives Oroonoko the opportunity to kill his enemy that escapes him in Behn, the killing of Imoinda in Ferriar derives much of its momentum (as it does in Southerne) from Imoinda herself, after which Oroonoko eschews revenge in favor of killing himself. In all this, Ferriar means to transfer full responsibility for his Prince's tragedy to the colonists and slaveholders, one of whom states upon the Prince's death, "the guilt is ours;/For deeds like these are slavery's fruit" (Ferriar 1788: 52).

Ferriar's Prince's enforced killing of Imoinda is staged with considerably more ceremony than it is in Behn, and witnesses the resurgent echo of an Othello who, unlike Shakespeare's, is not given over to a "lust of the blood":

> Thou tremblest still. O most accursed Fiends,
> That make this cruelty an act of love.
> Must I deface this idol of my heart?
> Is it for me to strike the living bloom
> From that dear cheek, and murder in that bosom
> Ten thousand tender doating thoughts of me?
>
> (Ferriar 1788: 51)

The corrective echo of Othello's "And makest me call what I intend to do/A murder, which I thought a sacrifice" (5.2.65–6), in which Ferriar's Prince blames not Imoinda but the merciless slaveholders for the action he undertakes, is only one instance of Ferriar's strategic redeployment of Shakespeare in his adaptation of *Oroonoko*. His appropriation of Hamlet's "I have heard that guilty creatures" speech (*Hamlet*, 2.2.589–93) as an epigraph to his play reveals his intention to have the play itself function as a mousetrap both for guilty slaveholders and for readers who countenance the trade in slaves. And his conflated delegation to slaveholders of the role Caliban delegates to Prospero in *The Tempest* (see 1.2.334–46), and Gloucester delegates to the gods in *King Lear* (4.1.36–7)—"You are a white man—you take me for a mischievous beast, and fawn upon me, that you may strike safely. You entrap us for your use, and murder us for your sport" (Ferriar 1788: 52)—demonstrates an acute understanding of how recognizable monuments of the literary past may be put to productive work under pressure of the "present time." Indeed, Ferriar's appropriations of Southerne and Shakespeare may be said to constitute a pre-emptive strike in the struggle of contemporary postcolonial writers to take charge of, and to redirect, the traffic in signs and markers that makes works like *The Tempest*, *Othello*, and Behn's *Oroonoko* complicit in the circulation of racist and colonialist stereotypes.

7

"LIKE OTHELLO": TAYEB SALIH'S *SEASON OF MIGRATION* AND POSTCOLONIAL SELF-FASHIONING

> Othello was my grandfather.
>
> (W.E.B. Du Bois)

In the statement from which my epigraph is drawn, W.E.B. Du Bois was not attempting to claim a direct line of descent from Shakespeare's Moor. He was simply making a statement of fact: "Othello" was the *name* of Du Bois's grandfather, who was born in 1791 to a free black family near Great Barrington, Massachusetts, and died in 1872 (Sundquist 1996: 85). However Du Bois's great-grandparents came by this name for their son, one assumes that it had a resonance for them different from that of their other "splendidly named" children: Ira, Harlow, Chloe, Maria, and Lucinda.[1] What that difference was is lost to us, though it may be useful to note that three years prior to Othello's birth a self-styled "free Negro of Baltimore" employed the same name as a pseudonym in a plea "for gradual emancipation or immediate freedom with colonization in the western territory" of the United States published in the pages of the *American Museum* (Jordan 1968: 547). The anonymous author of this "Essay on Negro Slavery" presumably felt that the name Othello would serve to ennoble his plea, give it the exceptionality that was in short supply for the great mass of American Negroes, enslaved or free. "Othello" was a name to conjure with, a name that his white readership would probably register with respect, without worrying about the implications of the Moor's fifth-act descent into savagery and murder of his trusting white wife.

Should these have been his motives, "Othello" may well have shared with the name-givers of Du Bois's grandfather an attitude towards the

Moor later exemplified by Paul Robeson, in stage terms at least, the most prominent black twentieth-century Othello. Robeson considered Othello "a great Negro warrior," who was motivated to kill Desdemona by "the destruction of himself as a human being, of his human dignity" (Duberman 1988: 274). Like the free Negro of Baltimore, Robeson readily appropriated the name of the Moor to add probity and distinction to his actions, titling the publishing and recording ventures he undertook in the 1950s "Othello Associates" and "Othello Recording Corporation," respectively. For Robeson, the name was honorific; it signaled by association a sense of his own exceptionality and of the potential exceptionality of other African-Americans, Othello serving as that man "of royal siege" from whom they, in turn, could be said to have fetched their "heritage."

As the preceding chapter indicates, this identification with Othello negotiated by African-American men raises a daunting array of problems and questions, one of which concerns the provenance of the Moor himself: a composite representation of an Arab-African mercenary fabricated by an English playwright in 1604 and played almost exclusively by white actors in and out of blackface for the first 340 years of his stage history. Othello was, in fact, "Africanized" *and* "Orientalized" at his inception, cast in the role of "extravagant and wheeling stranger" in a play that assembles and puts to work a mass of early modern (mis)conceptions about both the African and the Arab-African *Other*. While the sheer singularity of Shakespeare's deployment of a charismatic black protagonist provides an understandable basis for the naming of Du Bois's grandfather, for the choice of pseudonym by the free Negro of Baltimore, and for Robeson's identification with Othello, these appropriations of Othello's name operate primarily in the service of identity-building and work within specifically African-American cultural formations. As such, they embrace Shakespeare's starting conception of Othello's greatness of soul and approve long-prevailing critical views of his undeserved victimization at the hands of a demonized Iago. They thus fail to address, much less contest, all that Shakespeare has arguably transacted in the name of the Moor (and of Moors) in the course of his play, as if the glamor of the name could be divorced from a plot that delivers Othello to a fate that is altogether more complicated and problematic. It is not, I would submit, until Tayeb Salih "writes back" to *Othello* in *Season of Migration to the North* that the specifically Orientalist proportions of Othello's construction, and its implications for a very different kind of self-fashioning, are made plain.

1.

We move, in this chapter, to the discussion of a work first published in
Arabic in 1966 and subsequently translated into English for inclusion in
the Heinemann African Writers series in 1969. Published ten years after
the Sudan's establishment as a sovereign state, the novel focuses on a
stretch of time that reaches back to the "reconquest" period and establishment of the Anglo-Egyptian Condominium at the turn of the
century and extends forward to the 1950s when the transition to independence had become a foregone conclusion.[2] One of only a few
Sudanese literary works translated into English, the novel is as deeply
grounded in Arabic literary conventions as in those of the West. But,
like many works of the postcolonial "emergence" period of the 1950s
and 1960s, Achebe's *Things Fall Apart* pre-eminent among them, *Season
of Migration* is clearly designed to function in responsive relation to some
of the most influential texts of the colonial period, *Othello* serving as its
most obvious point of reference, though *Heart of Darkness* also plays an
influential role in Salih's structuring of his plot and disposition of his
characters. In fact, as Barbara Harlow notes, *Season of Migration* puts
Arabic literary conventions to work in the very act of responding to
such texts:

> The *Season of Migration to the North* is generically a novel, a form
> imported by the Arabs from the West. But it participates as
> well in what, in Arabic literary terms, is called *mu aradah*, liter-
> ally "opposition," "contradiction," but meaning here a
> formula whereby one person will write a poem, and another
> will retaliate by writing along the same lines, but reversing the
> meaning. Tayeb Salih's use of the "novel" form might be taken
> as a literary practice of this sort. It is a rereading of
> Shakespeare's *Othello*, a restatement of the tragedy, a reshaping
> of the tragic figure of the Moor.
>
> (Harlow 1979: 162–3)[3]

As a novel specifically sited at that "season" when the colonized Arab-
African intellectual begins to retrace the steps of the European
conqueror back to the imperial "center," *Season of Migration* also restates,
reshapes, and reverses the voyage of Marlow into the heart of darkness,
converting it, in Edward Said's words,

> into a sacralized *hegira* from the Sudanese countryside, still
> weighted down with its colonial legacy, into the heart of

Europe, where [the novel's protagonist] Mustafa Sa'eed, a mirror image of Kurtz, unleashes ritual violence on himself, on European women, [and] on the narrator's understanding.

(Said 1994: 211)

Season of Migration speaks to us, as does *Heart of Darkness*, through the voice of a survivor of a crisis that is at once cultural and personal. Though the novel concerns the "migration north" to the heart of the imperial center and subsequent return south to the heart of the Sudan of its protagonist, Mustafa Sa'eed, it is the impact of that double migration on the narrator (who has made a similar migration of his own) that frames and defines its larger interests.[4] Mustafa serves as a kind of bridge for the narrator between the village culture of his grandfather that has been largely untouched by colonialism, and the incipiently postcolonial culture of the modern Sudan which he would like to think can sustain an unfractured relationship with precolonial conventions and traditions. Like Marlow in *Heart of Darkness*, the narrator of *Season of Migration* pits his starting sense of "wholeness" in direct competition with the dividedness of his protagonist, whose complexity is produced by an insular childhood lived entirely in estranged relation to his mother; his education in British schools in Khartoum and Cairo; his migration to England to study at Oxford; his irregular career as a daytime anti-colonial economist and nighttime "Othello" or seducer of white women; his trial and imprisonment for the murder of his English wife and for his complicity in the suicides of several other English women; and his subsequent effort to integrate himself into traditional Arab village and family life in a town at the bend of the Nile. Engagement with Mustafa and with the wife Mustafa leaves behind after his inexplicable death or disappearance eventuates in the narrator's own estrangement from the village and family life he had formerly embraced and in a sense of disillusionment with a culture he once felt could easily reassert itself in the wake of the receding colonialist presence.

The narrator's concern about this crisis in his own attitude toward his cultural traditions will, in the end, supersede his interest in Mustafa's double life as an apparently assimilated "black Englishman" and erotic terrorist or avenger—that is, as a repositioned version of Othello. In this respect, the novel anticipates some of Michelle Cliff's preoccupations in *No Telephone to Heaven*, whose rewriting of *The Tempest* is undertaken in the interests of breaking free of the colonialist paradigm that holds West Indian textuality in bondage to imperial influence. Indeed, *Season of Migration* first establishes its relationship to *Othello* in terms of denial, as if its protagonist is all too aware of how easily the Orientalist stereotype can be made to encapsulate and explain his situation and behavior, turning it and him into a cautionary example of the Arab-African's enslavement to his passions.

Mustafa Sa'eed will twice insist that he is "no Othello" in the course of the novel. He does so for the first time in response to his English lawyer's high-minded, but patronizing, attempt to displace the guilt of his crime by representing him as a latter-day Othello. According to his advocate: " 'Mustafa Sa'eed…is a noble person whose mind was able to absorb Western civilization but it broke his heart. These girls were not killed by Mustafa Sa'eed but by the germ of a deadly disease that assailed them a thousand years ago'." Recounting his reaction to this argument, Mustafa observes to the narrator:

> It occurred to me that I should stand up and say to them: "This is untrue, a fabrication. It was I who killed them. I am the desert of thirst. I am no Othello. I am a lie. Why don't you sentence me to be hanged and so kill the lie?"
>
> (Salih 1980: 33)

Mustafa Sa'eed's second denial of association with Othello occurs at the climax of a remarkably incisive speech he delivers to the narrator, in which he imagines himself a kind of avenging angel wreaking vengeance against Europeans for two thousand years of interventions in African affairs: "Yes, my dear sirs, I came as an invader into your very homes: a drop of the poison which you have injected into the veins of history. 'I am no Othello, Othello was a lie' " (95).

In addition to the significant shift from "*I* am a lie" to "*Othello* was a lie" (my emphasis), we register here a shift of attribution of the earlier reference to "the germ of a deadly disease" that Mustafa's lawyer holds responsible for the deaths of Mustafa's female victims. Dwelling on the efforts of the court to rise above itself and give him, the presumptive colonized Other, every benefit of the law, Mustafa confesses that he maintained "a feeling of superiority towards [the court], for the ritual was being held primarily because of me; and I, over and above everything else am a colonizer, I am the intruder whose fate must be decided" (94). Mustafa then launches into the peroration that will end by giving the lie to Othello and, presumably, make Mustafa himself the repository or embodiment of truth in this place where racial and colonial fantasies cross:

When Mahmoud Wad Ahmed was brought in shackles to Kitchener after his defeat at the Battle of Atbara, Kitchener said to him, "Why have you come to my country to lay waste and plunder?" It was the intruder who said this to the person whose land it was, and the owner of the land bowed his head and said nothing. So let it be with me. In that court I hear the rattle of swords in Carthage and the clatter of the hooves of Allenby's horses desecrating the ground of Jerusalem. The ships at first sailed down the Nile carrying guns not bread, and the railways were originally set up to transport troops; the schools were started so as to teach us how to say "Yes" in their language. They imported to us the germ of the greatest European violence, as seen on the Somme and Verdun, the like of which the world has never previously known, the germ of a deadly disease that struck them more than a thousand years ago. Yes, my dear sirs, I came as an invader into your very homes: a drop of the poison which you have injected into the veins of history. "I am no Othello, Othello was a lie."

(Salih 1980: 94–5)

Mustafa vividly recalls here the notoriously brutal commencement of the Sudan's career as a British protectorate, depicting a scene which even British historians have drawn with considerably more "pity and respect for the dignified and spirited young savage," the Emir Mahmoud, than the arrogant victor, Lord Kitchener, would show him (Magnus 1958: 122).

The exchange Mustafa recounts occurred immediately after the 1898 Battle of the Atbara that initiated the British reconquest of the Sudan, which would conclude some five months later in the near-massacre of 11,000 Sudanese at the Battle of Omdurman. As Philip Magnus writes regarding the aftermath of Atbara:

[Kitchener] took Mahmoud with him when he celebrated his victory by a ceremonial parade followed by a march through Berber…Dragging chains which were riveted round his ankles, and wearing a halter round his neck, the defeated enemy commander was made to walk, and sometimes run, behind the cavalry. His hands were bound behind his back, and he was driven forward by Sudanese guards who lashed him with whips when he stumbled, while the crowds pelted and reviled him. Kitchener rode on a white horse in triumph.

(Magnus 1958: 122)

Given Kitchener's self-positioning as a latter-day Tamburlaine riding in triumph through Berber, the proud Mahmoud's reduction to the proportions of a slave whose sufferings are positively Christ-like, and Kitchener's subsquent desecration of the bones of the Mahdi in Omdurman, it is hard to credit the young Winston Churchill's claim that Omdurman represented "the most signal triumph ever gained by the arms of science over barbarians."[5]

It may be equally hard to credit the idiosyncratic stance Mustafa Sa'eed takes toward this event when he aggressively resists identification with the (allegedly) silent victim of Kitchener's astonishing presumption.[6] For Mustafa wants it to "be with me" as it was with *Kitchener*, not with Mahmoud Wad Ahmed or, for that matter, with Othello. Summoning up a panoramic history of Western intrusions in the affairs of Arab-Africa and the Arab Mideast that begins in Carthage and ends in the institutionalization of British power in Egypt, Palestine, and the Sudan, Mustafa takes example from the victor to avenge in the victor's homeland all that the victor has wasted and plundered over the course of two millennia. He does so, moreover, by establishing the existence of a corrupt bloodline between victor and victim that links both to the fatal contagion of plunder and revenge.

In both the first and last passages quoted above, the "germ of [this] deadly disease" is something that "assailed" or "struck" the female victims of Mustafa and the European invaders of Arab-Africa "a thousand years ago" (Salih 1980: 33, 94–5). But whereas in the first passage the disease seems to be something like a self-destructive craving for, or nagging curiosity about, the exotic, a form of compulsive Orientalizing, in the second passage the disease is directly linked to a penchant for violence whose germs have, through the medium of imperialism, infected the subjects of Empire as well. Mustafa rejects the first diagnosis, effectively assuming responsibility for the deaths of the women he has seduced, but advances the second himself, which would appear to make him more the medium, than the self-determining agent, of the reactive violence he visits upon his European victims, hence, less responsible for his behavior than he initially appears to insist.

Bound up in these competing diagnoses is Mustafa's likeness, or unlikeness to Othello, and the question of who or what is, or is not, "a lie" and what being "a lie" signifies in this context. In Mustafa's first formulation he is a "desert of thirst," "no Othello," and "a lie." In the second, he is an invasive poison contaminated by Europe, "no Othello," and it is Othello, not Mustafa, that is "a lie." What do we make of this?

First off, we need to know what Mustafa thinks being Othello would signify. In the first instance, where Mustafa assumes responsibility for his actions, Othello is positioned as the opposite of the "desert of thirst" and "lie" Mustafa insists he is. Presumably, in his delegated status as "a noble person whose mind was able to absorb [the] civilization [that] broke his heart," Othello constitutes some kind of truth. This reading of Othello adverts to conventional assessments of his character in which guilt for Desdemona's death is displaced to Iago, the embodiment of at least one kind of disease specific to Europeans, if not the one Mustafa's lawyer has in mind. But if Othello is "true," what can we maintain to be "false" about Mustafa? Is it his lack of nobility? Or is it merely a kind of bad faith, peculiar to himself and not exemplary of the condition of other deluded Moors?

The second formulation is superficially at odds, but consistent, with the first. Othello remains the opposite of the "desert of thirst" if we see this thirst as equivalent to the insatiable need of the colonized subject to avenge his contamination by Europe. He thus remains the noble mind seduced by Iago and the medium of a violence not proper to himself. But what, then, does it mean for Othello to be a lie? Is he a lie insofar as he constitutes the West's fabrication of a Moor and of a Moor's sensibility? A lie because even in his last moments he fashions himself the loyal servant of Venice? Whose Othello are we talking about anyway? Shakespeare's Moor or the mythologies that have developed around him? Are the two, in any event, distinguishable? Or, as Barbara Harlow has it: "Whose is the lie? And who Othello? Who Mustafa Sa'eed?" (1979: 163).[7]

The contexts of the two denials are worth re-examining. In the first, the interpretation of Mustafa as a "noble mind" whose "heart" was broken by the West is advanced by Mustafa's English advocate: an interpretation rejected by Mustafa who insists on his agency in bringing about the deaths of the women in question. By describing himself in this context as "a lie," he is not necessarily implying that Othello constitutes an opposing truth. Instead, as in *Heart of Darkness*, we appear to be confronted here with a choice of lies, Othello being one, Mustafa another. The lie that Mustafa claims himself to be may even be identified with that aspect of Othello which, far from being "noble" or embodying a truth, is best explained by Fanon's (1967) notion of the "white mask" which the man of "black skin" constructs for himself. Whereas Othello continues to wear this mask to the end, Mustafa, at least in the company of the narrator, takes his off to reveal a heart as bitter as Iago's. In this first passage (Salih 1980: 33), then, Mustafa both acknowledges and disclaims complicity with this masquerade, this lie, proclaiming himself something more challenging and dangerous than Othello: "a desert of thirst."

As we move back to the second passage and the unanswered questions I've raised, we may conclude that, by proclaiming Othello a lie, Mustafa is attempting to demystify the mythologies of Othello. Positioned as and at the climax of Mustafa's indictment of Western imperialism, Mustafa's identification of Othello as a lie functions as a conclusive commentary on the evidence assembled in the speech. Given the documentedly duplicitous nature of Western imperial interests, their capacity to make Arab-Africans seem like strangers in their own houses and violators of concords they never agreed to, Othello operates as both a cautionary construction and sentimental fantasy of the West: a noble mind undermined by a predictably primitive heart that remains cloyingly faithful to the colonizing interests that destroy him.

Mustafa, however, is decidedly *Other*: he is the intruder, the invader, a "drop of poison," self-constituted avenger of the ships that carried guns and trains that carried troops, the man whose "mind cuts like a knife" and is heartless to the women he seduces and destroys, the man taught to say "Yes" who chooses to say "No," a fantasy that the West has not yet dreamed or cultivated except in the predominantly reactive and ultimately containable form of the Othello complex. Resisting identification with the sentimental assessment of Othello as a man whose heart was broken by Western civilization, Mustafa aggressively promotes his identification with the implicitly racist construction of Othello's resurgent savagism, but redefines that construction in terms of a savagism re-equipped to function in the service of an historically justified "holy war" against the West, indeed, remodels it on the style of Kitchener's amazing presumption, fashioning a composite Anglo-Arab-African self that embodies all the contradictions of the colonial and postcolonial conditions.

2.

The two denials, and the incisive, counter-imperial conclusion they point to, are, however, complicated by a third reference to Othello that intervenes between them as Mustafa recounts his predatory seduction of Isabella Seymour, one of his first English victims. This seduction is literally transacted by Mustafa's self-consciously parodic appropriation of the style and persona of Othello, as that style and persona are revealed in the Moor's recounting of his wooing of Desdemona. As they drink tea, Mustafa tells Isabella "fabricated stories about deserts of golden sands and jungles where non-existent animals called out to one another" (Salih 1980: 38). When asked at the end of his recitation to identify himself, Mustafa glibly states, "'I'm like Othello—Arab-

African'," adding "My face is Arab like the desert of the Empty Quarter, while my head is African and teems with a mischievous child-ishness" (38).

Throughout this episode, Mustafa teasingly exploits what he takes to be the European's limitless store of misconceptions about Arabs and Africans alike: "I told her that the streets of my country teemed with elephants and lions and that during siesta time crocodiles crawled through it" (38). But in so doing, he also experiences an answering responsiveness to these fantasies, feeling himself "transformed in [Isabella's] eyes into a naked, primitive creature, a spear in one hand and arrows in the other, hunting elephants and lions in the jungles" (38). His inability to resist defining himself in ways he knows have already been defined for him by the Orientalist imagination is revealed by the subject positions he assumes for himself out of the hearing of his audience and victims. At one instance, he calls himself "a thirsty desert, a wilderness of southern desires" (38) and at another reflectively states, "You, my lady, may not know, but you—like Carnarvon when he entered Tutankhamen's tomb—have been infected with a deadly disease which has come from you know not where and which will bring about your destruction, be it sooner or later" (39). Mustafa is, appar-ently, as caught up as his victims are in a web of fantasies and misrepresentations that prevents anything like a mutually forthright understanding or transaction to occur. And, despite the control Mustafa exerts over his many victims, the compulsiveness with which he pursues his conquests indicates the extent to which he depends on these same constructions to establish a sense of his own power, identity, and self-worth.

Though Mustafa plays the predator or, in his words, the "colonizer" in the series of doomed relationships he engages in prior to his marriage, positions are reversed in his climactic wooing of and marriage to Jean Morris. Jean leads him on only to turn him off; she plays the dominatrix and makes him a victim of her sexual wiles in every bit the way Iago "seduces" Othello into imaginative commitment to his pornographic fantasies. Indeed, what attracts him to Jean Morris in the first place is her very contempt for the man she caustically calls *Mr.* Mustafa Sa'eed, her refusal to be caught up in the exoticized trap he has laid for his earlier conquests, to be taken in by the lies he has cultivated. In a particularly telling scene, Jean systematically destroys many of the expensive "Oriental" artifacts Mustafa has assembled in his London flat as much for their beauty as for their erotic utility, as if she means to test the extent of Mustafa's capacity for humiliation and self-abasement. In what at times seems a domestic reproduction of the battles of Omdurman and Atbara, Jean transforms Mustafa himself into a stranger in his own home in a "murderous war in which no quarter is given" (160), going so far as to tear "to bits" a rare Arabic manuscript, "filling her mouth with pieces of paper which she chewed and spat out" (157), in a grotesque parody of the West's desecration of the East.[8]

Once they are married, Jean openly engages in a series of affairs; she revels in leaving physical evidence of her lovemaking behind for Mustafa to discover, including a handkerchief. And, finally, when the day of reckoning comes, she positively encourages Mustafa to take her life, positioning her own murder as a form of erotic surrender or sexual climax. She is, in short, nothing like Desdemona but functions, instead, as a provocatively sexual, female avatar of Iago, medium and agent of Mustafa's demise, in much the way that Lula functions in Amiri Baraka's *Dutchman*, the most incisive African-American rewriting of *Othello*. As in *Dutchman*, it is the black Othello figure whose victimization figures most prominently in an exchange which effects the reversal of his claim to exceptionality, agency, and control.[9] Though Jean is the one who is literally destroyed, her status in the novel as avenging angel of the West makes her demise negligible in comparison to the fate visited on Mustafa. One aspect of this fate is to make the man who has been playing at being Othello actually inhabit and act out the most sinister part of the role, thereby transforming what he knows to be a lie into the semblance of a truth.

The sexual and personal humiliation he endures at the hands of Jean Morris makes Mustafa Sa'eed's self-styling as the consummate Orientalized seducer seem, in the end, a form of compulsive role-playing that masks a deeper anxiety about his status as an Arab-African in London. The "facts" of the case as Mustafa presents them reveal a man slavishly obedient to the will of the alien invader, capable of sacri-ficing all that is most precious to him to satisfy her desires: a state of affairs that brings Mustafa considerably closer to the orbit of Othello than he initially allowed. The anxious positioning of the avowedly counter-colonizing avenger begins to emerge in the first part of the scene that ends in Mustafa's recounting of his murder of Jean Morris. This scene opens on the narrator's discovery of the special room Mustafa has annexed to his otherwise inconspicuous house in the Sudanese village to which he retreats after his release from imprison-ment in England. This is a "rectangular room" with a "triangular roof" and "green windows" that houses a quintessentially English library, furnished with a "real English fireplace," "two Victorian chairs covered in a figured silk material," and lavishly carpeted with Persian rugs

(136)—a room that is, in short, "the exact counterpart of Sa'eed's former Oriental bedroom in London" (Takieddine-Amyuni 1980: 16).

Finding "the four walls from floor to ceiling...filled, shelf upon shelf, with books and more books and yet more books," the narrator remarks, "What a fool he was! Was this the action of a man who wanted to turn over a new leaf?," and resolves to "bring the whole place down upon his head" by setting it on fire (Salih 1980: 136). However, before he can do so, he provides an inventory of Mustafa's collection that indicates Mustafa's status as a remarkably cosmopolitan scholar and intellectual, a reader of everything from Plato to Gibbon to Wittgenstein and Freud, even of Mannoni's *Prospero and Caliban*, and author of impressive volumes of his own, provocatively entitled *Colonialism and Monopoly*, *The Cross and Gunpowder*, and *The Rape of Africa* (137). As the titles of Mustafa's own works indicate, he was in his professional life as an economist a vigorous critic and accomplished anatomizer of Western imperialism. Yet, as the narrator remarks, this anomalously plush library set down in the Sudanese desert contains "not a single Arabic book"; the closest it comes to is a copy of *"The Koran* in English," an observation that leads him to conclude: "A graveyard. A mausoleum. An insane idea. A prison. A huge joke" (137–8).

In his own assessment of this scene, Edward Said suggestively associates Mustafa Sa'eed's "secret library" of European books with "Kurtz's skull-topped fence" in *Heart of Darkness* (Said 1994: 211). Where the latter illustrates the depths of African savagery to which Kurtz has descended, the library may be said to represent the extent of Mustafa's submersion in European states of mind and feeling, of his contamination by Western culture and civilization. It also represents, given the expressly anti-colonial stance of his scholarly writings, the fatal and irreconcilable split in his character and commitments that retrospectively helps to explain both his chronic unease and his sudden disappearance. Like the final speech Othello delivers in Shakespeare's play, which witnesses his slippage between two essentially opposed subject positions, Mustafa Sa'eed's library, cut off from the rest of his house and the village that surrounds it by a locked iron door, testifies to the strength of European culture's hold over him within the very space he has chosen to effect his decolonization. The self-styled counter-colonizing avenger is brought up short here to indulge, and play witness to, his own conquest and colonization, which is nowhere more graphically figured than in his English translation of the Koran.

The narrator greets his discovery of Mustafa's contradictions with much the same combination of indignation and reflexivity Marlow brings to his disillusionment with Kurtz. Poring over Mustafa's books, pictures, letters, and memorabilia, he concludes that:

> It was no coincidence…that he had left me the key to this wax museum. There was no limit to his egoism and conceit; despite everything, he wanted history to immortalize him. But I do not have the time to proceed further with this farce…At the break of dawn tongues of fire will devour these lies.
>
> (Salih 1980: 154)

Yet, at the exact moment he comes to this resolve, his eyes are drawn to a portrait of Jean Morris and his mind rehearses Mustafa's detailed account of their violent courtship and marriage. What remains of the novel after Mustafa's voice graphically depicts Jean's murder is a four-page coda that finds the narrator submerged in the waters of the Nile, "half-way between north and south…unable to continue, unable to return," resolving finally to "choose life" but doing so "like a comic actor on a stage," screaming for help "with all my remaining strength" (167, 169).[10]

3.

Although the novel and its closure are too complex to reduce to any ready formula, one must ask what it is exactly that cues the narrator's rage, disillusionment, and decision to enter the river "naked as when my mother bore me" (166) instead of setting Mustafa's library afire as he had planned? In terms of the novel's verbal preferences, it would appear that what most inflames the narrator is the discovery of "these lies," which he associates with the varied contents of Mustafa's "secret room," with his books, first and foremost. But why should the narrator be so surprised by the library's contents, by Mustafa's books, particularly given Mustafa's established persistence in calling himself a lie? To answer such questions, it is first necessary to establish the narrator's position as he stands at the door of the library, ready to begin the novel's last movement.

The narrator comes to the door of the library with his world "turned suddenly upside down," filled, he states, with feelings of hatred and revenge for the "adversary" who waits within, though it is clear both to himself and the reader that the lines of opposition are no longer so neatly drawn. The murder-suicide executed by Mustafa's widow, Hosna Bint Mahmoud; the sexual mutilations endured by her and revisited on the body of the elderly second husband who has been forced upon her;

and the collective revilement of this, "the only woman I have ever loved," by the residents of the village, including his grandfather—all have sundered the narrator from a world he thought was his own, in which he "felt not like a storm-swept feather but like that palm tree, a being with a background, with roots, with a purpose" (2). Failing to make the choice that was offered him, to step into Mustafa's shoes in order to care for and protect the wife and children he left behind, the narrator plays passive witness to the Arab village's paternalistic contempt for women, to its dissemination of an indigenous poison or disease arguably as insidious as the infection spread by Europeans and as native to it as the firmly rooted palm tree.[11] The immediate consequence is an alienation that profoundly unsettles both his sense of self and related sense of place:

> Now I am on my own: there is no escape, no place of refuge, no safeguard. Outside, my world was a wide one; now it had contracted, had withdrawn upon itself, until I myself had become the world, no world existing outside of me. Where, then, were the roots that struck down into times past? Where the memories of death and life? What had happened to the caravan and to the tribe? Where had gone the trilling cries of the women at tens of weddings, where the Nile floodings, and the blowing of the wind summer and winter from north and south?
>
> (Salih 1980: 134)

In the heart of what he had accounted as light, he now finds darkness, and it is from this darkness that he enters Mustafa's secret room, there to encounter not Mustafa Sa'eed, but "a picture of me frowning at my face from a mirror," and, from "an oasis of light" (135), to encounter additional mirror images of England and the West writ large.

In this face-to-face encounter with these overlapping reflections, the narrator discovers the extent of Mustafa's dependence on the West for the intellectual sustenance which the privileged "simplicity" of Arab village life could not afford: a discovery that unsettles the complacent illusions about that life which he had heretofore cultivated. Like the "deadly disease" that infected "Carnarvon when he entered Tutankhamen's tomb," the productions of Western culture enmesh the narrator as he enters Mustafa's "mausoleum" and wrap him in the same fatal embrace of doubleness or dividedness that beset Othello. Unmoored from the firm standing he had maintained in his culture that had allowed him to emerge from seven years in England, three of

which were devoted to the study of "an obscure English poet," in order
to teach pre-Islamic literature" in his emerging nation's secondary
schools (57), the narrator is overwhelmed by the sheer bulk of the
room's holdings: "Books on economics, history and literature. Zoology.
Geology. Mathematics. Astronomy. The Encyclopaedia Britannica."
But "not a single Arabic book" (137). The room literally bulges with the
West's claim to mastery of the human sciences and with Mustafa's
apparent accession to that claim. And it threatens to overawe its new
occupant, so recently schooled in examples of his own culture's
brutality.

This simultaneous dislodging from any ground of certainty and challenge to accede to the arrogant assertiveness of the West precipitate the
narrator's flight into the waters of the Nile from which he issues his
closing cry for help. But there remains in his complex response one
more matter to elaborate: the charge of duplicity he levels against
Mustafa. What exactly is it about Mustafa's library that makes him
seem a lie?

Throughout the novel, the narrator cultivates two seemingly
opposed, but ultimately related, ideas about Mustafa. On the one hand,
he appears to accept Mustafa's promotion of himself as a counter-
colonizing avenger of the West's crimes against Arab-Africa as well as
his decision to commit himself, upon his return to the Sudan, to a
productive family life lived within the traditional protocols of the Nile
village. On both these grounds, Mustafa emerges as a figure who, like
the narrator, has managed to resist contamination by the West and to
commit himself to the work of incipiently postcolonial nation-building.
On the other hand, the narrator records a number of alternative views
from a series of acquaintances which depict Mustafa as both a mercenary and opportunist, a willing convert to the ways of the West.

One of his sources, a "retired Mamur," recalls that Mustafa "was the
spoilt child of the English" and "the first Sudanese to be sent on a
scholarship abroad." He was nicknamed " 'the black Englishman' " out
of "a combination of admiration and spite" for his expert capacity to
speak English which "in our day…was the key to the future: no one had
a chance without it" (53). This same man notes that he, himself,
remained behind at Gordon Memorial College—a school founded by
the infamous Lord Kitchener—which "was actually little more than an
intermediate school where they used to give us just enough education
for filling junior government posts" (53). By way of contrast, "The
English District Commissioner was a god who had a free hand over an
area larger than the whole of the British Isles and lived in an enormous
palace full of servants and guarded by troops" (53).[12]

Another acquaintance observes that Mustafa Sa'eed was "the first Sudanese to marry an Englishwoman, in fact he was the first to marry a European of any kind," and adds: "He married in England and took British nationality...he played an important role in the plottings of the English in the Sudan during the late thirties. He was one of their most faithful supporters" (55–6). This same character's assertion that Mustafa is "now a millionaire living like a lord in the English countryside" is, however, so misinformed that it casts doubt on his other presentments. An Englishman in the same company, who is unsure of "the truth of what was said concerning the role Mustafa Sa'eed had played in the English political plottings in the Sudan," petulantly claims that Mustafa "was not a reliable economist," was "one of the darlings of the English left," and "built quite a legend of a sort round himself—the handsome black man courted in Bohemian circles" (57–8). Finally, a former student of Mustafa's confirms his status as a successful womanizer at the same time as he resituates him in the camp of activists committed to the decolonization of Africa:

> "You remind me of a dear friend with whom I was on very close terms in London—Dr Mustafa Sa'eed...In 1928 he was President of the Society for the Struggle for African Freedom of which I was a committee member. What a man he was! He's one of the greatest Africans I've known. He had wide contacts. Heavens, that man—women fell for him like flies. He used to say 'I'll liberate Africa with my penis,' and he laughed so widely you could see the back of his throat."
>
> (Salih 1980: 120)

Mustafa Sa'eed emerges from this series of observations as a contradictory figure whose exceptionality and notoriety make it difficult to separate fact from fiction. But, given their repeated emphasis on Mustafa's easy and intimate commerce with his country's English overlords and the pride he took in his sexuality, the comments contribute an overriding impression of Mustafa as a conscientiously assimilated opportunist attempting, like the British in the Sudan, to live well above the aspirations of his countrymen or, better yet, trying, like a latter-day Othello made cynical by his easy access to the salons and bedrooms of the metropolis, to reap the greatest harvest from his well-cultivated exoticism.

The narrator's growing skepticism about Mustafa's anti-colonial credentials pointedly echoes his established disillusionment with the opportunism of "the new rulers of Africa"—men who are:

smooth of face, lupine of mouth, their hands gleaming with
rings of precious stones, exuding perfume from their cheeks, in
white, blue, black and green suits of fine mohair and expensive
silk rippling on their shoulders like the fur of Siamese cats, and
with shoes that reflect the light from chandeliers and squeak as
they tread on marble.

(Salih 1980: 118–19)

As the narrator observes: "Had [Mustafa] returned in the natural way
of things he would have joined up with this pack of wolves. They all
resemble him: handsome faces and faces made so by comfortable
living" (120). It is, in fact, one of these same ministers who claimed
membership with Mustafa in the Society for the Struggle for African
Freedom and gloatingly quoted his resolve to "liberate Africa with [his]
penis."

This moment in the novel, in which the narrator recounts his participation in a pan-African conference on educational methodologies,
occupies a pivotal space in Salih's assessment of the postcolonial condition and of the role that men like the narrator and Mustafa Sa'eed play
in shaping it. The significance of the novel's engagement with *Othello*
largely rests on its concern with the impact of the West on the identity
formations of those few individuals who by training, education, or
circumstance are, like Othello, compelled to live in an undefined space
between East and West, North and South.[13] The narrator has heretofore maintained that he has managed to avoid the damaging
dividedness of this condition, that it is not with him as it is with Mustafa
Sa'eed:

He had said that he was a lie, so was I also a lie? I am from
here—is not this reality enough? I too had lived with them.
But I had lived with them superficially, neither loving nor
hating them. I used to treasure within me the image of this
little village, seeing it wherever I went with the eye of my
imagination.

(Salih 1980: 49)

In this passage, as elsewhere in the novel, the narrator claims immunity
from the infection of Westernism that has so fatally undermined
Mustafa. Far from hearing "the rattle of swords in Carthage and the
clatter of hooves...desecrating the ground of Jerusalem," the narrator
had, during his sojourn in England, insulated himself through a combination of nostalgia, indifference, and denial against any incursion the

West might attempt to make against his sense of wholeness and integrity:

> Sometimes during the summer months in London, after a downpour of rain, I would breathe in the smell of [this little village], and at odd fleeting moments before sunset I would see it. At the latter end of the night the foreign voices would reach my ears as though they were those of my people out here...I would imagine the faces over there as being brown or black so that they would look like the faces of people I knew.
>
> (Salih 1980: 49)

This insularity leads him to discount the differences between East and West—"Over there is like here, neither better nor worse" (49)—and to discount as well the idea that the long-sustained occupation of the Sudan by the British will have corrosive effects on the postcolonial dispensation:

> The fact that they came to our land, I know not why, does that mean that we should poison our present and our future? Sooner or later they will leave our country, just as many people throughout history left many countries. The railways, ships, hospitals, factories and schools will be ours and we'll speak their language without either a sense of guilt or a sense of gratitude. Once again we shall be as we were—ordinary people—and if we are lies we shall be lies of our own making.
>
> (Salih 1980: 49–50)

Salih has the narrator deliver this passage in a deceptively comforting manner as if common sense and a strongly-rooted sense of oneself could comprise an antidote to the consequential history of Anglo-Arab relations and to the fatal dividedness of characters like Mustafa. A few sentences later, however, the narrator again encounters the mental image of Mustafa Sa'eed, who "has, against my will, become a part of my world, a thought in my brain, a phantom that does not want to take itself off" (50). And the message this phantom delivers is the "fear that it is just conceivable that simplicity is not everything" (50).

The narrator's valorization of simplicity, his calm assessment that "Over there is like here" and that the departure of the British from the Sudan will make no palpable difference in the way people live their lives, is arguably as symptomatic of his internal or psychic colonization as is the destructive double life Mustafa Sa'eed led. As the retired

Mamur observes: "Has not the country become independent? Have we not become free men in our own country? Be sure, though, that they will direct our affairs from afar. This is because they have left behind them people who think as they do" (53). Although the narrator operates throughout the novel as a voice of reason, compassion, and restraint, the very sanity of his "no fault" approach to experience may be as much the product of his careful schooling at the hands of the British as the result of his continued devotion to home and country. It was, in fact, the aim of Lord Kitchener—conqueror of Khartoum, desecrator of the bones of the Mahdi, and founder of the Gordon Memorial College—to instill the same sense of complacency in educated Sudanese with which the narrator anticipates the departure of the British. This much and more—including a belief in the salutary effects of the study of literature—is made plain in a commendatory letter sent to Kitchener by Lord Salisbury on 21 November 1898:

> The reconciliation of the races which inhabit the Nile Valley to a Government that, in its principles and in its methods must be essentially Western...will tax the resources of the present generation of Englishmen, and of those who come after for many years...
>
> The only method by which that reconciliation can be attained is to give to the races whom you have conquered access to the literature and knowledge of Europe.
>
> Your scheme, therefore, for establishing a machinery by which European knowledge can be brought to the inhabitants of the Valley of the Nile, is not only in itself wholly admirable; but it represents the only policy by which the civilizing mission of this country can effectively be accomplished.
>
> (quoted in Magnus 1958: 144, 146)

It is to disrupt the complacency of the narrator with this "scheme" that Salih sends the "phantom" of Mustafa Sa'eed to haunt him with the message that "simplicity is not everything" and also brings him face-to-face with "the facts about the new rulers of Africa" and with the new lies that are being sponsored in the name of what another character calls "the superstition of industrialization, the superstition of national-ization, the superstition of Arab unity, [and] the superstition of African unity" (Salih 1980: 59). Indeed, Salih relentlessly disburdens the narrator of every illusion he has maintained about his culture, particu-larly regarding the probity of the village life of his father and grandfather, which comes crashing down when Mustafa's widow murders herself and Wad Rayyes, the second husband forced upon her by the elders of the village.

Like the narrator, Salih himself considers this event "the most important thing that [occurs] in *Season of Migration*" and calls it "the real horror" (Berkley and Ahmed 1982: 49). For Salih as for the narrator, "here" continues to matter considerably more than "there"; it is this difference in commitment that most distinguishes them from Mustafa, who is condemned to respond to the siren call of the West. As Mustafa says to the narrator in their last interview before his disappearance:

> That distant call still rings in my ears. I thought that my life and marriage here would silence it...Rationally I know what is right: my attempt at living in this village with these happy people. But mysterious things in my soul and in my blood impel me towards faraway parts that loom up before me and cannot be ignored. How sad it would be if either or both of my sons grew up with the germ of this infection in them, the wanderlust. I charge you with the trust because I have glimpsed in you a likeness to your grandfather.
>
> (Salih 1980: 66–7)

In linking his fate to that of "the vagrant and all wheeling stranger," Othello, "it is possible to say," as Salih elsewhere observes, "that Mustafa Sa'eed has been connected with a delusion or phantom" (Berkley and Ahmed 1982: 40): a factitious construction of the Arab-African character and sensibility. But it is one of the novel's bitter ironies that the firmer course Mustafa hopes his sons will take, a course carved out by the "happy people" of the Nile village, is shown to be as riddled with contradictions as Mustafa. Although he is assuredly "no Othello," the narrator is himself positioned at the novel's end "half-way between north and south" (Salih 1980: 167), willing himself back into existence, but sounding, for all rights and purposes, "like a comic actor shouting on a stage" (169).

That such a position may, in the end, prove redemptive is indicated by an earlier section of the novel that brings North and South into productively hybridized communion when a group of lorry drivers and bedouins attracted by the lights of their trucks become "a huge cara-vanserai of more than a hundred men [and women] who ate and drank and prayed and got drunk" (113). There in the center of the great desert, beers are drunk "to the good health of the Sudan," "the night and the desert resounding with the echoes of a great feast, as though we were some tribe of genies" (114):

We clapped, stamped on the ground, and hummed in unison, making a festival to nothingness in the heart of the desert. Then someone produced a transistor radio which we placed in the centre of the circle and we clapped and danced to its music…The men imitated the loud trilling cries women utter at festivities and the horns of the cars all rang out together.

(Salih 1980: 114)

The driver of the narrator's lorry,

who had kept silent the whole day,…raised his voice in song: a sweet, rippling voice that you can't imagine is his. He is singing to his car just as the poets of old sang to their camels:

How shapely is your steering-wheel astride its metal stem.
No sleep or rest tonight we'll have till Sitt Nafour is come.

(Salih 1980: 113)

For his own part, the narrator declares:

On such a night as this you feel you are able to rise up to the sky on a rope ladder. This is the land of poetry and the possible—and my daughter is named Hope. We shall pull down and we shall build, and we shall humble the sun itself to our will; and somehow we shall defeat poverty.

(Salih 1980: 112–13)

This demonstration of the hybridizing resilience and resourcefulness of Sudanese culture proves decidedly ephemeral in the context of the narrator's enforced return to his native village to contend with the murder-suicide of Mustafa's widow and with his own disillusionment. But the fact that such an event can occur at all within sight of "the peaks of the mountains of Kerari overlooking Omdurman" (115)—that is, in the shadow of Arab-Africa's most momentous defeat—also proves entirely pertinent to the narrator's awakening "from the nightmare" (168) put into motion by the Othello-like dividedness of Mustafa Sa'eed and exacerbated by the inflexibly conservative social practices of the Nile village. The complexity of Mustafa and the "simplicity" of the Nile village represent, in the end, equally false alternatives for the narrator, who must learn to resist the "self-Orientalizing" tendencies implicit in each: the one embodied by the attempt to emulate the West, the other by the effort to become more "authentically" Islamic.[14]

Fashioning a self between the banks of North and South will require not only "force and cunning" (169) but also, as the caravanserai suggests, freedom from the disabling ghosts of history and the falsely enabling "superstitions" of postcoloniality alike. This is not assuredly a freedom easily obtained, and, when obtained, leaves no sure ground to stand upon. The rejection of the dividedness of the Northward-leaning Othello is coterminous with rejection of the "wholeness" of the Nilotic grandfather and the rootedness he represents. But this double rejection, Salih seems to suggest, is precisely what is needed if a daughter named Hope is to survive her own season of migration and help "a land of poetry and the possible" thrive.

CONCLUSION

Decolonizing Shakespeare: *My Son's Story*, *Children of Light*, and late imperial romance

However uncertain the position—and positioning—of the narrator at the end of *Season of Migration*, Salih's novel decisively arrests the traffic in signs and markers that allows the originary act of misrepresentation that is *Othello* to underwrite succeeding acts of misrecognition. Having demonstrated the damaging and distorting effects of *Othello*'s "afterlife" on both sides of the colonial divide, the novel effectively closes the door to the library that is emblematic of the Sudanese intellectual's submission to the siren call of Europe during the colonial period. As it turns its face to the South, however, *Season of Migration* does not map out or endorse a privileged avenue of relief or escape from the "betweenness" of the postcolonial condition. Like Ngũgĩ in *A Grain of Wheat* and Michelle Cliff in *No Telephone to Heaven*, Salih ultimately fastens on the immediate problems and pressures of the post-independence period; on the effort to fashion selves and societies within the compass of competing models of social organization and of established traditions that either have eroded or have gone unexamined during the long season of colonialism. And, like Ngũgĩ in particular, he indicates that there is no particularly crucial role for Shakespeare to play at this juncture in Third World postcolonial societies.

This delegation of Shakespeare to the largely superseded domain of anti-colonial applications has a number of possible consequences, including the bard's own liberation from an interpretive consensus that has colonized his plays just as surely as the plays have imposed themselves on subjects, both colonial and domestic, who have grown up in the shadow of Othello, Caliban, and Jack Cade. A decolonized or decommissioned Shakespeare, freed from his service to imperial interests and from the circuit of countertextual applications such service inspires, could presumably be remobilized to address ancillary concerns about social or sexual redefinition—as he is in Gus Van Sant's *My Own*

Private Idaho and in a host of gender-bending contemporary productions—or be reassigned to the domain of popular culture where he may
serve as an instantly recognizable icon and article of consumption, and
as a rich repository of plots for updated adaptations and make-overs.
He might, alternatively, be redeployed to reveal how dependent on him
we in the West remain for self-validating constructions of ourselves, as
he is in Robert Stone's *Children of Light*. Shakespeare could even be
productively repositioned to reflect his comparatively diminished status
in, and relevance to, a changing social order, as is the case in Nadine
Gordimer's novel, *My Son's Story*, whose protagonist's self-promoting
embrace of Shakespeare becomes increasingly irrelevant the more
involved he becomes in the struggle against apartheid. The destruction
of this character's collection of Shakespeare in the same conflagration
that destroys his home in an integrated suburb seems, in fact, particularly pertinent to the differently focused efforts at decolonization
undertaken by Ngũgĩ and Salih.

In the process of examining this repositioning of Shakespeare in
South Africa, I want also to assess the deployment of Shakespeare in
Children of Light—a novel published shortly after George Shultz declared
that the United States had no intention of becoming "the Hamlet of
nations" by a novelist who has been characteristically preoccupied with
Cold War politics and paranoia.[1] What in particular do we make of
Stone's provocative reconfiguring of his Lear and Rosalind figures?, of
his staging of "Rosalind" as Lear and of "Lear" as Orlando in the
context of a novel that deploys Shakespeare as both a commonly available and strategically privatized language of commentary and
interaction? Would it be stretching our sense of the postcolonial too far
to see this conspicuously gendered transposition as symptomatic of
changes in social and political consciousness set into motion by move-
ments of racial and national liberation?, to see it, then, as a byproduct
or symptom, if not exactly an embodiment, of postcolonial appropriation? Or would this move need to be construed as another instance of
First World "colonizing" of a characteristically Third World model of
literary production?, as an act transacted through the interpretive grid
of U.S. national formations, hence, as a critical version of what John
McClure has termed "late imperial romance"?

1.

The "children of light" of Stone's novel, the actress Lee (Lu Anne)
Verger and the screenwriter/actor Gordon Walker, are presented as
refugees or "survivors" from the pastoral space of the 1960s. Their

"fall" into the corrupt present of Hollywood—where neither does their best work—is partly figured by the prominence of Shakespeare at earlier, more promising stages of their careers. The signal moment of Lu Anne's career was her performance as Rosalind in a production of *As You Like It* staged in New Haven—"that production...where everybody in it became rich and famous" (Stone 1992: 80). It is a moment to which she—and everyone acquainted with her career—repeatedly refers. At the start of the novel, Walker has just returned to Los Angeles after an abbreviated run as Lear in a regional theater production in Seattle. His identification with the part has, apparently, extended beyond the run of the production and finds him in a state of drug- and alcohol-fueled disintegration, declaiming lines from *King Lear* into a bathroom mirror, largely oblivious to his family, his marriage in shambles.

Against the advice of his agent and other associates (who chorically embody roles in *Lear* delegated to the Fool and Kent), he decides to visit Lu Anne on the Baja, California set of *The Awakening*, whose screenplay he had written with Lu Anne in mind many years before. He finds her there abandoned by her husband and children and at the exact point of departure for a climactic schizophrenic episode which the film's director—Walter Drogue, *fils*, son of the legendary Walter Drogue, *père*—hopes won't happen until filming is completed. Instead of attempting to protect or preserve her, Walker—an "assassin" who is "full of shit," according to the novel's all-licensed Shelley, a mutual friend of Walker and Lu Anne—feeds her "great lines" of Shakespeare and cocaine and helps push her past the breaking point.

In a double climax, the first part of which is clearly modeled on Shakespeare, Stone stages a "storm scene" abetted by a site-specific *chubasco* on an abandoned film set (now no more than a hovel) in the wilds of Baja in which Lu Anne rages at her demons like Lear and Edgar combined, tearing her clothes from her body and rending her flesh, while Walker, Kent-Gloucester-and-Fool-like, tries, ineffectually, to rein her in. On their return to *The Awakening* set, the intertextual transaction becomes even more complicated as Lu Anne, now apparently subsumed in the role of Edna Pontellier but spouting lines from *Antony and Cleopatra* that Walker has supplied as directives, walks into the sea to her death while Walker flails about in an alcoholic haze. The novel ends some months later in a post-memorial service barroom scene where Shelley excoriates Walker for precipitating Lu Anne's demise, and comments, upon his departure, "Men have died from time to time and worms have eaten them, but not for love," and another companion approvingly adds, "Great line."

Shakespeare makes a number of other cameo appearances in the novel, his words summoned up at the sight of the worm in a bottle of mezcal ("I wish you joy of the worm"), as an epitaph for a screenwriter whose drugged-out body has been welded into an oil drum ("He's home, man, he's in Abraham's bosom"), and his name inscribed on the bill of a gofer's cap. But he plays an ongoing role in the novel's staging of Walker and Lu Anne's relationship to the protocols of Hollywood filmmaking. For Gordon, and particularly for Lu Anne, there is not, nor has there ever been, any reliable separation between acting and life. Caught up as they have been for years enacting what they consider to be the spurious visions of life generated by the film industry, they consider the scenarios spun out by the Bard to constitute a deeper, more reliable version of the real or authentic. Hollywood for them is second-hand mimicry, Shakespeare the thing itself; the relationship resembles the postcolonial configuration of margin and center (though in this case it is margin that colonizes center). But in rejecting (if only intellectually) the hollowness of Hollywood for the presumed solidity of Shakespeare, the characters do little more than privilege one script over another, playacting their way through an anthology of remembered lines and scenes that supplies them with a shared language in which they may stage their mutual disintegrations.

In the novel's "storm scene," for example, the characters act out a "dream of passion" that allows Lu Anne to play all the roles—Edgar, Lear, Rosalind—that give shape and substance to a madness that has her spinning out of control. Walker never fully participates in Lu Anne's passion; he is a reluctant player and audience, drawn in against his will, though he has sworn otherwise: " 'I would die for you,' he said. It was true, he thought, but not really helpful. He was the kind of lover that Edna Pontellier was a mother" (231–2). In fact, we might consider Walker—given his status as author of the scenes Lu Anne enacts and as a man who "hath ever but slenderly known himself" (5)—as more deeply implicated than Lu Anne in the shallow scenarios he has scripted for Hollywood, including the script for *The Awakening* itself, whose margins he has filled with high-flown directives drawn from *Antony and Cleopatra* about the sublimity of Edna's embrace of death, comments which Lu Anne considers fatuous:

> *She moves like Cleopatra,* Walker had written, *as though impelled by immortal longings*. The lines of direction were addressed only to her, a part of their game of relentless Shakespeareanizing, half

purely romantic, half higher bullshit. He meant he wanted Edna going out like the Queen in *Antony & Cleo*, Act V, scene 2.

> *She senses a freedom the scope of which she has never known. She has come beyond despair to a kind of exaltation.*

*　　　*　　　*

Of course, that was the spirit of the book and its ending. But exaltation beyond despair? She had never found anything beyond despair except despair.

(Stone 1992: 120)

Although she trails the words of Shakespeare in her wake when she follows Edna's lead and takes her own culminating walk into the water—" 'See the world, Walker? How it goes?' "; " 'Give me my robe,' she said. 'Put on my crown' "; " 'Immortal longings,' she said" (251)—Lu Anne goes well beyond the protocols of suffering drawn up by Shakespeare and Walker alike. Reluctant to accept her invitation to join her, Walker himself fails, in the end, to enact the ritual and take the medicine he prescribes.[2]

This sequence might help us better gauge the resonance of Shelley's concluding appropriation of Rosalind's comment that bold lovers like Orlando have never died for love. In the play Rosalind speaks with a pragmatic authority she has not really had the experience to claim. Lu Anne considers her the sanest of women, but also eagerly absorbs her in the terms of her own lunacy: "I am Rosalind who can strike you lame with reasons and be mad without any" (26–7). Shelley quotes her out of hard-won knowledge about men, especially men like Walker. In so doing, Shelley—herself a cynical Hollywood player—appears to recuperate Shakespeare's capacity to speak knowingly about experience, though her companion's rejoinder could be said to reposition her comment as but one of many clever pieces of Hollywood dialogue, or "great lines" (in a novel in which "lines" just as often find their way up people's noses).

Shakespeare is being simultaneously colonized and cannibalized here, his words and parts appropriated in fragmented form both to shore Stone's characters against their ruin and to help them enact it. Shelley wields Rosalind's line like a knife, helping her carve her way through a world of self-serving men. (In the novel's concluding scene, Shelley announces that the agency she has just established will only cater to women clients.) Walker continues to play and to quote Shakespeare as a way of assuring himself that there really is more to him than everybody thinks, that his "literariness" will always redeem his seductions. And although her knowledge of Shakespeare appears to be more informed than Walker's—"I am myself no more than good bones. A rag, a hank of hair and good bones" (214), she says to an admirer— Lu Anne travesties and supersedes it in service to her massive delusions.[3]

Unlike the other, more expressly politicized appropriations of Shakespeare we have examined, those delegated by Stone to his characters do not appear to be underwritten by any particular national or cultural agenda. It is, however, revealing that Lu Anne chooses in the end the path to death sketched out by the American writer Kate Chopin in her protofeminist novel *The Awakening*. In a novel that is something of an intertextual nightmare, in which even Edna's walk into the water is discussed in the context of a film anthology of watery deaths the Drogues have had specially edited for the occasion, Chopin's novel, rooted as it is made to be in Lu Anne's own Louisiana heritage, ultimately emerges as the nightmare of choice.

2.

The use to which Shakespeare is put in *My Son's Story* bears some resemblance to Stone's climactic subordination of *As You Like It* to *The Awakening* insofar as Shakespeare is superseded here by preoccupations that are more integral to the South African struggle against apartheid. The novel's narrator is named Will by its protagonist, Sonny, a schoolteacher who, in the course of the novel, will be forced out of his job in order to embrace on a full-time basis his increasing commitment to political activity. Will, we learn, "was named for Shakespeare, whose works, in a cheap complete edition bound in fake leather, stood in the glass-fronted bookcase in the small sitting-room and were no mere ornamental pretension to culture." In a voice that occasionally sounds too much like Gordimer's, Will goes on to tell us that "Sonny read and reread them with devotion; although the gilt lettering had been eaten away by fishmoth, and the volume he wanted had to be selected blindly, his hand always went straight to it" (Gordimer 1990: 6).

As a way of emphasizing the functional, as opposed to "ornamental," basis of Sonny's devotion, the narrator notes that "Sonny and his wife did not covet" the furnishings and housewares available to "their kind"—"bedroom 'schemes' and lounge 'suites'" marketed under such exotic names as "Granada" or "Versailles"—because "with an understanding of Shakespeare there comes a release from the gullibility that makes you prey to the great shopkeeper who runs the world and would sell you cheap to illusion" (11). But given Will's repeated, and occasionally perverse, resistance to embracing his father's devotion to Shakespeare—"He sees me with *Sportsday*, under his nose, instead of *King Lear* that he can quote reams of. An ungrateful child is sharper than a serpent's tooth" (46)—it is difficult to gauge the tone of this passage's affirmation of the liberatory function of reading Shakespeare. Are we really meant to believe that "an understanding of Shakespeare" can free "their kind" from the idols of the marketplace? Or is Will merely skeptically parroting one of his father's sermons on the freedom conferred by great art?

However effective Shakespeare might be in helping him distinguish illusion from reality, Sonny comes to consider Shakespeare largely irrelevant to the needs of the political struggle to which he commits himself. As he begins to feel a greater "accountability" to "the need to bring together the school and the community in which it performed an isolated function—education as a luxury, a privilege apart from the survival preoccupations of the parents," his reading choices change:

> He bought books that kept him from Shakespeare. He read them over and over in order to grasp and adapt the theory that recognized social education of the community, the parents and relatives and neighbours of the pupils, as part of a school's function. He started a parent–teacher association and an advisory service for parents…For the uplift of the community he enterprisingly approached the Rotary Club and Lions' Club in the white town with respectful requests that they might graciously send their doctors, lawyers, and members of amateur theatre and music groups to lecture or perform in the school hall.
>
> (Gordimer 1990: 9)

This chapter suggestively ends with a passage that notes that "The lover of Shakespeare never had the right to enter the municipal library and so did not so much as think about it while white people came out before him with books under their arms," walking below the "motto above the pillared entrance: CARPE DIEM" (12).

As Sonny proceeds in the course of the novel to make that motto his own, both on the political and erotic front, Shakespeare recedes from the former, but continues to play a prominent role in the "privatized" domain of Sonny's adulterous relationship with Hannah, a white fellow traveler. Other books, other voices, begin to overlay his release from gullibility, Kafka's for one—who "explained the context of the schoolteacher's life better than Shakespeare"—Rosa Luxemburg's for another (see Karen Johnson 1995: 133). Although he continues to resist the social and political formulations of his fellow activists and sloga-neers—"he went to Shakespeare for [definitions] with more authority than those given on makeshift platforms in the veld" (Gordimer 1990: 23)—Sonny eventually submits to the unambiguous demands of the political struggle: "As he loved the magnificent choices of Shakespearean language, the crudely reductive terms of political concepts were an embarrassment to him, but he had to use them, like everybody else" (47–8).

From this point forward in the novel, Shakespeare becomes compart-mentalized as the private language Sonny shares with Hannah, as the password of a relationship that the novel stages and assesses with some ambiguity. One is particularly led to wonder whether the unambigu-ously strong ties shared by two equally committed activists is something to be affirmed or celebrated, especially by contrast with the proto-bourgeois values of the presumably uncommitted wife and children? If so, why is their commitment to the struggle and to themselves ulti-mately outflanked by the even more risky ventures undertaken by the neglected wife and daughter? Does the Shakespearean password itself— "Sermons in stones and good in everything"—drawn as it is from the pastoral confines of As You Like It, indicate that the lovers have taken a fallback position of their own in bourgeois consciousness, creating a pastoral space for themselves that is not in fact supportive of, but antag-onistic to, their political professions and convictions? Gordimer is too subtle to provide a clear-cut answer to such questions, but utopian enough to associate sexual expressiveness with political liberation (see, for example, her earlier novel, A Sport of Nature). She has, in any event, hedged her bets by giving us a narrator whose criticism of the relation-ship is grounded in loyalty to his mother and a denouement that finds "good in everything" the novel unravels.

The positioning of Shakespeare in the novel seems comparatively more fixed and certain. Although Will's eventual emergence as a composite Hamlet/Horatio/Shakespeare figure—he announces in the end that "I have that within that passes show" and that "What he did— my father—made me a writer"—indicates Shakespeare's continued sponsorship of the novel's "mixed race" South African family romance, it is only within the span of such relationships, and of their extramarital extensions, that Shakespeare appears to sustain his relevance. What motivates Will's mother and sister—Aila and Baby—to expend them-selves in the struggle for black liberation transcends, and remains completely untouched by, Sonny's love of language and devotion to his books, which are translated into "Flocks of papery cinders" in the novel's concluding conflagration. Even Sonny seems to notice this, although, as Will notes of his choice of words, "And then of course the old rhetoric took up the opportunity" to elaborate on the obvious:

> We can't be burned out, he said, we're that bird, you know, it's called the phoenix, that always rises again from the ashes. Prison won't keep us out. Petrol bombs won't get rid of us. This street—this whole country is ours to live in. Fire won't stop me. And it won't stop you.
>
> (Gordimer 1990: 274)

In this last allusion to Shakespeare, the figure of the phoenix arguably becomes subdued to the "dyer's hand," the element which it works in, as literary reference cedes primacy and place to the material conditions that underwrite it: prison, petrol bombs, "this whole country," and the fire that won't stop.

3.

More broadly, what Gordimer is doing throughout *A Son's Story* is at once putting Shakespeare in his place and opening up a space for Shakespeare to inhabit in the suburbs of political consciousness, in the pastoral confines of social definition where Sonny need not resent Hannah's deployment of their romantic mantra—"Sermons in stones and good in everything"—"as a password, in the mouth of a third person" (164) devoted not to Shakespeare, but to the struggle. It could, indeed, be said that both Gordimer and Stone position their characters' appropriations of Shakespeare as versions of pastoral, operating not only as an occasionally clarifying source of knowledge about experience but as a liberating medium of self-expression. Although in each instance familiarity with Shakespeare mystifies as much as it clarifies— deluding Sonny and Walker into unexamined and humanly destructive convictions about their own integrity, and leading Lu Anne into a hall-of-mirrors distortion of her relationship to Rosalind—Shakespeare continues to exist apart from what they make of him as a reliable repository for other kinds of applications, Shelley's, for instance.

What keeps Shakespeare at some remove from more direct political applications in these texts is his general confinement to the domain of "privatized" romantic or family encounters and crises. The appropriative deployment of plays like *As You Like It*, *King Lear*, and, to a lesser extent, *Hamlet* in these novels signals a change in emphasis from the

Third World postcolonial preoccupation with more expressly politically and racially charged works like *Othello* and *The Tempest*. Although much social and political mileage can—and has been—made from *Lear* (see, e.g., Chapter 2), none of these plays lends itself directly to recent postcolonial themes and preoccupations. Yet the clash between the private domains these plays explore and the public domains that press against them in the novels in question opens up a space where the politics of their appropriative deployment can arguably be identified and felt.

The staging ground of this clash between public and private is politicized in very different ways. Stone positions personal encounters as taking place against the backdrop of a public sphere to which his characters are largely oblivious. To the extent that he can be said to have one, Walker's politics, for example, are an existential style of high-minded irresponsibility; "the political sincerities that remained to him were petty complaints" (Stone 1992: 7). Although Walker tells his agent that he "could spend the rest of [his] life doing *Lear*" and that "the fucking thing is bottomless" (15), Stone tells his readers that Walker "had been living at the Chateau Marmont since the closing of *Lear*" (8), having chosen one of Los Angeles's most prestigious hotels to recover from his extended bout as "unaccommodated man." He does Shakespeare to persuade himself of his moral and professional integrity but lives off the takings of his mercenary Hollywood gigs. In a similar vein, Walker revels in his familiarity with Third World cultures and landscapes but, like the semi-demonized Drogues of this world, treats them as little more than "locations" peopled by anonymously serviceable natives and predictably corrupt officials who can be relied on to forgive any excess in exchange for ready cash. The storm scene he and Lu Anne stage in Baja is a luxury only people fed fat on Hollywood excess could afford to play: a day trip whose cost rivals the yearly income of the farmers who store corn cobs and manure in the abandoned set.[4]

In this as in other respects, Stone's characters live out a peculiarly American variant on postcolonial experience—grounded not on the U.S.'s status as a former colony but on its emergence as an unofficial empire—that John McClure identifies as "late imperial romance." As McClure writes, "to foreground the drama of metropolitan self-discovery is to repeat with a difference the original insult of imperialism, which always values metropolitan 'discoveries' over local sufferings" (McClure 1994: 98). From this perspective, Walker and Lu Anne's chronic Shakespearizing is as much a form of late imperial substance abuse as is their fondness for whiskey and cocaine; each is underwritten by Walker's opportunistic trafficking in scripts and productive of the same kind of distortions. This is not to say, however, that Walker's Shakespeare functions in the same way as Stone's, or, for that matter, Shelley's, in whose hands Shakespeare speaks against the grain of Walker's (mis)appropriations of words and people alike.

Assessing the postcoloniality of Gordimer's deployment of Shakespeare is considerably more complicated. As Rosemary Jolly has observed, in a recent essay on the problems involved in applying the term "postcolonial" to any of the literatures, or tribal or ethnic groups, of South Africa, we are engaged here in a negotiation of identifying, naming, and critical appropriation that is vexed at every level of signification (see Jolly 1995: 21–4). The state of internal colonization that the great mass of black and "mixed race" South Africans still labor under even after apartheid's dismantling, for example, might make applying the term "postcolonial" to their condition seem like a bitter Orwellian joke.[5] In *My Son's Story*, however, Gordimer traces out a series of displacements that correspond in some measure to the presumptive movement from a state of internal colonization to that of incipient decolonization on the part of her mixed-race protagonists. She does so in part by "marking" each house successively inhabited by Sonny or members of his family with the signs of "a deeper historical displacement" (Bhabha 1994: 13). The first house in the ghetto is, as Homi Bhabha has noted, "the house of the collusiveness of the coloureds in their antagonistic relations to the blacks" (1994: 13). During their period of residency here, Sonny's "coloured" family is "spell-stopped," as it were, by Sonny's Prospero-like paternalism, held in a state of ignorance of the real conditions that govern their relations with white and black alike: "We didn't have any particular sense of what we were—my sister and I. I mean, my father made of the circumscription of our life within the areas open to us a charmed circle" (Gordimer 1990: 20).

This "charmed circle" is breached by Sonny's engagement in a more racially inclusive political struggle that occasions the un-Prospero-like surrender of his passion for his books. A new passion is kindled by Sonny's adulterous relationship with Hannah, which largely takes place in what Will calls the "lying house," a space that could be said to represent a detour from the political struggle, cued in part by a shared fondness for Shakespeare. The final move, to the "silent house" in the integrated suburb, culminates in that house's principled abandonment by his wife and daughter and in the conflagration which destroys Sonny's books and leaves in their wake the phoenix-like prospect of continuing progress to a state that approximates the postcolonial condition of betweenness.

In this series of displacements, another is enacted that finds the "mixed" voice of the white South African writer (colonized by England, but colonizer of black and colored South Africans) giving way to the "mixed race" voice of Will whose "first book" we are said to be reading (Gordimer 1990: 277). A final, troubling irony obtains, however, at the novel's end, when Will modestly confesses that a poem he has written and sent his once-again detained father, though personally satisfying, is "not Shakespeare" (276) and that the book he has written is one he "can never publish" (277). Like Oroonoko, Will becomes here both locus and victim of a double colonialist inscription. Named for Shakespeare, but incapable of compassing anything close to Shakespeare's achievement, he is also, in the end, merely a character put to work in a fiction, the imaginary resolution of a prevailing social contradiction: the product, in short, of a white South African version of late imperial romance only lately (and uncertainly) splintered by a new (dare we call it postcolonial?) black South African dispensation.

NOTES

INTRODUCTION

1 As Gauri Viswanathan observes in her study of the relationship between literary study and British rule in India, "the surrogate functions that English literature acquired in India offer a powerful explanation for the more rapid institutionalization of the discipline in the Indian colony than in the country where it originated" (1989: 7).

2 My preference for the use of an unhyphenated "postcolonial" differs from that of Mishra and Hodge, for whom the act of dropping the hyphen signals the movement from a politically neutral to an oppositional political stance (see Mishra and Hodge 1991: 407). In my employ, the term "anti-colonial" more accurately renders a work's oppositional positioning; the hyphenated "post-colonial" demarcates a specific political/temporal condition, that is, post-independence; and the unhyphenated "postcolonial" signifies an historically indeterminate state of betweenness, what Peter Hulme refers to as an ongoing "*process* of disengagement" (Hulme 1995: 120).

3 Despite the cautiousness of Buell's approach to the postcolonial, he has been roundly criticized for daring to propose that "early American writers be understood as postcolonial." As Amy Kaplan writes, such a proposal "not only overlooks the history of American imperialism, but in a sense colonizes postcolonial theory by implicitly positing the U.S. as the original postcolonial nation" (Kaplan 1993: 21 n. 17). Anne McClintock responds with even greater indignation to the positing of America's "paradigmatic" postcoloniality in *The Empire Writes Back*, "Whereupon, at a stroke, Henry James and Charles Brockden Brown, to name only two on their list, are awakened from their *tête-è-tête* with time and ushered into 'the postcolonial scene' alongside more regular members like Ngũgĩ wa Thiong'o and Salman Rushdie" (McClintock 1995: 12). Of the many problems with this kind of thinking—how can Henry James, of all writers, *not* be considered postcolonial?—is that it "mistakenly perpetuates an old game with the highest scores now awarded for such things as native authenticity and rejection of European languages rather than for beauty and truth: as a result we get arguments that Achebe is postcolonial, Soyinka not; Lamming is, Naipaul not. Such games do us no credit. If 'postcolonial' is a useful word, then it refers to a *process* of disengagement from the whole colonial

syndrome, which takes many forms and probably is inescapable for all those whose worlds have been marked by that set of phenomena: 'postcolonial' is (or should be) a descriptive, not an evaluative term" (Hulme 1995: 120).

4 But see Stuart Hall: "Australia and Canada, on the one hand, Nigeria, India, Jamaica on the other, are certainly not 'post-colonial' *in the same way*. In terms of their relation to the imperial center, and the ways in which...they are 'in but not of the West', they were plainly all 'colonial', and are usefully designated now as 'post-colonial', though the manner, timing and conditions of their colonisation and independence varied greatly. So, for that matter, was the U.S., whose current 'culture wars', conducted throughout with reference to some mythicised Eurocentric conception of high civilisation, are literally unintelligible outside the framework of America's colonial past" (Hall 1996: 245–6).

5 According to Mishra and Hodge, "At the heart of the oppositional post-colonial are three fundamental principles—principles which are as much points of difference between White settler colonies and the rest—which may be summarized as (a) racism, (b) a second language, (c) political struggle. For the category of the post-colonial to work in any other fashion it must become a 'complicit post-colonialism' and therefore effectively post-modern" (1991: 410).

6 This is clearly a space-clearing gesture on Weisbuch's part, as he, himself, seems to admit in citing a series of examples to the contrary (see Weisbuch 1986: 17). The fact is that, while occasional attacks on Milton's and Shakespeare's function as models for U.S. writers by Melville, Emerson, Thoreau, and, particularly, Whitman could be said to constitute a "minority opinion," it was an opinion that was both long-sustained and widely distributed.

7 This statement is made by William Alger in his 1877 biography of the American actor, Edwin Forrest, whose career figures prominently in the first chapter of this book. The passage from which the statement is drawn is worth quoting in full: "A nation beginning its career as a colony is naturally dependent on the parent country for its earliest examples in culture. Some time must elapse: wealth, leisure, and other conditions favorable to spiritual enrichment and free aspiration must be developed, before it can create ideals of its own and achieve aesthetic triumphs in accordance with them. Such was the case with America. Its mental dependence on England continued long after its civil allegiance had ceased" (1877: 1:193).

8 Cf. Buell: "Although the 13 American colonies never experienced anything like the political/military domination colonial India did, the extent of cultural colonization by the mother country, from epistemology to aesthetics to dietetics, was on the whole much more comprehensive—and partly because of the selfsame comparative benignity of the imperial regime" (1992: 415).

9 See Michael Bristol's discussion of the founding of the Folger Library in *Shakespeare's America, America's Shakespeare* (1990: 70–89). Michael Dobson notes that Bristol's "lament that the 'Shakespearizing' of America has marked the defeat of its revolutionary ideals, registering its fall into a 'Europeanized' system of social hierarchies, seems misplaced, not only because no innocently egalitarian, pre-Shakespearean America seems to

have existed, but because Shakespeare's position in American culture has been...so visibly that of a trophy" (Dobson 1992b: 203). Dobson also observes that "The adoption after the revolutionary war of Shakespeare as a figure simultaneously for America's claim to a stake in the European Renaissance and for America's claim to embody the ultimate triumph of the English-Speaking Peoples has as its final concomitant the claiming of England itself after World War II, the refashioning of the parent country in the archaic image projected onto it by the colony" (1992b: 203).

10 See, e.g., José Enrique Rodó's *Ariel* (1900), which implicitly casts the U.S. as the great Caliban to the North in conflict with the idealistic Ariel of a Latin America that functions as an outpost of European culture in the New World, and Roberto Fernández Retamar's more recent reidentification of an insurgent Latin America with Caliban in his essay of that name (1971). For Fernández Retamar, the move Rodó makes is a mistake. The imperializing tendencies of the U.S., made brutally evident in the war of 1898, identify it more with what might be called "the Prospero function," with Latin America playing slave to its master, an alternately servile and defiant Caliban. For U.S. writers of the nineteenth century, as we will see, *The Tempest* and its cast of characters had considerably less import than a play like *2 Henry VI*, which concentrated not on a plantation model of human relations but on a struggle between classes, the one representing insurgent democratic forces, the other the feudal impulse to over-awe and dominate.

11 As Ania Loomba has recently observed in the course of "[highlighting] the *multiple* relationships to the dominant, alien culture that can and do exist in any 'colonised' society": " 'National' culture, in the case of 'Third World' societies, is all too often understood as constituted by the overtly anti-colonial," such that "the terms 'national' and 'nationalist' are taken to be identical" (Loomba 1997: 110).

12 West Indian or Caribbean appropriations of *The Tempest* are too numerous to cite here but include work by the Barbadians, E.K. Brathwaite and George Lamming; the Martinican, Aimé Césaire; the Cuban, Roberto Fernández Retamar; and the Jamaican-American, Michelle Cliff, among others.

13 Cf. Benita Parry: "To dismantle colonialist knowledge and displace the received narrative of colonialism's moment written by ruling-class historiography and perpetuated by the nationalist version, the founding concepts of the problematic must be refused" (1987: 28).

14 See Stanley Wells's five-volume collection of Shakespeare travesties and burlesques (1978).

15 As Marianne Novy observes in the Introduction to the first of her two estimable anthologies on women's "re-visions" of Shakespeare: "Explicit feminist protest against Shakespeare emerged fairly recently out of a tradition that more often appropriated Shakespeare for women. Earlier rewritings of his plots made woman-centered points subtly while some contemporary rewritings make them more boldly" (Novy 1990: 2).

16 According to Peter Hulme, for many insistence on so narrow an assessment of the postcolonial "represents some kind of badge of merit, a reward for having purged one's writing of the evils of colonialism" (Hulme 1995: 120).

17 As W.J.T. Mitchell has observed: "The United States may well be the first nation in history to realize that it has been an empire only as it ceases to be one...Our national self-concept has always been resolutely anti-imperialist, from our origins in a colonial rebellion against the British Empire to our most recent stands against the 'Evil Empire.' Even the Monroe Doctrine, an imperial manifesto if ever there was one, represents itself as an anti-imperialist policy, a shield for 'free' countries in the Americas from the threat of European imperialism" (Mitchell 1992: 14). The profoundly compromised and deluded nature of the United States' sense of itself as anti-imperialist standard-bearer—which has prompted Carlos Fuentes to call it "the Jekyll and Hyde of our wildest continental dreams: a democracy inside, an empire outside" (Fuentes 1988: 16)—should not, in short, blind us to the fact that there once was a basis for lodging such a claim.

1 NATIVISM, NATIONALISM, AND THE COMMON MAN IN AMERICAN CONSTRUCTIONS OF SHAKESPEARE

1 This might not have been Van Sant's intention until the final stages of shooting and editing his film. In his working screenplay, Van Sant indicates that Scott's abandonment of Mike will not be as final as it is made to appear in the film (see Van Sant 1993: 186–7). In a brilliantly detailed and venturesome essay entitled "Elizabethan World Pictures," Curtis Breight contends that Van Sant privileges "the lower-class world to reveal its inhabitants as social victims of institutional power. In this respect he captures what mainstream criticism of the *Henriad* tends to suppress—Shakespeare's increasing concern with human casualties of elite struggle and military violence" (Breight 1997: 302). Breight suggestively adds that "Van Sant's interpretation...not only valorises the victims of a given social order (contemporary America) but also suggests how this order is the end-product of imperial history" (1997: 302).
2 See Robert Willson (1992) for a discussion of *Idaho* and other recent "recontextualizations" of Shakespeare on film. See Curtis Breight's earlier essay, "Branagh and the Prince" (1991), for an incisive appraisal of Branagh's conservative agenda and royalist affiliations.
3 As in *1 Henry IV*, Scott offers his audience an early indication of his imminent "change": "When I turn twenty-one, I don't want any more of this life. My mother and father will be surprised at the incredible change. It will impress them more when such a fuck up like me turns good than if I had been a good son all along. All the past years I will think of as one big vacation. At least it wasn't as boring as schoolwork. All my bad behavior I'm going to throw away to pay my debt. I will change when everybody expects it the least" (Van Sant 1993: 140). Prior to this point, the screenplay reveals the possible impact of Scott's deception on Mike in a planned (though not executed) voice-over of Mike's thoughts: "It was almost as if Scott was on some sort of crusade or mission,...He was the great protector of us all, and the great planner. He gave us hope in the future" (Van Sant 1993: 127).
4 As Jonathan Goldberg writes in his wonderfully suggestive chapter on the *Henriad* in *Sodometries*: "Although the response to him has not been unani-

mous, most critics in this century have found it all but impossible to resist the attractions of the prince" (Goldberg 1992: 145). See Jonathan Crewe (1990) for a particularly rich problematization of Hal's alleged reformation.

5 Levine grounds his conclusion on the premise that "It is difficult to take familiarities with that which is not already familiar; one cannot parody that which is not well known" (Levine 1988: 15–16). I would submit that the parodies and burlesques need only have assumed a general familiarity with the highly stylized *manner* of Shakespearean drama and a correspondingly general acquaintance with the characters, plots, and most memorable passages of individual plays. Levine fails to take adequate account of another piece of evidence he is otherwise conscientious in discussing, namely, the fact that the early nineteenth-century taste for Shakespeare was whetted on bowdlerizations of Shakespeare's texts which might be considered parodies in their own right. Levine does note several incidents that indicate that "Shakespeare was by no means automatically treated with reverence," nor "accorded universal acclaim," but concludes that "these and similar incidents were exceptions to the general rule: from the large and often opulent theaters of major cities to the makeshift stages in halls, saloons, and churches of small towns and mining camps, wherever there was an audience for the theater, there Shakespeare's plays were performed prominently and frequently" (Levine 1988: 20). This conclusion strikes me as altogether too optimistic.

6 Brougham's version of Portia's "Quality of mercy" speech begins, "The quality of mercy is so strained/In this, our day, and all our prisons drained/by legislative pardons that our city/Will need, I fear, a Vigilance Committee/To stem the current of outrageous crime/That leaves blood marks upon the banks of time" (Wells 1978: 5:113). This surprisingly sophisticated play ends with Shylock's pardon and Lorenzo's sudden announcement that he has "turned Jew" (Wells 1978: 5:116).

7 See Joyce Green Macdonald's (1994) illuminating account of *Othello* travesties and black and blackface acting in the nineteenth century.

8 I appropriate the quoted phrase from Timothy Murray's review of *Shakespeare's America, America's Shakespeare* which fails to note that Bristol's alleged indifference "to any detailed account of American contestatory discourses and practices" (Murray 1994: 268) is dictated by his overarching commitment to the study of American institutional and archival practices.

9 Cf. Stephen J. Brown (1978: 234–5). Discussions of Whitman's views on Shakespeare can be found in Brown, Dunn (1939: 266–74), Falk (1942), Harrison (1929), Stirling (1949: 61, 74–5), Stovall (1952a, 1952b), and Thaler (1941: 15–19, 45–62). Stovall and Thaler are particularly good on the (alleged) shifts of Whitman's points of view.

10 Robert Falk offers the following comment regarding the same passage: "Thus Whitman rates individuality, as expresssed in the great feudal characters of Shakspere [*sic*], above the spirit of democracy which underlines the poems of Burns" (1942: 95).

11 Like Whitman's, Melville's reluctance to worship at the shrine of Shakespeare is at least partly indebted to the Young America movement of the 1830s, whose "discussion of democracy, nationalism, and literature…established the terms of intellectual life" for the two men who,

according to Thomas Bender, "were both democrats and Democrats" (Bender 1987: 151). However, as Bender notes, while "Melville absorbed the ideals of intellectual life promoted by Young America,…he differed from most of them in an important way. They were so anxious to celebrate the literature of democracy that they forgot what Melville did not: a metropolitan intellectual must be a critic as well as a celebrant of American literature and democracy" (Bender 1987: 152).

12 See Sollors (1986: 119–39) for a more wide-ranging assessment of mid-nineteenth-century literary appropriations of the figure of the noble Indian, including *Metamora*, and of "the demolition campaign" launched against them by John Brougham in burlesques like *Metamora; or, The Last of the Pollywogs* (1847) and *Po-ca-hon-tas; or, The Gentle Savage* (1855).

13 According to William Alger: "the tragedian had urged on the editor the writing of a play for him on the theme of Jack Cade and his rebellion. He afterwards induced Conrad to reconstruct his play of Aylmere, which in its original form was not suited to his ideas" (Alger 1877: 1:323). The actual role played by Leggett in this negotiation remains unclear. As early as 18 December 1834, we find Leggett claiming that he has just been labeled "the Jack Cade of the [New York]*Evening Post* by the rival *Courier & Enquirer*" (Leggett 1970: 1:128). He makes this claim in a wide-ranging article of that date entitled "Utopia-Sir Thomas More-Jack Cade" (Leggett 1970: 1:125–34). Equally interesting is a letter of Leggett's dated 24 October 1838, sent from "Aylemere, New Rochelle," Aylemere evidently serving as the name of his house. In this letter, Leggett writes that "To be an abolitionist, is to be an incendiary now, as three years ago, to be an anti-monopolist, was to be a leveller, and a Jack Cade" (Leggett 1970: 2:336).

14 There are, strictly speaking, *two* Jack Cade plays that are attributed to Conrad. The first, and longer version, was published as *Aylmere, or Jack Cade* with a collection of Conrad's other "poems" in Philadelphia in 1852. Given Conrad's comments to the effect that "The tragedy, as originally written comprises much that was not designed for, and is not adapted to, the stage," and that he "is indebted" to "the judgment and taste of Mr. Forrest…for the suggestions which prepared 'Aylmere' for the stage" (Conrad 1869: 15), it would appear that the play published in London by T.H. Lacy in 1869 under the title *Jack Cade: The Captain of the Commons* more closely approximates the acting version. The latter play is appreciably shorter and reduces the first play's traditional five-act structure to four acts. I have chosen to conflate both versions in my quotations from the play(s) by bracketing passages from the 1852 version that were removed from the 1869 version. I supply dual page references for the benefit of other interested parties. Page citations for Conrad's unrevised historical notes refer to the later, more accessible edition published by Lacy.

15 This delegation to Aylmere of qualities more often associated with royalty or aristocrats may, of course, represent Conrad's effort to recover from history what history has made of the lives of noble commoners. If it is reasonable to assume that Whitman's preference for Shakespeare's, as opposed to Burns's, characters was informed by a sense of the eternally lost potentiality of feudal peasants and commoners, it may be equally reason-

able to infer that Conrad was attempting to apply a form of revolutionary optimism to a cast of characters excluded in their own time from the opportunity to transform their subjection into a form of self-mastery. See Helgerson (1992: 193–245) for a provocative discussion of citizen drama and Shakespeare's histories.

16 The reviewer prefaces this statement with the remark that "The powerful representation of such a play must produce a corresponding impression upon any audience; how strong its appeal to the sympathies of an *Irish* audience, may be better imagined than described" (Alger 1877: 1:405). Forrest demonstrated his keen awareness of the nature of these sympathies in his farewell speech to the Cork audience which expressed the "hope that the dark cloud that overhangs this fair country will soon pass away" and "that Ireland and her people will long enjoy the prosperity and happiness they are so eminently entitled to, and which are so much to be desired" (Alger 1877: 1:407). He made an even more conspicuous demonstration of his solidarity with Irish nationalist aspirations on his last night in Dublin. As Alger writes: "The Lord-Lieutenant of Ireland entered the theatre with a noble party, escorted by a military company with martial music. The audience rose with the curtain, and joined the whole dramatic corps in singing 'God save the Queen.' Forrest never once during the play [*Damon & Pythias*] looked toward the vice-regal box; and in the bows with which he acknowledged an honorary call from the audience at the close, he studiously avoided seeing the group of titularly-illustrious visitors. He was a democrat; he liked the Irish and disliked their English rulers, and he would not in his own eyes appear a snob" (Alger 1877: 1:409). One may also discern in the American's gesture of solidarity with his Irish hosts a hint of the lost anti-colonial potential of the formerly revolutionary United States.

17 Conrad's quotation is drawn from Leggett's 1834 article, "Utopia-Sir Thomas More-Jack Cade" (Leggett 1970: 1:128–33).

18 And for good reason, as Leggett's article of 24 December 1836 and a good many others demonstrate. Entitled "Your Napkin is Too Little," the piece draws its inspiration from Othello's sadly ironic response to Desdemona's effort to soothe him. In it Leggett writes: "We take the liberty to use this phrase in reference to the conduct of those political journalists who, on one side as well as the other, seek to tie up the abolition question within the limits of party, and treat it as if it were a subject on which men were divided by the same lines that divide them on the ordinary political topics of the time" (Leggett 1970: 2:147). It is worth noting here that Whitman "had always been a great admirer of William Leggett, linking him with Jefferson as 'the great Jefferson and the glorious Leggett'" (Stovall 1952a: 463).

19 Such attitudes were not restricted to the ignorant or unwashed. We find, for example, in the minutes of an 1837 banquet given in Forrest's honor, one Mr. Charles Ingersoll, "chairman of the Committee of Invitation," offering the following "sentiment" to his distinguished guests: "Who sees an American audience crowd to an American play and turn from Shakspeare to call for Metamora and the Gladiator [two earlier "prize plays"], and does not acknowledge in this fond prejudice the germ of excellence? Patriotism itself is a blind preference of our own earth; and shall there be

no patriotism in letters?...Give us, then, *nationality*, which is but a phase of patriotic feeling; give us excess of it" (Alger 1877: 1:337).

20 See Levine (1988: 60–3) for a brief summary of theater riots and disorders provoked by political and nationalist themes.

21 Officers of the Order "were given American Indian titles, such as Sachem for the president, and the membership was pledged to vote only for native-born citizens and to combat Catholics and foreigners whenever the occasion offered" (Moody 1958: 132), a protocol that bears some resemblance to Forrest's appropriation of the cause of Native Americans in *Metamora*, the first of the prize plays.

22 The use of the term, "base-born miscreants," in the placard is more than a little ironic. Although in the broadest sense an obvious example of how a Shakespearized English had established a foothold in the popular imagination, the term also closely echoes Jack Cade's angry characterization of his unfaithful followers as "recreants and dastards" who "delight to live in slavery to the nobility" in *2 Henry VI* (4.8.26–7). More interestingly still, the argument of the placard appropriates and transposes the strategy Clifford employs to win over Cade's followers when he reminds them of the memorable victories of Henry V over the French (*2 Henry VI*, 4.8.33–51). In this instance, "English ARISTOCRATS AND FOREIGN RULE" take the place of the French, while the "iron hearts of '76" take the place of Henry.

23 A more clearly intentioned effort to arouse nationalist sentiment informed Forrest's tour of Ireland in 1846. As Alger notes, "the acting of Forrest, the magnetic power of his personality, the patriotic sentiments and stirring invectives against tyranny with which his Spartacus and Cade abounded, conspired to arouse a wild enthusiasm in his passionate and imaginative audiences" (Alger 1877: 1:404–5). See note 16 above for additional commentary on Forrest's Ireland tour. As for audience identification with Macbeth, it is worth considering whether the nineteenth-century American audience's well-known preference for *Richard III* and *Macbeth* was founded upon their status as "tragedies of usurpation." As Michael Dobson notes, both plays "were among the entertainments regularly presented [in New York] by and for the British army between 1777 and 1783, who accused the rebels of treason against the Bard as well as against the State" (1992b: 195–6).

24 An edition of the *Journal* dated 26 May 1849 adds that "At the basis of this recent riot...there was 'a protest at *the degree too much* of ostentation by the wealthier'" (Moses 1929: 264).

25 The sad fate of the short-lived African Company (1821–23), an all-black troupe that performed *Richard III*, *Othello*, and a wide variety of contemporary plays in New York City before being summarily suppressed, surely discredits the notion of Shakespeare functioning as "common property" for *all* Americans. For discussions of the abbreviated career of the African Company and their chief actor, James Hewlett, see Yvonne Shafer (1977: 387–95) and Herbert Marshall and Mildred Stock (1968: 28–47). Joyce Green Macdonald offers a much more incisive appraisal of the African Company's suppression in her essay on *Othello* travesties and blackface acting (1994: 234–7), noting that "The African Company raid is an early example of the use of Shakespeare as a tool for enforcing cultural and

political hegemony" (1994: 236). In 1823, the same year as the African Company's demise, Edwin Forrest coincidentally became "the first actor who ever represented on the stage the southern plantation Negro with all his peculiarities of dress, gait, accent, dialect, and manner" (Hutton 1891: 103).

26 One of these patrons was Herman Melville, who in *Moby Dick* transacted what remains the most ambitious, sustained, and successful American appropriation of Shakespeare. Melville was, along with Washington Irving and Evert A. Duyckinck (former editor of the *Democratic Review* and formerly a supporter of Edwin Forrest), one of forty-seven leading New Yorkers who signed a letter of encouragement and support to Macready immediately prior to the outbreak of the riot (see Moody 1960: 270–1). For an exhaustive account of Melville's appropriations and annotations of Shakespeare that renders anything I might have to say about them superfluous, see Julian Markels (1993).

2 SHAKESPEARE AT HULL HOUSE: JANE ADDAMS'S "A MODERN LEAR" AND THE 1894 PULLMAN STRIKE

1 Addams's attack on Pullman was considered too vehement to allow for publication at the time of its writing. Read as a paper to the Chicago Woman's Club and the Twentieth Century Club of Boston, "it was not published until 1912, when it finally appeared in *Survey*" (Lasch 1965: 106). It was republished three years later as a chapter in *Satellite Cities* (1915), a study of industrial suburbs by Graham Romeyn Taylor. According to Addams's earliest biographer, "Of all the literature that grew out of the Pullman strike, and the American Railway Union strike that followed...hardly anything remains now in any general public consciousness except this paper,...[which] began to make Jane Addams a figure of national importance in the philosophy of social progress" (Linn 1935: 166–7).

2 Quotations from "A Modern Lear" are drawn from the collection of Addams's essays edited by Christopher Lasch (1965).

3 As Trachtenberg observes, "Anger and bitterness—at the successive wage cuts at Pullman, the intervention of the government on the side of the railroad companies—[had] brought Chicago to near hysteria in June and July of 1894, just one year after the wonders of [the World's Columbian Exposition or Chicago World's Fair]" (Trachtenberg 1982: 223).

4 Trachtenberg suggestively notes that the town of Pullman and the Chicago World's Fair "replicate each other in illuminating ways, and [that] the events of the year after the dismantling of the Fair also dismantled the notion that in culture alone resides a power to enforce obedience, to teach acquiescence and consent. In the end, it took armed federal troops to rescue Pullman from the failure of its ideal" (Trachtenberg 1982: 225).

5 See Buder: "From July to November 1893 the number of employees in Pullman dropped from 4,500 to 1,100. To make matters worse the company took several hundred of its own cars off the roads and placed them in storage while construction of new palace cars was halted." Pullman

subsequently "decided to acquire contracts even at loss," a move that led to a restoration of the workforce to 3,100 men by April 1894, however at reduced wages (Buder 1967: 149).

6 Ely's article was entitled "Pullman: A Social Study" and was published in *Harper's Monthly*, 70 ([1885]: 452–60). A 30-year-old Assistant Professor of Economics at the time of its writing, Ely was commissioned to write the article by Henry Mills Alden, editor of *Harper's*, after Alden had become frustrated with the results of earlier commissions which "read like a promotional puff for the Pullman company" (Buder 1967: 100). Hugh Dalziel Duncan, a more recent commentator on Pullman, writes that "In Pullman human relations were completely feudal. Architectural planning served to sustain autocratic capitalistic power, whose measure of success was profit. The model town of Pullman and the Pullman shops were controlled by different agencies all responsible to the Pullman Corporation…The *Pullman Journal* supported all policies of George Pullman and published nothing that would reflect on the merits of paternalism. Free speech was denied. Labor agitators and radical speakers were barred from the town by denying them the right to rent public halls" (Duncan 1989: 169–70).

7 Addams employs this phrase at the end of the following passage in *Democracy and Social Ethics*: "The family, like every other element of human life, is susceptible of progress, and from epoch to epoch its tendencies and aspirations are enlarged,…The family in its entirety must be carried out into the larger life. Its various members together must recognize and acknowledge the validity of the social obligation" (1907a: 78–9).

8 Levine notes traces of the same kind of condescension in Addams's estimate of workers that she attributes to George Pullman: "[The workers] were not children, owing gratitude to their employer for decent housing— which returned four per cent on costs. They would not, as Jane Addams thought they should, include in their vision of a just society benevolent cooperation with George Pullman,…they wanted more money and more self-determination. In this George Pullman had no place, for he already had too much of both. In asking the workers to be more mature, she was condescending" (Levine 1971: 164–5).

9 According to Jackson Lears, "Addams's effort to create a 'fuller life' for factory hands paralleled the longings of her own class for more intense experience; in a way it was a projection of these longings…Determined to revitalize their own lives, reformers became convinced they could revitalize working-class lives as well." Lears less convincingly concludes that "This was a key moment in the reformation of capitalist cultural hegemony: humanitarian reformers, even the perceptive Addams, began unwittingly to accommodate themselves to the corporate system of organized capitalism. Assuming that education alone could overcome alienated labor, Addams ended in an intellectual position scarcely different from the unctuous paternalism of the 'job enrichment' programs now run by giant corporations" (Lears 1981: 80).

10 Helen Epstein has suggestively noted in her recent biography of Joe Papp that the influence of Addams's Hull House theater and dance programs was strongly felt in "the after-school drama clubs and all school musicals" of the New York City public schools, which gave the future founder of the

New York Shakespeare Festival and Public Theater the opportunity "to bridge the gap between Elizabethan English and Brooklynese, school and street" (Epstein 1994: 34–5), and gave other Americans the chance to encounter Shakespeare in the accents and rhythms of their own neighborhoods.

11 The limits of Addams's progressivism are exhaustively explored by Rivka Shpak Lissak, who concludes that though "Hull House leaders did not have a pluralist view of society during the years 1890 to 1919...their concept of a humanitarian social democracy and their benign policies of assimilation created a dynamic that unintentionally paved the way for a more pluralist view of society in the 1930s" (Lissak 1989: 184).

12 I bring my epigraph to bear at this turn to suggest a connection between Addams's association of Shakespeare with conservative social values and the ambit of associations within which Shakespeare circulated in the colonial schools and culture of Erna Brodber's Jamaica.

13 In answer to the not always friendly question, "Who Funded Hull House?," Kathryn Kish Sklar contends that though Addams did, indeed, "rely heavily on Chicago's elite,...most of her funding came from three key sources—...her own inheritance;...Mary Rozet Smith, who became her life partner,...and her close friend, Louise deKoven Bowen" (Sklar 1990: 95). Although Sklar makes a powerful case for "the gendered components of Addams's fund raising" (Sklar 1990: 95), for the freedom of choice Addams was able to exercise in choosing sources of support, and for the "minimal donations" and "lukewarm support" of "prominent Chicago businessmen" (Sklar 1990: 104–5), she appears to understate the relationship between Hull House policies and the city's power elite. As Sklar herself confesses, "No other donor came close to [the] record" of Bowen, whose "eminently respectable standing among Chicago's wealthiest families brought a protective mantle to the settlement and paved the way for other wealthy donors." She adds that "Bowen's affiliation lent credibility to Addams's claims that Hull House aired all sides of 'the social question'" (Sklar 1990: 107–8).

14 It may be objected that Debs's condescending and transparently sexist dismissal of Addams discounts Addams's considerable courage in presenting such a paper in the first place and understates the disturbing effect the paper had on the captains of culture and commerce alike. Reliant as Hull House was on the generosity of men like George Pullman and on the support of legislators of public opinion, the fact that "Mr. Pullman himself resented it bitterly," that nine editors successively rejected its bid for publication, and that "it was greeted with a heavy fire of newspaper comment all over the United States" when it was finally published in the pages of *Survey* in 1912 (Linn 1935: 167), indicates that Addams's attack on Pullman's paternalism had struck a very raw nerve indeed.

3 SHAKESPEARE, 1916: *CALIBAN BY THE YELLOW SANDS* AND THE NEW DRAMAS OF DEMOCRACY

1 The quotation is drawn from a review of the production published 3 June 1916 in the *New York Dramatic Mirror*. Green summarizes the largely favorable accounts of the production in the following manner: "Though faulted

in audibility—the spoken units of the Masque Proper and the Inner Scenes just did not seem to carry—there was enough eyefilling spectacle to compensate" (Green 1989: 69).

2 For an exhaustive account of the rise and fall of the *Spectatorium* project, see Percy MacKaye 1927: 2:342–436.

3 Pullman was, in fact, Steele MacKaye's chief patron for the Chicago project and maintained a personal relationship with him that ended in MacKaye's death aboard one of Pullman's own railway cars outside Timpas, Colorado on 25 February 1894 (see MacKaye 1927: 2: 458–61).

4 Although the aims of Steele and, particularly, Percy MacKaye were professedly democratic and often focused on patriotic themes or on commemorations of socially transformative events like the French Revolution, the elaborate "synthesis of the arts" that both men envisioned was also inspired by the ambitious, and decidedly undemocratic, designs of Richard Wagner (see Franck 1964: 156) and depended heavily on patronage relationships with the rich and powerful. Like the entrepreneurs of today's entertainment industry, who spend millions on the development of ever more ingenious special effects, Steele MacKaye sought to assure that his investments in innovative stage machinery would repay the work and expense put into them by securing patents for "a curtain of light, a cloud creator, a sliding stage, [and] a floating stage," among other inventions (Franck 1964: 156).

5 MacKaye nonetheless calls, in "The Drama of Democracy" (1909), not for "a revival of old forms, not an emulation of Elizabethan blank verse, but a fresh imagining and an original utterance of modern motives which are as yet unimagined and unexpressed. Not a revival, but a new birth; not a restoration, but a renaissance of poetic drama" (MacKaye 1909: 116). Yet, as the text of *Caliban* makes plain, MacKaye is everywhere uncritically tied to the "old forms" and to "an emulation of English blank verse" rooted so deeply in "English tradition and language" that it is difficult to tell how he thought a "*new* drama" as native to America as "our American elms" could emerge from it. Although his summons echoes the calls for a national drama made some eighty years earlier by Edwin Forrest and William Leggett, in practice MacKaye, like Robert Taylor Conrad, the author of *Jack Cade*, would draw his imaginative "nutriment" from an originary English, and almost exclusively Shakespearean, seedbed. As James Bloom notes, "A retrospective attachment to a secure literary canon pervades [MacKaye's] works, which include an adaptation of Hawthorne's 'Feathertop' for the stage, a libretto based on 'Rip Van Winkle' ..., versedramas entitled 'The Canterbury Pilgrims,' 'Jeane d'Arc,' and 'Sappho and Phaon'" (Bloom 1992: 55).

6 As scholars like Harry Berger, Jr. have noted, Shakespeare explores in *The Tempest* the susceptibility of the artist himself to the mystifications of his art, the way in which his godlike command of his resources distances him from the very auditors he seeks to instruct and transform (see Berger 1968). In MacKaye's masque, however, Prospero's dual status as consummate artist and moral legislator is never probed, questioned, or qualified. His identity is merged entirely with "King Shakespeare," who commands the summit of

dramatic art, and functions as the figure to whom all history moves in a manner that is made to resonate with Christian Messianic traditions.

7 The iconography here is endlessly suggestive, the combination of scroll and staff at once identifying Prospero with the lawgiver Moses, the immortal playwright Shakespeare, and Christ the Messiah.

8 As William Green observes, "Caliban will learn by attending the theater, by watching pageants illustrating the history of the theater, and by seeing relevant scenes from Shakespeare's plays" (1989: 63).

9 Green contends that "This scene is selected to make Caliban aware of the horrors of the war and to get him [in the words MacKaye delegates to Miranda] 'to recoil to reason and to love'," but that "listening to this speech…has a reverse effect on him" (Green 1989: 66). In MacKaye's text, however, Miranda makes no mention of "the horrors of war," contending instead that the play teaches "how noblest natures/Are moved to tiger passions—by a painting/Called Honor, dearer than their brothers' lives," and that Caliban, "Born of a tiger's loins, seeing that picture,/May recognize an image of [himself]/And so recoil to reason and to love" (MacKaye 1916: 136).

10 As William Green notes, in the official program MacKaye supplies Caliban with an additional speech to close the masque addressed to "you, my fellow dreamers in the dark,…you millions that are me," which indicates that Shakespeare "can show us the way to realize our dreams" (Green 1989: 67). Green adds that Caliban also "calls upon the crowd of performers and pageant participants to kneel with him in tribute to Shakespeare" (1989: 67).

11 Although MacKaye would undoubtedly be classified a liberal in relation to most members of his class and caste, his representation of Caliban was consistent with the way the threat of the immigrant and immigration was constructed by the "race-thinkers" of his time. According to Edward A. Ross, for example, "the blood now being injected into the veins of our people is 'sub-common'. To one accustomed to the aspect of the normal American population, the Caliban type shows up with a frequency that is startling…These oxlike men are descendents of those who *always stayed behind*" (Ross 1914: 285). Like MacKaye, "the race-thinkers were men who rejoiced in their colonial ancestry, who looked to England for standards of deportment and taste, who held the great academic posts or belonged to the best clubs or adorned the higher Protestant clergy" (Higham 1955: 139).

12 Few steps are not, assuredly, the same as none. Among several exceptions, one may note MacKaye's deployment of "boys from the band of the Hebrew Orphan Asylum" as "buglers and drummers" in "the Egyptian segment of the First Interlude" (Green 1989: 68).

13 An inventory of such events might include the numerous occasions on which labor unrest was violently suppressed; the rise of vigorous labor organizations like the IWW; the entrance of America to the world-imperial stage in the Spanish–American War; the assassination of President McKinley in 1901; J.P. Morgan's temporary takeover of the U.S. economy in 1907; and, even, what Henry James termed "the Hebrew conquest of New York" (James 1907: 132). For a lively review of some of the more significant events in the first fourteen years of the century, see Walter Lord (1960).

14 Among the plays mined by MacKaye are *Antony and Cleopatra*, *Troilus and Cressida*, *The Merry Wives of Windsor*, *The Merchant of Venice*, *Romeo and Juliet*, *As You Like It*, *The Winter's Tale*, *Henry V*, and *Henry VIII*. MacKaye's staging of the first ghost scene from *Hamlet* seems motivated more by MacKaye's preoccupations with his father than by any discernible relevance it might have to Caliban.

15 An even closer connection may be drawn between Beveridge's pronouncement and a speech assigned to the figure of Thomas Carlyle in Albert Hatton Gilmer's tercentenary masque, *King Shakespeare*, performed in Boston in 1916. As "Carlyle" states: "Before long there will be a Saxondom covering great spaces of the globe. Now what can keep all these together, so that they do not fall out and fight, but live in peace, in brotherlike intercourse, helping one another? This King Shakespeare is the noblest, gentlest yet strongest of all rallying signs. Wheresoever English men and women are, they will say to one another, 'Yes, this Shakespeare is ours: we produced him, we speak and think by him; we are of one blood and kind with him! It is a great thing for a nation that it get an articulate voice to speak forth melodiously what the heart of it means'" (Gilmer 1916: 13). The same year witnessed the production of Isabelle Fiske Conant's *Will O'the World* (1916), a tercentenary masque performed on the grounds of Wellesley College. A year later *Caliban* itself traveled to Boston. As MacKaye writes, "at the Harvard Stadium, under auspices of the Governor of Massachusetts, the Mayor of Boston, and the Red Cross, five thousand citizens from nineteen sections of Greater Boston took part in the same masque for three weeks, publishing their own *Caliban* newspaper for their city-of-actors behind the scenes" (MacKaye 1927: 2:480).

16 For a representative sampling of the kind of material produced under the auspices of the Americanization movement, see Chancellor (1916), Grant (1916), Mahoney and Herlihy (1918), Mintz (1923), and Ross (1914).

17 MacKaye was hardly alone in employing the occasion of the tercentenary to promote Shakespeare's association with Anglo-Saxon values. See, e.g., Albert Hatton Gilmer's contemporaneous masque, *King Shakespeare*. MacKaye's *New Citizenship*—which he planned to have performed in Lewisohn Stadium as well as in other appropriate venues across the nation—was prompted by what he termed the "groping chaos of citizenship" represented by the approximately three million "foreign born white persons...over 21 years of age" who were "unnaturalized" and, hence, not yet "Americanized" (MacKaye 1915: 6–7). While MacKaye's attitude toward "the multitudinous desires and colorful temperaments of the world races" (MacKaye 1915: 13) is as condescendingly chauvinistic here as is his approach to Caliban in the tercentenary masque, he initially resists the melting-pot model of assimilation in favor of a more creative approach to the reconciling of differences. According to MacKaye, "the ideals of *the new citizenship*...stand not for the levelling away of all world-cultures to leave bare an American mediocrity, but for the welcoming of all world-cultures to create an American excellence: not for a national melting-pot to reduce all precious heritages to a cold puddle of shapeless ore, but for a national studio to perpetuate them in new creative forms of plastic life" (MacKaye 1915: 14). But MacKaye is not in the end entirely faithful to these high-

minded ideals which, in the ritual-proper, are repeatedly made to defer to a more strident privileging of quintessentially American values and practices. This is nowhere better evidenced than in the "fourth address" MacKaye assigns to a "representative citizen" which is assembled from excerpts of a speech given to new citizens of Philadelphia by Woodrow Wilson in 1915. In this address, the citizen asserts that "You cannot dedicate yourselves to America unless you become with every purpose of your will thorough Americans" and that "You cannot become thorough Americans if you think of yourselves in groups" because "America does not consist of groups" (MacKaye 1915: 82).

18 Riis was considerably more optimistic about the prospects for maturation of the new European immigrants than was Madison Grant, author of *The Passing of the Great Race* (1916), for whom the immigrants comprised "a large and increasing number of the weak, the broken and the mentally crippled of all races drawn from the lowest stratum of the Mediterranean basin and the Balkans, together with hordes of the wretched, submerged populations of the Polish Ghettos" (Grant 1916: 80).

19 Lippman wrote these words in a sketch entitled "All the MacKayes" published in the *International* for January 1911. The sketch is quoted in full by Percy MacKaye (1927) in the Epilogue to his two-volume celebration of his father's life.

20 MacKaye comes uncomfortably close here to echoing the sentiments of Madison Grant, one of the most notorious racialists of the period. In addition to claiming the superiority of the Nordic race, Grant contends that "true aristocracy is government by the wisest and best" (Grant 1916: 7) and calls attention to the threat against the "native American aristocracy" of the city of New York embodied "by layer after layer of immigrants of lower races" (Grant 1916: 5).

21 According to the self-styled proletarian writer, Michael Gold, the predominantly Jewish garment workers of early twentieth-century New York "*lived* with Shakespeare" (Gold 1990: 88, my emphasis).

22 It is important to note that the Americanization movement was a defensive project undertaken out of a sense of crisis by men who felt their grip on power and self-identity in jeopardy. As Madison Grant writes in the last paragraph of *The Passing of the Great Race*: "We Americans must realize that the altruistic ideals which have controlled our social development during the past century, and the maudlin sentimentalism that has made America 'an asylum for the oppressed,' are sweeping the nation toward a racial abyss. If the Melting Pot is allowed to boil without control, and we continue to follow our national motto and deliberately blind ourselves to all 'distinctions of race, creed, or color,' the type of native American of Colonial descent will become as extinct as the Athenian of the age of Pericles, and the Viking of the days of Rollo" (Grant 1916: 228).

23 I am referring here to the New York Shakespeare Festival's 1995 production of *The Tempest* directed by George C. Wolfe. In that production, the actor playing Caliban conspicuously failed to speak the lines, "I'll be wise hereafter/And seek for grace" (5.1.298–9), which embody Caliban's willing resubmission to Prospero's power and mastery. That the ethnically divided (and divisive) battle for an American Shakespeare continues to rage

unabated is indicated by John Simon's withering review of one of the last productions in the Public Theater's "Shakespeare Marathon," Karin Coonrod's two-part staging of the three parts of *Henry VI*. In addition to being annoyed at "how American everything" sounds by contrast with an early announcement in BBC English, Simon is particularly exercised by the Public's penchant for non-racially specific casting, and calls one black actress "a sort of overweight Whoopi Goldberg without the charm" (Simon 1997: 50). Alternatively, Curtis Breight has recently observed that "the national and international flavour of the last decade's 'Shake-cinema'...as well as the fact that even Hollywood displays multiple attitudes to Shakespearian raw materials, might indicate that Shakespeare is not just some ideological tool by which a single dominant group reproduces its own cultural and economic hegemony" (Breight 1997: 297).

4 PROSPERO IN AFRICA: *THE TEMPEST* AS COLONIALIST TEXT AND PRETEXT

1 For the Shultz quotation and for provocative remarks about political uses of Shakespeare, I am indebted to Donald K. Hedrick, whose paper "How to Find Authors" was presented at the ideology seminar of the World Shakespeare Congress (West Berlin, 1986).

2 Shultz's apparent belief that *Hamlet* teaches a lesson in decisiveness was, ironically, shared by Chris Hani, a former "leader of the South African Communist Party and hero of the township youth," who observed in a 1988 interview that "I want to believe that I am decisive and it helps me to be decisive when I read *Hamlet*" (quoted in David Johnson 1996: 201). As Johnson indicates, this pragmatic approach to Shakespeare may be considered the byproduct of the positivist transmission of Shakespeare practiced in the colonial educational institutions of South Africa.

3 In *The Conquest of America*, Tzvetan Todorov distinguishes "two component parts" in Columbus's attitude toward the Amerindians which, he contends, "we shall find again in the following century and, in practice, down to our own day in every colonist in his relations to the colonized." The colonist either "conceives the Indians...as human beings altogether, having the same rights as himself; but then he sees them not only as equals but also as identical, and this behavior leads to assimilationism, the projection of his own values on the others. Or else he starts from the difference, but the latter is immediately translated into terms of superiority and inferiority...What is denied is the existence of a human substance truly other, something capable of being not merely an imperfect state of oneself" (Todorov 1984: 42).

4 This is not to suggest that Ngũgĩ has no interest in linking the two subjects. The betrayals of their fellow Gikuyu by the "loyalist" member of the homeguard, Karanja, and by the informer, Mugo, are both motivated, to some extent, by a desire to please Thompson and are represented by Ngũgĩ as symptomatic of the colonial pathologies of identification or transference. As Ngũgĩ writes, "to Karanja, John Thompson had always assumed the symbol of whiteman's power, unmovable like a rock, a power that had built the bomb and transformed a country from wild bush and forests into

modern cities, with tarmac highways, motor vehicles on two or four legs, railways, trains, aeroplanes and buildings whose towers scraped the sky—and all this in the space of sixty years" (Ngũgĩ 1968: 136). Snubbed towards the end of the novel by Thompson, Karanja displays in his very posture something closely akin to the dependency complex Mannoni considers characteristic of colonized peoples: "his gait, to an observer, conjuring up the picture of a dog that has been unexpectedly snubbed by the master it trusts" (Ngũgĩ 1968: 140). See Mannoni (1964: 76–7).

5   As for the accuracy with which Ngũgĩ renders the sentiments of embattled imperialists during the state of emergency and for a good while thereafter, one may take note of the words of one Father Trevor Huddleston approvingly drawn from the *Johannesburg Star* of 12 December 1952 by Fred Majdalany: "The strength of Mau Mau stems from the fact that it has achieved a unifying force by combining primitive tribal superstition and fear with political and economic aspiration...Mau Mau is a movement which in its origins and in its development is wholly evil. It is the worst enemy of African progress in Kenya. It has about it all the horror of 'the powers of darkness; of spiritual wickedness in high places'" (Majdalany 1962: 82).

6   As Jomo Kenyatta observes in his classic "inside" study of the Gikuyu, *Facing Mount Kenya*: "[Europeans] speak as if it was somehow beneficial to an African to work for them instead of for himself, and to make sure that he will receive this benefit they do their best to take away his land and leave him with no alternative. Along with his land they rob him of his government, condemn his religious ideas, and ignore his fundamental conceptions of justice and morals, all in the name of civilization and progress" (Kenyatta 1965: 305).

7   All quotations from *The Tempest* are taken from Frank Kermode's 1958 Arden edition.

8   Each of these critics writes in the unacknowledged shadow of Harry Berger, Jr., who has convincingly exposed the flaws in an uncritical identification of Prospero with Shakespeare, but whose portrayal of Prospero's motivations bears a remarkable resemblance to Mannoni's classic depiction of Prospero as the prototypical embodiment of colonialist psychology. Where Berger observes that "Shakespeare presents in Prospero the signs of an ancient and familiar psychological perplex connected with excessive idealism and the longing for the golden age; a state of mind based on unrealistic expectations; a mind therefore hesitant to look too closely at the world as it is" and capable of exercising "violent repressiveness" in the face of "the pressure of actual life" (Berger 1968: 258), Mannoni contends that "the colonial in common with Prospero lacks [an] awareness of the world of Others, a world in which Others have to be respected." And, he concludes, this lack of awareness of the Other is often "combined with an urge to dominate" (Mannoni 1964: 108). The difference between these seemingly overlapping points of view is that Berger makes Shakespeare an active partner in his critical distinction, implicitly assigning priority to Shakespeare's critical acuity, whereas Mannoni appears to implicate Shakespeare in the psychology of his dramatic surrogate.

9 Ngũgĩ's thinking here is clearly indebted to Frantz Fanon, who in *Black Skin, White Masks* (1967) eloquently argues against relative positions with respect to racism or colonialism. See, especially, Fanon (1967: 85–92).

10 I choose the term "virtuous activity" because it was favored by another, more successful Prospero in Africa, namely, Cecil Rhodes, who, according to his biographers, "would often quote from Aristotle: 'The utmost good of man is the virtuous activity of the soul and pursuit of the highest virtue throughout life'" (Lockhart and Woodhouse 1963: 203–4). It is entirely apposite to my argument that Fanon defined the South Africa that the virtuous Rhodes "fathered" as "A boiler into which thirteen million blacks are clubbed and penned in by two and a half million whites" (Fanon 1967: 87).

11 A good inventory of examples is supplied by Hallett Smith, who provides an example of his own making in his Introduction, where he remarks that "[Caliban's] yearning for freedom is in no way respectable, since if he had it he would use it for devilish purposes" (Smith 1969: 5). Another instance worth recording can be found in Norman Rabkin (1967). In the course of a seven-page commentary on *The Tempest*, Rabkin reiterates the oft-cited designation of Prospero as "a symbolic representation of Shakespeare himself" (Rabkin 1967: 204); likens Prospero's maturation to that of Odysseus when he decides to leave Phaeacia; and refers to Caliban as the embodiment of the "brutal, earthy, fleshbound, treacherous" aspects of nature and as a character whose "irremediable bestiality" exemplifies "certain facts [that] are absolute and finally beyond the distorting vision of a simple mind" (Rabkin 1967: 227–8). Apart from the revealing wording which he employs to objectify Caliban's intractability in the face of an admirably flexible Prospero, susceptible both to change and growth (and which may also be employed to exemplify the critic's ideological bias), Rabkin's reading of *The Tempest* may be considered representative.

12 See Hulme (1981) for a detailed discussion of *The Tempest*'s joint participation in Mediterranean and Caribbean discourse.

13 Shakespeare may have modeled his treatment of the colonial encounter on William Strachey's prior account of Sir Thomas Gates's successive encounters with the Virginia Indians which, as Harry Berger observes, "supplies a close analogue to Prospero's experience with Caliban" (Berger 1968: 261–2). In this account, Gates's initial resistance to any "violent proceeding" against the Indians ultimately cedes, after a particularly troubling example of the Indians' alleged intractability, to a resolve "to be revenged" against them, Gates having now "well perceived, how little a faire and noble intreatie workes upon a barbarous disposition" (quoted in Kermode 1958: 140).

14 For Ngũgĩ, of course, this would hardly represent an isolated example of colonialist brutality. In addition to the frequently brutal reprisals perpetrated by the British against the Mau Mau and their sympathizers, he could look back to examples like the following drawn from an account given by Francis Hall, English administrator of Gikuyuland in 1894, of Britain's effort to forge a new "white man's country": "We soon set to work, lit up a kraal and got the men warm again…we made a mess of all their villages and, as the other column was working about two miles off, the natives had a

warm time, but they wouldn't stand, so I had no chance of trying my war-rockets. The Major [Smith] with his one arm carried a shotgun and bagged a brace of them in the first kraal but I had no fun for a long time...We brought in 1,100 goats and loads of grain...but we didn't manage to do much execution as the brutes wouldn't stand" (quoted in Rosberg and Nottingham 1966: 14–15).

15 Both during and after the state of emergency precipitated by the Mau Mau insurrection, it was commonplace for the British to characterize leaders of the Gikuyu opposition, like Jomo Kenyatta and Dedan Kimathi, in the most uncivil terms, despite their ability to claim a linguistic and rhetorical equality. The same Dedan Kimathi, who could explain the basis of his opposition in the following manner—"we are not fighting for an everlasting hatred but are creating a true and real brotherhood between white and black so that we may be regarded as people and as human beings who can do each and everything" (Rosberg and Nottingham 1966: 299)—was else-where referred to as "a deranged and diseased criminal, fighting for survival like a trapped animal" (Majdalany 1962: 220). On the idea of "civility" with specific reference to Stanley, see Spurr (1985).

16 In *A Grain of Wheat*, the complicitousness of the "loyalist," Karanja, is generated out of the same kind of enforced respect for the seemingly natu-ralized system of power relations established by the British: "The whiteman is strong. Don't you ever forget that. I know, because I have tasted his power. Don't you ever deceive yourself that Jomo Kenyatta will ever be released from Lodwar. And bombs are going to be dropped into the forest as the British did in Japan and Malaya. And those in detention will never, never see this land again" (Ngũgĩ 1968: 130).

17 See Barker and Hulme, who throughout their essay try "to show how much of *The Tempest*'s complexity comes from its *staging* of the distinctive moves and figures of colonialist discourse" (Barker and Hulme 1985: 204).

18 Indeed, as he prepares to leave Kenya on the eve of independence, Thompson suggestively states, "Perhaps this is not the journey's end," before more insidiously asserting, "We are not yet beaten...Africa cannot do without Europe" (Ngũgĩ 1968: 144). As Ngũgĩ presents it, this seems more like a prescient anticipation of the neo-colonial future than a last bout of self-delusion.

19 See, e.g., Greenblatt, who, after entertaining several possible interpretations, concludes that "Shakespeare leaves Caliban's fate naggingly unclear. Prospero has acknowledged a bond; that is all" (Greenblatt 1970: 570–1).

20 Abdul JanMohamed, for example, makes a persuasive case for the "charac-teristic openness" of Isak Dinesen's colonial encounters in Kenya (JanMohamed 1983: 53). He considers Dinesen "a major exception to the...pattern of conquest and irresponsible exploitation" (1983: 57), not least because "she does not distance herself [from the native cultures surrounding her] through the notion of racial superiority" (1983: 60). However, one should note that Ngũgĩ, a native Kenyan, does not share JanMohamed's high opinion of Dinesen, as he makes abundantly clear in *Homecoming*, where he directly associates her with Prospero (Ngũgĩ 1983: 9).

21 In *The Stranger in Shakespeare*, Leslie Fiedler notes that some "exponents of *négritude*" actually make Caliban "the hero, not the villain of the piece,"

thus inverting "the racist mythology of their former masters" (Fiedler 1972: 248).

5 AFTER *THE TEMPEST*: SHAKESPEARE, POSTCOLONIALITY, AND MICHELLE CLIFF'S NEW, NEW WORLD MIRANDA

1 Shakespeare may well maintain a more privileged position in post-independence India than *Shakespeare Wallah* would indicate. As Jyotsna Singh notes, "All of Delhi University's approximately 140,000 students must study English literature for at least one year, among whom around 20,000 may read Shakespeare" (Singh 1989: 456). For a trenchant discussion of this subject, which also takes account of the demise of Shakespeariana (the acting troupe led by Geoffrey Kemble on which the fictional Buckingham Company is modeled), see Loomba (1992: 28–31). In a later essay that also discusses *Shakespeare Wallah* and the Kemble acting troupe, Loomba quotes some remarkably apposite passages from a lecture given by C.J. Sisson at King's College, London in November 1924. Sisson attributed "the declining popularity of Shakespearian adaptations after 1912" to "a conscious reaction against European culture, and in especial, English culture." He specifically noted that "a constant stream of [nationalist] propaganda" places Shakespeare "in the enemy ranks of protagonists of an alien civilisation seeking to impose itself upon an ancient people," and further noted "a tendency to exalt Sanskrit literature at the expense of English" (Loomba 1997: 123). See Viswanathan (1989) for a comprehensive study of the relationship between Indian English studies and British rule in India.

2 As Rob Nixon observes, these writers "seized upon *The Tempest* as a way of amplifying their calls for decolonization within the bounds of the dominant cultures. But at the same time these Caribbeans and Africans adopted the play as a founding text in an oppositional lineage which issued from a geopolitically and historically specific set of cultural ambitions. They perceived that the play could contribute to their self-definition during a period of great flux" (Nixon 1987: 558). See Alden T. Vaughan and Virginia Mason Vaughan (1991: 144–71) for a comprehensive inventory of postcolonial responses to/appropriations of *The Tempest*.

3 The operation of these touchstones is exemplified in recent essays by Brydon (1984), Donaldson (1988), Gilbert (1991), Greenstein (1984–85), Laframboise (1991), Yelin (1992), and Zabus (1985). The critical practice of speaking through the medium of Shakespearean analogy clearly bears more than a trace of the neo-colonialist gesture as works from an alleged periphery are reconstituted to fit the established canon's need for growth and replenishment. I would prefer to mark it as a stage in a process of critical reorientation to which scholars like myself—rooted in a value system in which Shakespeare "serve[s] as something like the gold standard of literature" (Nixon 1987: 560)—are trying to contribute.

4 Rob Nixon (1987) and Susan Willis (1986) have made much the same point in their own essays on Caribbean and African appropriations of *The Tempest*.

5 Ngũgĩ's career provides an exemplary case of a writer working through this problem. In 1977, after what he terms "seventeen years of involvement in Afro-European literature" (1986: 27), Ngũgĩ began to do all his imaginative writing in Gikuyu, reserving English for his more "explanatory" works.

6 See Brathwaite (1981) on "nation language"; also Wilenz, who notes that "the nation languages, emergent in the Caribbean, have been perceived solely as bastardized forms of English, not only by those who imposed their culture, but also by the colonial subjects who have been instructed by them" (Wilenz 1992: 263).

7 In discussing "how the ghosts of writers like Kipling and Forster still haunt the contemporary Indian novel in English," Sara Suleri notes that "Kipling's powerful transcultural fetish plays a secret role in the energies of Rushdie's abundant idiom, suggesting an ironic relation that deserves more careful reading." She adds that, "In place of the remorseless postcolonial paradigm of Prospero and Caliban, a new equation suggests itself: the complicity of comedy and shame that the postcolonial narrative must experience, when it acknowledges that it indeed descends from the jaunty adolescence of *Kim*" (Suleri 1992: 178).

8 Appiah describes postcoloniality as the condition of "a relatively small, Western-style, Western-trained group of writers and thinkers, who mediate the trade in cultural commodities of world capitalism at the periphery. In the West they are known through the Africa they offer; their compatriots know them both through the West they present to Africa and through an Africa they have invented for the world, for each other, and for Africa" (1991: 348). Appiah also notes that, although all African cultures "have been influenced, often powerfully, by the transition of African societies *through* colonialism,…they are not all in the relevant sense *post*colonial. For the *post-* in postcolonial…is the *post-* of the space-clearing gesture…and many areas of contemporary African cultural life…are not in this way concerned with transcending, with going beyond, coloniality (Appiah 1991: 348). The "postcolonial," as both term and gesture, is also rigorously problematized in the essay by Mishra and Hodge (1991), which I discuss in my Introduction.

9 As Stephen Slemon observes, "Hearne's point here is…that colonial discourse has 'preconstituted' social existence in the marginalised territories of Empire" (Slemon 1987: 10). Cf. John Dos Passos on the situation of American literature, ca. 1916: "As a result of [the] constant need to draw on foreign sources our literature has become a hybrid which, like the mule, is barren and must be produced afresh each time by the crossing of other strains" (Dos Passos 1916: 269).

10 These efforts, abetted by ongoing reforms in college and university curricula, have radically reoriented the ways in which many "First World" readers receive and interpret such landmarks of the high-colonial past. Tutored by writers like Césaire and Lamming, Achebe and Ngũgĩ, Walcott and J.M. Coetzee, to question the previously inviolate authority of these canonically (and politically) privileged texts, contemporary students of post-colonial writing are often discouraged from granting them the interpretive priority which their canonicity would appear to assure them. The canonical implications of this kind of contextual or contestatory reading are explored

by Attridge (1992) in an essay on *Foe* and the politics of the canon, and by Tiffin (1987) in an essay on postcolonial counter-discourse that also focuses on *Foe*.

11 Maria Helena Lima notes that "Cliff's decision...to rely primarily on standard English and only cursorily to employ patois, not only marks the class/culture division between her narrator and the Jamaican characters who populate her fiction, but also signals the primary audience for whom the novel is written" (Lima 1993: 37). However, Lima fails to register the defamiliarizing effect even the occasional use of patois probably has on the non-Jamaican reader. As Isabel Fonseca observes, the novel's employment of patois "suggests that the key to any language (and by extension its culture and its people) lies in its untranslatable words; inaccessibility not only dictates texture, but is a central theme" (Fonseca 1988: 364).

12 Belinda Edmondson contends that the *Jane Eyre* passage "engenders within the reader a full realization that the site of dialogue is not simply with an ambivalent white creole tradition but also with the European literary canon itself, which freezes the colonized subject in an eternal relation of subject/object" (Edmondson 1993: 184). In a similarly incisive essay, Fiona Barnes argues that in her "portrayal of Clare's rebellion, Cliff resists the domination of the 'master codes' of literary genres and/or historical narratives, and constructs new narrative paradigms for post-colonial subjects" (Barnes 1992: 28).

13 Edmondson notes that the *Jane Eyre* "passage is particularly important for the link it provides between Caliban and Bertha, the two gendered symbols of Caribbean independence and invisibility," both of whom "inhere within the identity of Clare" (Edmondson 1993: 184).

14 Lima cogently observes that "Cliff posits Clare's urge to return to the island in essentialist terms, representing her homeland, the landscape of her identity, as female. The land is infused with the spirit and passion of Clare's grandmother and mother in a deeply personal, almost biographical connection" (Lima 1993: 38).

15 As Cliff elsewhere observes, like Miranda's, "Pocahontas's name has often been considered synonymous with collaborator, traitor, consort of the enemy. The truth is more complicated. The daughter of Powhatan, she was kidnapped by colonists and held against her will. She was forced to abandon the belief system of her people and to memorize the Apostle's Creed, Lord's Prayer, and Ten Commandments. She was taken to England in 1616 and there displayed—a tame Indian, the forest behind her, cleansed by civilization" (Cliff 1990: 267).

16 According to Lima, "The truly revolutionary gesture [in *No Telephone to Heaven*] lies in Christopher's 'revenge' against Paul H.'s family, and the cautionary tale that it embodies if we read Christopher as Clare's alter ego" (1993: 42). Rather than serving as Clare's alter ego, Christopher seems instead a damaged and diminished Caliban-figure, the sad, deracinated embodiment of postcolonial self-hatred. Cliff, herself, indicates as much in a recent interview with Meryl Schwartz, stating that Christopher's "violent act is based in his self-loathing" (Cliff 1993: 613).

17 As Lauren Berlant writes, Cliff shows how "long after the high imperial moment has passed, Jamaica and other postimperial sites must nonetheless

continue to play the game of domination/castration beneath the caretaking skirt of the motherland (scenes of castration and sodomy are central to the novel's exhaustion of patriarchal national politics as a source of emancipatory federation)" (Berlant 1994: 148).

18 According to Brathwaite, "the idea of creolization as an ac/culturative, even an interculturative process between 'black' and 'white,' with the (subordinate) black absorbing 'progressive' ideas and technology from the white, has to be modified into a more complex vision in which appears the notion of *negative or regressive creolization*: a self-conscious refusal to borrow or be influenced by the Other, and a coincident desire to fall back upon, unearth, recognize elements in the maroon or ancestral culture that will preserve or apparently preserve the unique identity of the group" (Brathwaite 1977: 54).

19 Unlike Lamming, who responds to Prospero's gift of speech with an answering lyricism capable of charming Prospero himself, Cliff revels in the unpedigreed sounds of a language too inward to be entirely "overshadowed by a discourse of Empire." What Lamming aspires to in his groundbreaking work—that is, the decolonization of Caribbean "cultural history by replacing an imposed with an endemic line of thought and action" (Nixon 1987: 569)—Cliff comes close to realizing in "a heteroglossic Caribbean narrative" that "both enacts and describes the multiple struggles against cultural cannibalism and for decolonization on literary and geographical terrain" (Barnes 1992: 23).

20 As the published version of Greenaway's film indicates, *Prospero's Books* is thoroughly colonial in its postmodernism, modeling its representation of *The Tempest* exclusively on the visual and textual productions of the European Renaissance. The closest Greenaway gets to integrating New World imagery into his Mediterranean fantasy world is to have "four naked young women and a small, naked three-year-old female child—a group of the island's 'John White' Indians—look out from their shelter under a clipped box-hedge" (Greenaway 1991: 65). It is also worth noting that, while the figure of the film's Miranda was modeled on that of Botticelli's image of Spring (1991: 91), Greenaway's efforts to imagine what Sycorax looked like "when she was powerful in Argiers" were inspired by "Felicien Rops' Pornocrates" (1991: 83). See cited pages for respective images and captions.

21 In this respect, Cliff may be said to be operating within a different framework from that of the Francophone-Caribbean writers Jean Bernabé, Patrick Chamoiseau, and Raphael Confiant, who declare in their recent manifesto that "Creoleness is the cement of our culture and that it ought to rule the foundations of our Caribbeanness" and who define creoleness as "the *interactional or transactional aggregate* of Caribbean, African, Asian, and Levantine cultural elements, united in the same soil by the yoke of history" (1990: 891). This "praise of creoleness" is, significantly, undertaken in direct, corrective response to the residual claims of Négritude which Bernabé *et al.* dismissively identify as a "violent and paradoxical therapy" that "replaced the illusion of Europe by an African illusion" (1990: 889).

22 See Stephen Orgel's suggestive meditation on "the absent, the unspoken, that seems...the most powerful and problematic presence in *The Tempest*,

figured in the conspicuous absence from the play of Prospero's wife" (Orgel 1986: 50).

23 Cliff's move here is consistent with Jamaica Kincaid's even more aggressive repositioning of *The Tempest* at the end of "The Red Girl" chapter of her 1986 novel *Annie John*. In a sequence that draws equally on the protofeminist sisterhood of Titania and her Indian "vot'ress" in *A Midsummer Night's Dream* (2.1.121–37), Annie dreams that the boat on which the Red Girl is traveling to Anguilla "suddenly splintered in the middle of the sea, causing all the passengers to drown except for her, whom I rescued in a small boat. I took her to an island, where we lived together forever, I suppose, and fed on wild pigs and sea grapes. At night, we would sit on the sand and watch ships filled with people on a cruise steam by. We sent confusing signals to the ships, causing them to crash on some nearby rocks. How we laughed as their cries of joy turned to cries of sorrow" (Kincaid 1986: 70–1). In addition to replacing Shakespeare's pregnant "vot'ress" with the Calibanesque Red Girl, Kincaid has her characters do considerably more than "imitate" the "embarked traders on the flood." Drawing the rich cruise ships to their ruin, Annie and the Red Girl return the colonialist "favor" with interest, reveling in their power to reverse the flow of history.

6 ENSLAVING THE MOOR: *OTHELLO*, *OROONOKO*, AND THE RECUPERATION OF INTRACTABILITY

1 I owe my awareness of Okri's "Meditations" to Ania Loomba, who refers to them in her chapter on *Othello* in *Gender, Race, Renaissance Drama* (1992: 61–2), a book to which I am more generally indebted. Of the many associations to *Othello* drawn by commentators on the Simpson trial, see, in particular, an article published by Jimmy Breslin under the headings "Monsters of the Heart" and "Othello Goes Tabloid," which is illustrated by a provocative still from Olivier's film version of the play, the caption of which reads "All the rage: Othello strangles Desdemona" (Breslin 1994: 93).

2 See the rash of articles, chapters, and books on the play that have appeared in the last ten years, a list which includes work by Andreas (1992), Bartels (1990), Barthelmy (1987), Boose (1994), Lim (1993), Little (1993), Loomba (1992), Macdonald (1994), Neill (1989), Newman (1987), Orkin (1987), Parker (1994), and Vaughan (1994).

3 Cf. Newman: "Iago enjoys a privileged relation with the audience. He possesses what can be termed the discourse of knowledge in *Othello* and annexes not only the other characters, but the resisting spectator as well, into his world and its perspective. By virtue of his manipulative power and his superior knowledge and control over the action, which we share, we are implicated in his machinations and the cultural values they imply" (1987: 151).

4 Cf. Neill: "Iago lets horrible things loose and delights in watching them run; and the play seems to share that narcissistic fascination—or perhaps, better, Iago is the voice of its own fascinated self-regard. The play thinks abomination into being and then taunts the audience with the knowledge that it can never be *un*thought: 'What you know, you know'" (1989: 395). Also

compare Loomba: "Othello moves from being a colonised subject existing on the terms of white Venetian society and trying to internalize its ideology, towards being marginalized, outcast and alienated from it in every way, until he occupies his 'true' position as its other" (1992: 48). Barthelmy frames this "restatement" of Othello's "exclusion" in terms of Othello's "relapse" or "lapse into the stereotype" (1987: 161).

5 Notably Goreau, who writes: "Aphra's impassioned attack on the condition of slavery and defense of human rights in *Oroonoko* is perhaps the first important abolitionist statement in the history of English literature" (1980: 289). Ferguson construes Behn as articulating "a paradoxical perspective on England's colonizing venture, a perspective [she] would describe as *partially critical*" and "oscillating...between complicity with and critique of the emergent institution of New World slavery" (1993: 24). Newman concludes her powerful assessment of femininity and the monstrous in *Othello* by maintaining that "by making the black Othello a hero, and by making Desdemona's love for Othello, and her transgression of her society's norms for women in choosing him, sympathetic, Shakespeare's play stands in a contestatory relation to the hegemonic ideologies of race and gender in early modern England" (1987: 157). Orkin contends that Shakespeare cultivates racist constructions only to "explode" them (1987: 176): "Shakespeare is...working consciously against the colour prejudice reflected in the language of Iago, Roderigo, and Brabantio. He in fact reverses the associations attached to the colour white and black that are the consequence of racist stereotyping" (1987: 170). Orkin adds that "in its fine scrutiny of the mechanisms underlying Iago's use of racism, and in its rejection of human pigmentation as a means of identifying worth, the play, as it always has done, continues to oppose racism" (1987: 188).

6 Scholars who have registered and discussed connections between *Othello* and *Oroonoko* include Barthelmy (1987), Ferguson (1993), Gillies (1994), and Sypher (1942), Ferguson's being by far the best and most sustained treatment of the subject.

7 As Laura Brown observes, "The novella has been recognized as a seminal work in the tradition of antislavery writings from the time of its publication down to our own period" (1987: 42). The enlistment of *Oroonoko* in the cause of abolition does not, however, change the fact that, as Wylie Sypher long ago noted, "Mrs. Behn is repelled not by slavery, but by the enslaving of a prince" (1942: 110).

8 Cf. Neill: "Since the audience is exposed to these obscenities before it is allowed to encounter either Othello or Desdemona in person, they serve to plant the suggestion, which perseveres like an itch throughout the action, that the attractive public face of this marriage is only the mask of something unspeakably adulterate. The scenes that follow contrive to keep alive the ugly curiosity that Iago has aroused, even while the action concentrates on Othello's public magnificence, on Desdemona's courageous resistance to patriarchal authority, and upon idealized affirmations of the love between them" (1989: 396–7). Okri observes that "Othello is a character with only one road leading out of him, but none lead into him" and considers, by comparison, "Iago...a more authentic creation than Othello" (1987: 618–19).

9 Cf. Loomba: "Othello is described in terms of the characteristics popularly attributed to blacks during the sixteenth century: sexual potency, courage, pride, guilenessness, credulity, easily aroused passions; these become central and persistent features of later colonial stereotyping as well" (1992: 52).

10 See the suggestive connections drawn by Laura Brown between the characters and events depicted in the novel and contemporaneous developments in English political history (1987: 55–60). According to Brown, "For Behn and others, the colonies stage an historical anachronism, the repetition of the English revolution, and the political endpoint of Behn's narrative is the reenactment of the most traumatic event of the revolution, the execution of Charles I" (1987: 57). Brown also offers a concise assessment of the historical specificity of Behn's attribution to Oroonoko of characteristics commonly associated with Coromantines throughout the period in question (1987: 59–60).

11 In this, Gillies seems to be following Karen Newman's lead when she unaccountably employs Rymer's Iago-like attack on *Othello* to conclude that by this time (1693) "Shakespeare's heroic and tragic representation of a black man seemed unthinkable" (1987: 155): a conclusion that itself seems unthinkable given what Behn and Richard Southerne thought they were doing in 1688 and 1695, respectively, when the former wrote and the latter rewrote the story of Oroonoko. For comprehensive studies of the figure of the Moor and African on the seventeenth-century stage, see Barthelmy (1987), D'Amico (1991), Jones (1965), and Vaughan (1994).

12 For Gillies, "the difference between Othello and Oroonoko bespeaks a major paradigm-shift in the discursive construction of otherness between the beginning and end of the seventeenth century": "Shakespeare's Renaissance imagination of otherness is still heavily indebted to the ancient poetic geography. Behn's Restoration idea of the other, however, is essentially modern and can readily be grasped in terms of post-Renaissance forms of the discourses of race, slavery, the 'noble savage', [etc.]" (1994: 28). For such reasons, Gillies argues, "*Othello* has proved particularly intractable to approaches via the post-Elizabethan category of the 'Negro'" whose *otherness* "has none of the exoticism of the Elizabethan 'moor', none of his theatrically vital mix of danger and allure" (1994: 32–3).

13 Behn's otherwise unaccountable decision to call Oroonoko a "gallant *Moor*" (1973: 6), having already established his provenance as a native of "*Coromantien,* a Country of *Blacks* so called" (5), is symptomatic of the conflation of ethnic differences that was, I would argue, characteristic of the period. It also indicates how closely attuned her construction of Oroonoko was to Shakespeare's construction of Othello.

14 For more sustained discussions of Oroonoko's naming, see Ferguson (1993: 25, 45 n.31), Athey and Alarcon (1993: 425–6), and Hulme (1986: 241).

15 See Greenblatt's remarks about the advantages rendered early modern Europeans capable of improvisation, among whose number he identifies Iago (1980: 227–9).

16 Greenblatt suggestively notes that "Iago's attitude toward Othello is [effectively] colonial: though he finds himself in a subordinate position, the ensign regards his black general as 'an erring barbarian' whose 'free and open nature' is a fertile field for exploitation" (1980: 233).

NOTES

17 Cf. Sypher: "Her disgust is not with slavery, but with the treachery of the
    white man. She is a primitivist, not a humanitarian. We can say no more of
    many anti-slavery crusaders" (1942: 113).

18 Indeed, in Behn, Warren, and Ligon alike, the common run of black slaves
    are considered "a sort of sullen Fellows, that would drown or kill themselves
    before they would yield" or surrender after a defeat (Behn 1973: 64),
    evincing the kind of "obstinacy" (Warren 1667: 20) that marks the "primi-
    tive" temperament.

19 Cf. Ferguson: "Here Oroonoko woos his "'Great Mistress' and other
    English ladies as Othello wooed Desdemona with his eloquent story of his
    'most disastrous chances...moving accidents...hair breadth scapes i' th'
    imminent deadly breach'" (1993: 39).

20 In one of the presumptive sources of *Oroonoko*, George Warren writes that
    "there are several Nations which Trade and familiarly Converse with the
    People of the Colony, but those they live amongst are the *Charibes*, or
    Caniballs" (1667: 23). According to Warren the Surinam Indians are collec-
    tively "a people Cowardly and Treacherous" and the women among them
    "are generally lascivious" (1667: 23). He adds, however, that some are "so
    truly handsom" that he hopes that they will soon be taught to kiss (1667:
    23–4). Also, see Warren on the Indians' practices of decorative piercing and
    self-mutilation (1667: 24). For his part, Richard Ligon observes that the
    Surinam Indians "are very active men, and apt to learne any thing, sooner
    then the *Negroes*...they are much craftier, and subtiler then the *Negroes*; and
    in their nature falser; but in their bodies more active" (1657: 54). Like
    Warren, Ligon reserves a special place in his heart for Indian women,
    whom he romanticizes in an anecdote that will later become elaborated in
    the "noble savage" story of Inkle and Yarico (1657: 55). See Sypher (1942:
    122–37) for a discussion of the story's development and permutations.

21 In her discussion of this sequence, Ferguson invokes what she terms the
    "Aaron potential" to explain how sexual anxieties about Othello surface in
    Behn's representation of the threat embodied by "a sexually powerful black
    man...taking out terrible impulses of anger and revenge" (1993: 28–9).
    According to Ferguson, Aaron, who recently "resurface[d] in the black
    villain in Ravencroft's 1686 play *Titus Andronicus, or the Rape of
    Lavinia*...helps shape the plot of *Oroonoko*. The black hero's nobility may be
    instantly undermined by the powerful *fantasies* of the story's colonial
    women, fantasies that transform Othello into Aaron at the first 'news' that a
    black man is seeking freedom and political power" (1993: 29). She refines
    this insight by observing that "Behn makes use of *Othello* and its cultural
    resonances...by sensationalizing and rendering more visible precisely that
    aspect of Othello's relation to a metropolitan state which we might call the
    'Aaron potential'—the possibility, rendered fearsome by widespread preju-
    dices against black-skinned men, that a black slave will seize any chance to
    usurp the white leader's political and erotic places" (1993: 29). Although
    Ferguson's identification of the "Aaron potential" is suggestive, the condi-
    tion she addresses could with greater accuracy be called the "Othello
    potential." Though Othello and Aaron may be prejudicially considered
    brothers under the skin, they are, even within the evolving seventeenth-
    century discourse of blackness, as distinct in their fraternity as Cain and

Abel, or Edmund and Edgar. Othello, like Oroonoko, is cut from differently textured cloth than is Aaron, whose criminality, like Iago's, is compulsive and all-defining. What Behn is mining is less the potential for *evil* in Oroonoko, and by extension in Othello, than their *intractability*, their incapacity to be brought under reliable control and constraint, which, I would argue, is assumed from the start.

22 Athey and Alarcon contend that "In adopting [such practices]—which he previously thought too full of rage and malice, too horrible—Oroonoko is engaging a native, non-European code of honor and aligning himself with the only people he has seen who have successfuly resisted the treacherous colonists" (1993: 440–1 n. 26).

23 Cf. Athey and Alarcon: "Throughout the novel [Behn] wields a subtle rhetoric of allegiance that enables her to be against mutiny but for Oroonoko; against the corrupt colonists and the Lieutenant Governor but for colonization; against having her own throat cut but for the 'honorable' decapitation of Imoinda. Behn's depiction of colonial slavery constitutes the narrator as simultaneously white and metaphysically feminine; the narrator claims the power of political speech and the protections of citizenship for her person" (1993: 437).

24 As Anne Fogarty observes, "in the closing moments of the narrative [Oroonoko] is no longer seen as desirable. Instead, he has become an image of abjection and horror. His body is now a sign not of exotic otherness but of savagery" (1994: 13).

25 Brown remarks "the fascination with dismemberment that pervades the novella's relation with the native 'other'—both Indian and African—[and] that suggests a perverse connection between the female narrator and Oroonoko's executioners" (1987: 55). Ferguson similarly notes that Behn "deploys" her "Female Pen" "to describe, with an unnerving blend of relish and horror, the novella's concluding scenes of Oroonoko's dismemberment" (1993: 36). By contrast, Fogarty contends that "The grotesque and harrowing account of the pipe-smoking Oroonoko being slowly hacked to death acts as a final reminder of the gulf separating white women and slaves in a colonial society" (1994: 13). Gallagher offers a considerably less convincing assessment of the import of Oroonoko's dismemberment (1994: 83–5), remarking that "Oroonoko's kingship comes to consist in his godlike willing of the piecemeal alienation of his own body. In this contradictory manner, he proves that he still owns it" (1994: 84–5).

26 As Suvir Kaul observes, "Within the colonial system in Surinam, the form of Oroonoko's death is, in the fullest sense, meant to be exemplary" (1994: 85).

27 Cf. Athey and Alarcon: "As the 'Fruits of tenderest Love' rot in this otherwise fertile setting, and the 'noisom' stench of Imoinda's spoiling flesh rises over the New World landscape, the language of the travel narrative reasserts itself. The narrative consciousness intrudes on the scene to remind us that the ruined productivity of the enslaved female body points directly back to the transcendent productivity of the land, every inch yielding 'natural Sweets' " (1993: 436).

28 Although Ferguson wants to sustain an idea of Behn as at least "*partially critical*" of "England's colonizing venture" (1993: 24), she makes a more

convincing case for Behn's complicity in the slave economy in formulations like the following: "Playing a version of Othello to both her slaves, and thus dramatizing a complex mode of authorial 'ownership' of characters cast in the role of enthralled—and feminized—audience, Behn represents herself creating a paradoxical *facsimile* of freedom, for herself, her immediate audience, and by implication, her readers back home" (1993: 36–7). While Ferguson is specifically addressing here a strategy Behn adopts to beguile Oroonoko and Imoinda at the midpoint of the novel, the formulation stands as an astute characterization of Behn's positioning throughout the novel.

29 According to Kaul, Southerne "glosses over [Behn's] text's colonial coordinates and contemporaneity in favor of a much more assimilable account of great human, that is, transcultural, tragedy. Oroonoko's assimilation to the Othello-paradigm shifts the burden of the peculiar form of his death and his suffering from the nature of slavery and the plantation economy that define the contemporary historical moment onto a prior literary model of the tragedy of a natural aristocrat acted upon by baser intelligences who refuse to acknowledge his worth" (1994: 89).

30 Cf. Ferguson: "Behn not only kills the African woman off in the end but performs an ideologically significant gesture of cultural appropriation and justification by making the heroine voice, as if it were her own, a desire for death at the hands of a lover, a desire founded, moreover, on precisely the European ideal of female 'honor' as chastity which Behn mocks and interrogates in so many of her works. In thus making her nonwhite heroine participate verbally in the mystification of the complex causes of her death, Behn makes Imoinda into an interesting variation of the Desdemona who lies for love at the moment of her death" (1993: 40). Though Desdemona does "[lie] for love at the moment of her death," she also resists Othello with all the force she can muster. This is, I would submit, more in the way of a crucial difference than an "interesting variation."

31 A story told in several places recounts a visit made by the royal African himself to a production of Southerne's *Oroonoko*. As Laura Brown writes: "[*Oroonoko*'s] sentimental authenticity was confirmed and augmented by the famous occasion in 1749 when an African 'prince' and his companion, previously sold into slavery but ransomed by the British government and received in state in London, attended a performance of *Oroonoko*" (1987: 42). See Sypher (1942: 166–8) on this event and the literary responses prompted by it.

7 "LIKE OTHELLO": TAYEB SALIH'S *SEASON OF MIGRATION* AND POSTCOLONIAL SELF-FASHIONING

1 In the account of his background provided in his autobiography, Du Bois speaks of "a mighty family, splendidly named" and appends an exclamation point after listing Othello last in the series of names (Du Bois 1968: 62).

2 Salih "purposely situates his protagonist at a precise time in the history of the Sudan and of European Colonization in general"; "the time-span [of the novel] includes...the major phases of the history of the modern Sudan:

the Mahdist Movement of 1881, the Anglo-Egyptian rule beginning in 1889, and the birth of independence during Nasser's regime in 1955" (Takieddine-Amyuni 1980: 5, 7). As Balfour-Paul writes, "For most of the nineteenth century the Sudan…was formally part of the Ottoman Empire, brought within it by the ambitious and largely autonomous Khedives of Egypt and administered by them on the Sultan's behalf. The Mahdist revolt of 1881 was provoked primarily by the oppressions and inadequacies of this Khedival administration but can now be seen—indeed it quickly took that form, consciously or unconsciously—as an early 'independence movement'" (1991: 17). Britain's suppression of the Mahdist "revolt" was undertaken in the wake of its consolidation of control over Egypt and eventuated in 1899 in the establishment of an Anglo-Egyptian Condominium in the Sudan, "a device without historical precedent" (Balfour-Paul 1991: 16). For a concise account of Britain's relinquishment of control over the Sudan in the 1950s, see Balfour-Paul (1991: 16–48). See Magnus (1958: 118–60) for an account of Britain's defeat of the Mahdi under the leadership of Kitchener and of its consolidation of power in the Sudan.

3 My reading of *Season of Migration* is greatly indebted to Harlow's groundbreaking assessment of the novel in her 1979 essay in *Edebiyat*. My interest in the subject was first aroused by Jyotsna Singh's suggestive 1994 essay on "Othello's Identity."

4 Cf. Takieddine-Amyuni: "my thesis is that the Narrator, not Mustapha Sa'eed, is the hero [of the novel]; he also represents the third generation dramatized in the novel. He is not given a name since he stands for the enlightened contemporary Arab as Salih sees him" (1980: 15).

5 Quoted in Lindqvist (1996: 67) from Churchill's *The River War* (1899). According to Robert Giddings, "Two important mythologies were born at Omdurman: the almost god-like quality of Kitchener, and the invincible power of machine-gun fire" (1991: 186). See Magnus (1958: 118–37) for a fuller account of these proceedings.

6 According to Magnus, Mahmoud was not as passive in the face of Kitchener's aggression as Mustafa suggests. To Kitchener's question, "Why did you come here to burn and kill?," Mahmoud is reported to have responded: "I obeyed my orders, as you obey yours." Magnus adds that "as he was being dragged away Mahmoud shouted that his comrades would be avenged at Omdurman if Kitchener succeeded in getting there" (Magnus 1958: 122).

7 According to Harlow, "The question…'who is Othello?' as posed to the literary and Shakespearean tradition of the West does not necessarily remain the same question when presented to an Arab, North African, Sudanese, or even Turkish reader of William Shakespeare. Why should it have been *Othello* that was the first of Shakespeare's plays to be translated and performed in Turkey? The Turks are not Arabs. Indeed it was to fight the Turks, whose Ottoman Empire controlled virtually the entire Middle East, that the Arabs accepted to work for the British and French in the late nineteenth and twentieth centuries" (1979: 163).

8 As Takieddine-Amyuni observes, "Sa'eed's bedroom [resembles] Africa itself with its desert and its Snake God, the Nile. It is transformed into a parody of an altar with incense and burning sandalwood in the air, a silken

Isphahan prayer rug on the floor and a very precious Arabic manuscript on the table. The pseudo-religious vocabulary merges with a sado-masochistic jargon as the room is transformed into a 'theatre of war' and graveyard" (1980: 13). It is worth noting that Jean destroys the prayer rug, as well as the manuscript, in the course of their "murderous war," the rug being "the most valuable thing I owned, the thing I treasured most" (Salih 1980: 157).

9 According to James Andreas, "*Dutchman* may well represent the ultimate African American revision of *Othello*." Andreas also contends that in *Dutchman* Lula plays "the aggressor in a war overtly declared and waged between the races" and that "the true victim in the biracial sexual struggle is the black *male*" (1992: 50).

10 It remains unclear to me what we are to make of this apparent allusion to the first lines of Shakespeare's sonnet 23, "As an unperfect actor on the stage,/Who with his fear is put besides his part," apart from remarking its evocation of the narrator's own enduring dividedness between North and South, East and West.

11 As Sonia Ghattas-Soliman observes, "behind the conciliatory tone" of *Season of Migration* "one detects a strong attack on conservative practices that conflict with the spirit of Islam. All manifestations of abuse—from excessive paternal authority to man's self-indulgence—are at the expense of woman and are denounced and condemned" (1991: 102).

12 The Gordon Memorial College was officially opened by Kitchener in 1902. From the start, its curriculum was "consciously planned, not to give a liberal education, but to provide adequately trained government employees" (Holt 1961: 195). Edward Atiyah, a young Lebanese Oxford graduate who came to teach at the college in 1926, has this to say of it: "It was a military, not a human institution. It was a Government School in a country where the Government was an alien colonial government. The [British] Tutors were members of the Political Service. They were there in the dual capacity of masters and rulers, and the second capacity overshadowed the first. The pupils were expected to show them not the ordinary respect owed by pupils to their teachers, but the submissiveness demanded of a subject" (quoted in Holt 1961: 196). According to Holt, the first Sudanese students to come to Britain for post-secondary education arrived "just before the outbreak of the Second World War" and "were trained at the University College of the South-West (now the University of Exeter)" (1961: 198).

13 As Holt has observed, for "the great majority of this *elite*" both during and after the Condominium period, a "dislocation" obtained "between their Muslim, Arab tradition, nurtured from their earliest years by their environment, and appealing to their deepest emotions, and the academic and technical skills, laboriously acquired through the medium of a foreign language...Generally speaking, the Western-educated student has tended to solve the internal conflict by putting the two traditions into separate compartments of his being, applying the Western attitudes and response to the demands of his public and official life, and relaxing at other times into more congenial ways of thought and behaviour. Within Sudanese society, the tension takes the form of lack of understanding between the generations, a loss of authority by the older peoples, a tendency for the more

immature members of the educated *elite* to acquire habits of intellectual arrogance" (1961: 203–4).

14 I am here adapting and enlarging upon Said's discussion of how "the modern Orient…participates in its own Orientalizing" (1979: 325).

CONCLUSION—DECOLONIZING SHAKESPEARE: *MY SON'S STORY, CHILDREN OF LIGHT*, AND LATE IMPERIAL ROMANCE

1 My discussion of *Children of Light* is profoundly indebted to James Bloom's *The Literary Bent* (1997: 20–61).

2 Cf. McClure: "Walker…is troubled by 'murderous fantasies': he dreams of destroying the woman he loves. And he turns these fantasies into fiction, or at least a film script, for his actual lover. Working from Kate Chopin's *The Awakening*, he literally writes Lu Anne…into suicide. And she takes the part—over his protests but with his subtle cooperation—literally" (1994: 116).

3 Cf. Bloom: "Living up to their characters' eloquence, their 'great lines'…living through the trials that lend such lines credence kills Lu Anne and mortifies Walker. Their catastrophes call into question the availability of Shakespeare, our right to claim him as a contemporary. [The novel] seems both to rehearse the necessity of steeping ourselves in Shakespeare and to lament the inevitability of outgrowing him" (1997: 52).

4 Noting that Walker and Lu Anne work "against the backdrop of a Mexico reduced to little more than a series of 'locations'," McClure concludes that "What is missing in such scenes…is any serious attempt to represent Mexico." He adds: "Stone has ceased to think politically about the implications of the American presence, and one consequence is that Mexico and its people are reduced once again to their traditional roles as figures of futility, suffering and spirituality" (1994: 115). As I try to suggest, the failure of "any serious attempt to represent Mexico" is Walker's more than it is Stone's. Stone provides all the material we need to register the self-serving politics of Walker's thoughtlessly privileged exploitation of people and things, American and Mexican alike.

5 And, as Jolly notes, there is the case of the nationalist Afrikaners who, even as they set about colonizing black and coloured South Africans, "continued to see themselves as victims of English colonization" and thus continue to see themselves as "true postcolonials" (1995: 22).

WORKS CITED

Achebe, Chinua (1958) *Things Fall Apart*, London: Heinemann.

Addams, Jane (1907a) *Democracy and Social Ethics*, New York and London: Macmillan.

—— (1907b) *Newer Ideals of Peace*, Chautaugua, NY: Chautaugua Press.

—— (1965) "A Modern Lear," in Christopher Lasch (ed.) *The Social Thought of Jane Addams*, Indianapolis: Bobbs Merrill, 105–23 (orig. *Survey* 29 [2 November 1912]: 131–7).

——(1981, orig. 1910) *Twenty Years at Hull House*, New York: New American Library.

Alger, William (1877) *Life of Edwin Forrest*, 2 vols., Philadelphia: Lippincott (reprinted 1972 New York: Benjamin Blom).

Althusser, Louis (1971) "Ideology and Ideological State Apparatuses," in *Lenin and Philosophy and Other Essays*, trans. Ben Brewster, New York: Monthly Review Press.

Andreas, James R. (1992) "*Othello*'s African-American Progeny," *South Atlantic Review*, 57: 39–57.

Anonymous (1753) *The Royal African or Memoirs of the Young Prince of Annamboe*, London.

Appiah, Kwame Anthony (1991) "Is the Post- in Postmodernism the Post- in Postcolonial?," *Critical Inquiry*, 17(2): 336–57.

Ashcroft, Bill (1996) "On the Hyphen in 'Post-Colonial'," *New Literature Review*, 32: 23–31.

Ashcroft, Bill, Gareth Griffiths, and Helen Tiffin (1989) *The Empire Writes Back: Theory and Practice in Post-Colonial Literatures*, London and New York: Routledge.

Athey, Stephanie and Daniel Cooper Alarcon (1993) "Oroonoko's Gendered Economies of Honor/Horror: Reframing Colonial Discourse Studies in the Americas," *American Literature*, 65(3): 415–43.

Attridge, Derek (1992) "Oppressive Silence: J.M. Coetzee's *Foe* and the Politics of the Canon," in Karen Lawrence (ed.) *Decolonizing Tradition: New Views of Twentieth Century "British" Literary Canons*, Urbana and Chicago: University of Illinois Press, 212–38.

Baker, Jr., Houston A. (1986) "Caliban's Triple Play," in Henry Louis Gates, Jr. (ed.) *"Race", Writing, and Difference*, Chicago: University of Chicago Press, 381–95.

Balfour-Paul, Glen (1991) *The End of Empire in the Middle East: Britain's Relinquishment of Power in Her Last Three Arab Dependencies*, Cambridge: Cambridge University Press.

Barker, Francis and Peter Hulme (1985) " 'Nymphs and reapers heavily vanish': The Discursive Con-texts of *The Tempest*," in John Drakakis (ed.) *Alternative Shakespeares*, London and New York: Methuen, 191–205.

Barnes, Fiona R. (1992) "Resisting Cultural Cannibalism: Oppositional Narratives in Michelle Cliff's *No Telephone to Heaven*," *Journal of the Midwest Modern Language Association*, 25(1): 23–31.

Bartels, Emily (1990) "Making More of the Moor: Aaron, Othello, and Renaissance Refashionings of Race," *Shakespeare Quarterly*, 41(4): 433–54.

Barthelmy, Anthony (1987) *Black Face, Maligned Race: The Representation of Blacks in English Drama from Shakespeare to Southerne*, Baton Rouge and London: Louisiana State University Press.

Bate, Jonathan (1989) *Shakespearean Constitutions: Politics, Theatre, Criticism 1730–1830*, Oxford: Clarendon Press.

Baxandall, Lee (ed.) (1972) *Radical Perspectives in the Arts*, Baltimore: Johns Hopkins University Press.

Behn, Aphra (1973, orig. 1688) *Oroonoko, or The Royal Slave*, New York: W.W. Norton.

Bender, Thomas (1987) *New York Intellect*, New York: Knopf.

Bennett, Tony (1982) "Text and History," in Peter Widdowson (ed.) *Re-Reading English*, London: Methuen, 223–36.

Berger, Jr., Harry (1968) " 'Miraculous Harp': A Reading of Shakespeare's *Tempest*," *Shakespeare Survey*, 5: 253–83 (reprinted in Harry Berger, Jr. [1988] *Second World and Green World: Studies in Renaissance Mythmaking*, Berkeley and Los Angeles: University of California Press, 147–85).

Berkley, Constance E. and Osman Hassan Ahmed (1982) *Tayeb Salih Speaks: Four Interviews with the Sudanese Novelist*, Washington, D.C.: Office of the Cultural Counsellor, Embassy of the Democratic Republic of the Sudan.

Berlant, Lauren (1994) " '68, or Something," *Critical Inquiry*, 21: 124–55.

Bernabé, Jean, Patrick Chamoiseau, and Raphael Confiant (1990) "In Praise of Creoleness," trans. Mohamed B. Taleb Khyar, *Callaloo*, 13: 886–909.

Bhabha, Homi (1994) *The Location of Culture*, London and New York: Routledge.

Bloom, James (1992) *Left Letters: The Culture Wars of Mike Gold and Joseph Freeman*, New York: Columbia University Press.

——(1997) *The Literary Bent: In Search of High Art in Contemporary American Writing*, Philadelphia: University of Pennsylvania Press.

Boose, Lynda E. (1994) " 'The Getting of a Lawful Race': Racial Discourse in Early Modern England and the Unrepresentable Black Woman," in Margo Hendricks and Patricia Parker (eds.) *Women, "Race," and Writing in the Early Modern Period*, London: Routledge, 35–54.

Brantlinger, Patrick (1985) *"Heart of Darkness*: Anti- Imperialism, Racism, or Impressionism?" *Criticism*, 27(4): 363–85.

Brathwaite, Edward Kamau (1973) *The Arrivants: A New World Trilogy*, London: Oxford University Press.

——(1977) "Caliban, Ariel, and Unprospero in the Conflict of Creolization: A Study of the Slave Revolt in Jamaica in 1831–32," *Annals of the New York Academy of Sciences*, 292: 41–62.

——(1981) "English in the Caribbean: Notes on Nation Language and Poetry," in Leslie A. Fiedler and Houston A. Baker (eds.) *English Literature: Opening up the Canon*, Selected Papers from the English Institute, 1974, N.S. 4, Baltimore: Johns Hopkins University Press, 15–53.

Breight, Curtis (1991) "Branagh and the Prince, or a 'Royal Fellowship of Death'," *Critical Quarterly*, 33(4): 94–111.

——(1997) "Elizabethan World Pictures," in John J. Joughin (ed.) *Shakespeare and National Culture*, Manchester: Manchester University Press, 295–325.

Breslin, Jimmy (1994) "Monsters of the Heart," *Esquire* (October), 92–7.

Bristol, Michael (1990) *Shakespeare's America, America's Shakespeare*, London and New York: Routledge.

Brodber, Erna (1988, orig. 1980) *Jane and Louisa Will Soon Come Home*, London and Port of Spain: New Beacon Books.

Brown, Laura (1987) "The Romance of Empire: *Oroonoko* and the Trade in Slaves," in Felicity Nussbaum and Laura Brown (eds.) *The New Eighteenth Century*, London and New York: Methuen, 41–61.

Brown, Paul (1985) "'This Thing of Darkness I Acknowledge Mine': *The Tempest* and the Discourse of Colonialism," in Jonathan Dollimore and Alan Sinfield (eds.) *Political Shakespeare: New Essays in Cultural Materialism*, Manchester: Manchester University Press; Ithaca, NY: Cornell University Press, 48–71.

Brown, Stephen J. (1978) "The Uses of Shakespeare in America: A Study in Class Domination," in David Bevington and Jay L. Halio (eds.) *Shakespeare Pattern of Excelling Nature*, Newark, DE: University of Delaware Press, 230–8.

Brydon, Diana (1984) "Re-Writing *The Tempest*," *World Literature Written in English*, 23(1): 75–88.

Buder, Stanley (1967) *Pullman: An Experiment in Industrial Order and Community Planning, 1880–1930*, New York: Oxford University Press.

Buell, Lawrence (1992) "American Literary Emergence as a Postcolonial Phenomenon," *ALH*, 4(3): 411–42.

Burton, Richard F. (1961, orig. 1876) *The Lake Regions of Central Africa*, 2 vols., New York: Horizon.

Cartelli, Thomas (1983) *"Bartholomew Fair* as Urban Arcadia: Jonson Responds to Shakespeare," *Renaissance Drama*, N.S. 14: 151–72.

——(1995) "After *The Tempest*: Shakespeare, Postcoloniality, and Michelle Cliff's New, New World Miranda," *Contemporary Literature*, 36(1): 82–102.

Césaire, Aimé (1986, orig. 1969) *A Tempest*, trans., Richard Miller, New York: Ubu Repertory Theater Publications.

Chancellor, William E. (1916) *History and Government of the United States*, New York: American Book Co.

Chartier, Roger (1995) *Forms and Meanings*, Philadelphia: University of Pennsylvania Press.

Cliff, Michelle (1984) *Abeng*, New York: Penguin.

——(1989, orig. 1987) *No Telephone to Heaven*, New York: Vintage.

——(1990) "Clare Savage as a Crossroads Character," in Selwyn Cudjoe (ed.) *Caribbean Women Writers: Essays from the First International Congress*, Wellesley, MA: Calaloux Press, 263–8.

——(1991) Conference Presentation, in Philomena Mariani (ed.) *Critical Fictions: The Politics of Imaginative Writing*, Seattle: Bay Press, 66–71.

——(1993) "An Interview with Michelle Cliff" (by Meryl F. Schwartz), *Contemporary Literature*, 34(4): 595–619.

Cohen, Walter (1985) *Drama of a Nation: Public Theater in Renaissance England and Spain*, Ithaca, NY: Cornell University Press.

Cohn, Ruby (1976) *Modern Shakespearean Offshoots*, Princeton: Princeton University Press.

Conant, Isabelle Fiske (1916) *Will O'the World: A Shakespeare Tercentenary Masque*, Wellesley, MA: Wellesley College.

Conrad, Robert Taylor (1852) *Aylmere, or The Bondman of Kent and Other Poems*, Philadelphia: E.H. Butler.

——(1869) *Jack Cade, the Captain of the Commons*, London: T.H. Lacy [Lacy's acting edition of plays, vol. 83].

Craton, Michael (1974) *Sinews of Empire: A Short History of British Slavery*, Garden City, NY: Anchor/Doubleday.

Crewe, Jonathan (1990) "Reforming Prince Hal: The Sovereign Inheritor in *2 Henry IV*," *Renaissance Drama*, N.S. 21: 225–42.

D'Amico, Jack (1991) *The Moor in English Renaissance Drama*, Tampa: University of South Florida Press.

Davis, Allen F. (1973) *American Heroine: The Life and Legend of Jane Addams*, New York: Oxford University Press.

Davis, Merrell R. and William H. Gilman (eds.) (1960) *The Letters of Herman Melville*, New Haven: Yale University Press.

Dobson, Michael (1992a) *The Making of the National Poet: Shakespeare, Adaptation, and Authorship, 1660–1769*, Oxford: Clarendon Press.

——(1992b) "Fairly Brave New World: Shakespeare, the American Colonies, and the American Revolution," *Renaissance Drama*, N.S. 23: 189–207.

Donaldson, Laura (1988) "The Miranda Complex: Colonialism and the Question of Feminist Reading," *Diacritics*, 18(3): 65–77.

Dos Passos, John (1916) "Against American Literature," *New Republic*, 14 October 1916, 269–71.

Du Bois, W.E.B. (1968) *The Autobiography of W.E.B. Du Bois*, New York: International Publishers.

Duberman, Martin (1988) *Paul Robeson*, New York: Knopf.

Duncan, H. Dalziel (1989) *Culture and Democracy*, New Brunswick: Transaction Publishers.

Dunn, Esther Cloudman (1939) *Shakespeare in America*, New York: Macmillan.

Edmondson, Belinda (1993) "Race, Writing, and the Politics of (Re)Writing History: An Analysis of the Novels of Michelle Cliff," *Callaloo*, 16(1): 180–91.

Ely, Richard T. (1885) "Pullman: A Social Study," *Harper's Monthly*, 70: 45–60.

Emerson, Ralph Waldo (1903) *Representative Men*, Boston and New York: Houghton-Mifflin.

——(1971) "The American Scholar," in Alfred R. Ferguson and Robert E. Spiller (eds.) *The Collected Writings of Ralph Waldo Emerson*, vol. 1, Cambridge: Harvard University Press.

Epstein, Helen (1994) *Joe Papp: An American Life*, Boston: Little, Brown.

Falk, Robert (1942) "Shakespeare's Place in Walt Whitman's America," *Shakespeare Association Bulletin*, 17(2): 86–96.

Fanon, Frantz (1967, orig. 1952) *Black Skin, White Masks*, trans. Charles Lam Markmann, New York: Grove Press.

Ferguson, Margaret (1993) "Transmuting *Othello*: Aphra Behn's *Oroonoko*," in Marianne Novy (ed.) *Cross-Cultural Performances: Differences in Women's Re-Visions of Shakespeare*, Champaign: University of Illinois Press, 15–49.

Fernández Retamar, Roberto (1989) *Caliban and Other Essays*, trans. Edward Baker, Minneapolis: University of Minnesota Press.

Ferriar, John (1788) *The Prince of Angola*, Manchester.

Fiedler, Leslie (1972) *The Stranger in Shakespeare*, New York: Stein & Day.

Fogarty, Anne (1994) "Looks that Kill: Violence and Representation in Aphra Behn's *Oroonoko*," in Carl Plasa and Betty J. Ring (eds.) *The Discourse of Slavery*, London: Routledge, 1–17.

Fonseca, Isabel (1988) Review of Michelle Cliff, *No Telephone to Heaven*, *Times Literary Supplement*, 1–7 April 1988, 364.

Franck, Jane P. (1964) "Caliban at Lewisohn Stadium, 1916," in Anne Paolucci (ed.) *Shakespeare Encomium*, New York: City College, 154–68.

Froude, James Anthony (1888) *The English in the West Indies*, New York: Scribner's.

Fuentes, Carlos (1988) "Prologue" to José Enrique Rodó, *Ariel*, trans. Margaret Sayers Peden, Austin: University of Texas Press.

Gallagher, Catherine (1994) *Nobody's Story: The Vanishing Acts of Women Writers in the Marketplace, 1670–1820*, Berkeley: University of California Press.

Ghattas-Soliman, Sonia (1991) "The Two-Sided Image of Women in *Season of Migration to the North*," in Kenneth Harrow (ed.) *Faces of Islam in African Literature*, Portsmouth, NH: Heinemann, 91–103.

Giddings, Robert (1991) "Cry God for Harry, England and Lord Kitchener," in Giddings (ed.) *Literature and Imperialism*, New York: St. Martin's, 182–219.

Gilbert, Helen (1991) "The Boomerang Effect: Canonical Counter-Discourse and David Malouf's *Blood Relations* as an Oppositional Reworking of *The Tempest*," *World Literature Written in English*, 31(2): 50–64.

Gillies, John (1994) *Shakespeare and the Geography of Difference*, Cambridge: Cambridge University Press.

Gilmer, Albert Hatton (1916) *King Shakespeare: A Masque of Praise for the Shakespeare Tercentenary*, Boston: Ginn & Co.

Gold, Michael (1990, orig. 1930) *Jews Without Money*, New York: Carroll and Graf.

Goldberg, Jonathan (1992) *Sodometries: Renaissance Texts, Modern Sexualities*, Stanford: Stanford University Press.

Gordimer, Nadine (1990) *My Son's Story*, New York: Penguin.

Goreau, Angeline (1980) *Reconstructing Aphra: A Social Biography of Aphra Behn*, New York: Dial Press.

Grant, Madison (1916) *The Passing of the Great Race; or, The Racial Basis of European History*, New York: Scribner's.

Green, William (1989) *"Caliban by the Yellow Sands*: Percy MacKaye's Adaptation of *The Tempest*," *Maske und Kothurn*, 35: 59–69.

Greenaway, Peter (1991) *Prospero's Books*, New York: Four Walls Eight Windows.

Greenblatt, Stephen J. (1970) "Learning to Curse: Aspects of Linguistic Colonialism in the 16th Century," in Fredi Chiapelli (ed.) *First Images of America: The Impact of the New World on the Old*, Berkeley: University of California Press, 561–80 (reprinted in Stephen J. Greenblatt [1990] *Learning to Curse*, London: Routledge, 16–39).

——(1980) *Renaissance Self-Fashioning: From More to Shakespeare*, Chicago and London: University of Chicago Press.

Greenstein, Susan M. (1984–85) "Miranda's Story: Nadine Gordimer and the Literature of Empire," *Novel*, 18: 227–42.

Hall, Stuart (1996) "When was 'the Post-Colonial'? Thinking at the Limit," in Iain Chambers and Lidia Curti (eds.) *The Post-Colonial Question*, London and New York: Routledge, 242–60.

Hamner, Robert (1984) "Colony, Nationhood and Beyond: Third World Writers and Critics Contend with Joseph Conrad," *World Literature Written in English*, 23(1): 108–16.

Harlow, Barbara (1979) "Othello's Season of Migration," *Edebiyat*, 4(2): 157–75.

Harrison, Richard Clarence (1929) "Walt Whitman and Shakespeare," *PMLA*, 44: 1201–38.

Hearne, John (1990) *"The Wide Sargasso Sea*: A West Indian Reflection," in Pierette M. Frickey (ed.) *Critical Perspectives on Jean Rhys*, Washington, D.C.: Three Continents Press, 186–93.

Helgerson, Richard (1992) *Forms of Nationhood: The Elizabethan Writing of England*, Chicago: University of Chicago Press.

Hibbert, Christopher (1984) *Africa Explored: Europeans in the Dark Continent, 1769–1889*, London: Penguin.

Higham, John (1955) *Strangers in the Land: Patterns of American Nativism 1860–1925*, New Brunswick, NJ: Rutgers University Press.

Holt, P.M. (1961) *A Modern History of the Sudan*, New York: Grove.

Howe, Irving (1976) *World of Our Fathers*, New York and London: Harcourt-Brace.

Hulme, Peter (1981) "Hurricane in the Caribbees: The Constitution of the Discourse of English Colonialism," in Francis Barker *et al.* (eds.) *1642: Literature and Power in the Seventeenth Century*, Proceedings of the Essex Conference on the Sociology of Literature, July 1980, Colchester: University of Essex, 55–83.

——(1986) *Colonial Encounters: Europe and the Native Caribbean, 1492–1797*, London and New York: Routledge.

——(1995) "Including America," *Ariel*, 26(1): 117–23.

Hutton, Laurence (1891) "The American Stage Negro," *Curiosities of the American Stage*, London: Osgood.

Jackson, Shannon (1996) "Civic Play-Housekeeping: Gender, Theatre, and American Reform," *Theatre Journal*, 48: 337–61.

James, Henry (1968, orig. 1907) *The American Scene*, Bloomington, IN: Indiana University Press.

JanMohamed, Abdul (1983) *Manichean Aesthetics: The Politics of Literature in Colonial Africa*, Amherst: University of Massachusetts Press.

Johnson, David (1996) *Shakespeare and South Africa*, Oxford: Clarendon Press.

Johnson, Karen Ramsey (1995) " 'What the Name Will Make Happen': Strategies of Naming in Nadine Gordimer's Novels," *Ariel*, 26(3): 117–37.

Johnson, Lemuel (1990) "A-beng: (Re)Calling the Body In(To) Question," in Carole Boyce Davies and Elaine Savory Fido (eds.) *Out of the Kumbla: Caribbean Women and Literature*, Trenton, NJ: Africa World Press, 111–42.

Jolly, Rosemary (1995) "Rehearsals of Liberation: Contemporary Postcolonial Discourse and the New South Africa," *PMLA*, 110(1): 17–29.

Jones, Eldred (1965) *Othello's Countrymen*, London: Oxford University Press.

Jordan, Winthrop D. (1968) *White Over Black: American Attitudes Toward the Negro*, Chapel Hill: University of North Carolina Press.

Kahn, Otto H. (1916) *Art and the People*, New York: Shakespeare Tercentenary Celebration Committee.

Kaplan, Amy (1993) "Left Alone with America: the Absence of Empire in the Study of American Culture," in Amy Kaplan and Donald Pease (eds.) *Cultures of U.S. Imperialism*, Durham, NC: Duke University Press, 3–21.

Kaul, Suvir (1994) "Reading Literary Symptoms: Colonial Pathologies and the *Oroonoko* Fictions of Behn, Southerne, and Hawkesworth," *Eighteenth-Century Life*, 18(3) (n.s.): 80–96.

Kenyatta, Jomo (1965) *Facing Mt. Kenya*, New York: Random House.

Kermode, Frank (ed.) (1958) *The Tempest* (by William Shakespeare), Arden edition, London: Methuen.

Kincaid, Jamaica (1986) *Annie John*, New York: New American Library.

Knight, G. Wilson (1966, orig. 1947) *The Crown of Life: Essays in Interpretation of Shakespeare's Final Plays*, New York: Barnes & Noble.

Laframboise, Lisa (1991) " 'Maiden and Monster': The Female Caliban in Canadian *Tempests*," *World Literature Written in English*, 31(2): 36–49.

Lamming, George (1971) *Water with Berries*, London: Longman.

—(1984, orig. 1960) *The Pleasures of Exile*, London: Allison and Busby.

Lasch, Christopher (ed.) (1965) *The Social Thought of Jane Addams*, Indianapolis: Bobbs-Merrill.

—(1967) *The New Radicalism in America: 1889–1963*, New York: Vintage Books.

Lears, Jackson (1981) *No Place of Grace: Antimodernism and the Transformation of American Culture 1880–1920*, New York: Pantheon.

Leggett, William (1970, orig. 1840) *A Collection of the Political Writings of William Leggett*, ed. Theodore Sedgwick, 2 vols., New York: Arno Press.

Levine, Daniel (1971) *Jane Addams and the Liberal Tradition*, Madison: State Historical Society of Wisconsin.

Levine, Lawrence W. (1988) *Highbrow/Lowbrow: The Emergence of Cultural Hierarchy in America*, Cambridge: Harvard University Press.

Ligon, Richard (1657) *A True and Exact History of the Island of Barbados*, London.

Lim, Walter S.H. (1993) "Representing the Other: *Othello*, Colonialism, Discourse," *Upstart Crow*, 13: 59–78.

Lima, Maria Helena (1993) "Revolutionary Developments: Michelle Cliff's *No Telephone to Heaven* and Merle Collins's *Angel*," *Ariel*, 24(1): 35–56.

Lindqvist, Sven (1996) *"Exterminate All The Brutes"*, trans. Joan Tate, New York: New Press.

Linn, James Weber (1935) *Jane Addams: A Biography*, New York and London: D. Appleton-Century.

Lissak, Rivka Shpak (1989) *Pluralism and Progressives: Hull House and the New Immigrants, 1890–1919*, Chicago: University of Chicago Press.

Little, Arthur L. (1993) "'An Essence That's Not Seen': The Primal Scene of Racism in *Othello*," *Shakespeare Quarterly*, 44(3): 304–24.

Lockhart, J.G. and C.M. Woodhouse (1963) *Cecil Rhodes: The Colossus of Southern Africa*, New York: Macmillan.

Loomba, Ania (1992) *Gender, Race, Renaissance Drama*, Delhi: Oxford University Press.

—(1997) "Shakespearian Transformations," in John J. Joughin (ed.) *Shakespeare and National Culture*, Manchester: Manchester University Press, 109–41.

Lord, Walter (1960) *The Good Years: From 1900 to the First World War*, New York: Harper.

McClintock, Anne (1995) *Imperial Leather: Race, Gender and Sexuality in the Colonial Contest*, New York and London: Routledge.

McClure, John A. (1994) *Late Imperial Romance*, London and New York: Verso.

Macdonald, Joyce Green (1994) "Acting Black: *Othello*, *Othello* Burlesques, and the Performance of Blackness," *Theatre Journal*, 46: 233–46.

McDonald, Russ (1991) "Reading *The Tempest*," *Shakespeare Survey*, 43: 15–28.

MacKaye, Percy (1909) *The Playhouse and the Play*, New York: Macmillan.

—(1915) *The New Citizenship*, New York: Macmillan.

—(1916) *Caliban by the Yellow Sands: Shakespeare Tercentenary Masque*, Garden City, NY: Doubleday.

——(1927) *Epoch: The Life of Steele Mackaye*, 2 vols., New York: Boni and Liveright.

Magnus, Philip (1958) *Kitchener: Portrait of an Imperialist*, London: John Murray.

Mahoney, John J. and Charles M. Herlihy (1918) *First Steps in Americanization: A Handbook for Teachers*, New York: Houghton-Miflin.

Majdalany, Fred (1962) *State of Emergency: The Full Story of Mau Mau*, London: Longman.

Mannoni, Octave (1964, orig. 1950) *Prospero and Caliban: The Psychology of Colonization*, trans. Pamela Powesland, New York: Praeger.

Markels, Julian (1993) *Melville and the Politics of Identity*, Urbana and Chicago: University of Illinois Press.

Marsden, Jean I. (ed.) (1991) *The Appropriation of Shakespeare: Post-Renaissance Constructions of the Works and the Myth*, New York: St. Martin's Press.

Marshall, Herbert and Mildred Stock (1968) *Ira Aldridge: The Negro Tragedian*, Carbondale, IL: Southern Illinois Press.

Mason, Jeffrey D. (1991) "The Politics of *Metamora*," in Sue Ellen Case and Janelle Reinelt (eds.) *The Performance of Power*, Iowa City, IA: University of Iowa Press.

Mintz, Frances Sankstone (1923) *The New American Citizen: A Reader for Foreigners*, New York: Macmillan.

Mishra, Vijay and Bob Hodge (1991) "What is Post(-)Colonialism?," *Textual Practice*, 5(3): 399–414.

Mitchell, W.J.T. (1992) "Postcolonial Culture, Postimperial Criticism," *Transition*, 56: 11–19.

Moody, Richard (1958) *The Astor Place Riot*, Bloomington, IN: Indiana University Press.

——(1960) *Edwin Forrest*, New York: Knopf.

Moses, Montrose J. (1929) *The Fabulous Forrest: The Record of an American Actor*, Boston: Little, Brown.

Mukherjee, Arun P. (1990) "Whose Post-Colonialism and Whose Post-Modernism," *World Literature Written in English*, 30(2): 1–9.

Murray, Timothy (1994) "American Shakespeare, or, the Bourgie-Woogie Blues," *American Quarterly*, 46(2): 267–75.

My Own Private Idaho (1991) dir. Gus Van Sant, prod. Laurie Parker, with Keanu Reeves and River Phoenix, Fine Line.

Naipaul, V.S. (1981, orig. 1962) *The Middle Passage*, New York: Vintage.

Neill, Michael (1989) "Unproper Beds: Race, Adultery, and the Hideous in *Othello*," *Shakespeare Quarterly*, 40(4): 383–412.

Newman, Karen (1987) "'And Wash the Ethiop White': Femininity and the Monstrous in *Othello*," in Jean E. Howard and Marion O' Connor (eds.) *Shakespeare Reproduced: The Text in History and Ideology*, New York and London: Methuen, 141–62.

Ngũgĩ wa Thiong'o (1968) *A Grain of Wheat*, London: Heinemann.

——(1983, orig. 1972) *Homecoming: Essays on African and Caribbean Literature, Culture, and Politics*, Westport, CT: Lawrence Hill.

—(1986) *Decolonising the Mind: The Politics of Language in African Literature*, Portsmouth, NH: Heinemann.

Nixon, Rob (1987) "Caribbean and African Appropriations of *The Tempest*," *Critical Inquiry*, 13: 557–78.

Novy, Marianne (ed.) (1990) *Women's Re-Visions of Shakespeare*, Urbana and London: University of Illinois Press.

Okri, Ben (1987) "Meditations on Othello," *West Africa*, 23–30 March 1987, 562–4, 618–19.

Orgel, Stephen (1986) "Prospero's Wife," in Margaret W. Ferguson, Maureen Quilligan, and Nancy J. Vickers (eds.) *Rewriting the Renaissance: The Discourses of Sexual Difference in Early Modern Europe*, Chicago: University of Chicago Press, 50–64.

Orkin, Martin (1987) "Othello and the 'Plain Face' of Racism," *Shakespeare Quarterly*, 38: 166–88.

Parker, Patricia (1994) "Fantasies of 'Race' and 'Gender': Africa, *Othello*, and Bringing to Light," in Margo Hendricks and Patricia Parker (eds.) *Women, 'Race,' and Writing in the Early Modern Period*, London and New York, 84–100.

Parry, Benita (1987) "Problems in Current Theories of Colonial Discourse," *Oxford Literary Review*, 9(1/2): 27–58.

Pratt, Mary Louise (1985) "Scratches on the Face of the Country; or, What Mr. Barrow Saw in the Land of the Bushmen," *Critical Inquiry*, 12(1): 119–43.

Prospero's Books (1991) dir. Peter Greenaway, prod. Kees Kasander, with John Gielgud, Michael Clark, Isabelle Pasco, Allarts.

Rabkin, Norman (1967) *Shakespeare and the Common Understanding*, New York: Free Press.

Riis, Jacob (1890) *How the Other Half Lives*, New York: Charles Scribner's Sons.

—— (1902) *The Battle with the Slum*, New York: Macmillan.

Rodó, José Enrique (1988, orig. 1900) *Ariel*, trans. Margaret Sayers Peden, Austin: University of Texas Press.

Rosberg, Carl G. and John Nottingham (1966) *The Myth of "Mau Mau": Nationalism in Kenya*, New York: Praeger.

Ross, Edward A. (1914) *The Old World and the New*, New York: Century.

Said, Edward (1979) *Orientalism*, New York: Vintage.

—(1994) *Culture and Imperialism*, New York: Vintage.

Salih, Tayeb (1980, orig. 1969) *Season of Migration to the North*, trans. Denys Johnson-Davies, Colorado Springs, CO: Three Continents Press.

Shafer, Yvonne (1977) "Black Actors in the Nineteenth Century American Theatre," *CLA Journal*, 20(3): 387–400.

Shakespeare Wallah (1965) dir. James Ivory, prod. Ismail Merchant, with Shashi Kapoor, Felicity Kendal, Madhur Jaffrey, Merchant Ivory Productions.

Simon, John (1997) "Ill Will," *New York*, 6 January 1997, 50–1.

Sinfield, Alan (1992) *Faultlines: Cultural Materialism and the Politics of Dissident Reading*, Berkeley and Los Angeles: University of California Press.

Singh, Jyotsna (1989) "Different Shakespeares: The Bard in Colonial/Post-Colonial India," *Theatre Journal*, 41(4): 445–58.

——(1994) "Othello's Identity, Postcolonial Theory, and Contemporary African Rewritings of *Othello*," in Margo Hendricks and Patricia Parker (eds.) *Women, "Race," and Writing in the Early Modern Period*, London and New York: Routledge, 287–99.

——(1996) *Colonial Narratives/Cultural Dialogues: "Discoveries" of India in the Language of Colonialism*, London and New York: Routledge.

Sklar, Kathryn Kish (1990) "Who Funded Hull House?," in Kathleen D. McCarthy (ed.) *Lady Bountiful: Women, Philanthropy, and Power*, New Brunswick: Rutgers University Press, 94–115.

Slemon, Stephen (1987) "Monuments of Empire Allegory/Counter-Discourse/Post-Colonial Writing," *Kunapipi*, 9(3): 1–16.

Smith, Hallett (ed.) (1969) *Twentieth Century Interpretations of "The Tempest,"* Englewood Cliffs, NJ: Prentice-Hall.

Sollors, Werner (1986) *Beyond Ethnicity: Consent and Descent in American Culture*, New York: Oxford University Press.

Southerne, Richard (1976, orig. 1695) *Oroonoko*, Lincoln, NE: University of Nebraska Press.

Spivak, Gayatri Chakravorty (1986) "Three Women's Texts and a Critique of Imperialism," in Henry Louis Gates, Jr. (ed.) *"Race," Writing, and Difference*, Chicago: University of Chicago Press, 262–80.

Spurr, David (1985) "Colonialist Journalism: Stanley to Didion," *Raritan*, 5(2): 35–50.

Stanley, Richard and Alan Neame (eds.) (1961) *The Exploration Diaries of H.M. Stanley*, London: William Kimber.

Stirling, Brents (1949) *The Populace in Shakespeare*, New York: Columbia University Press.

Stone, Robert (1992, orig. 1986) *Children of Light*, New York: Vintage.

Stovall, Floyd (1952a) "Whitman, Shakespeare, and Democracy," *JEGP*, 51:4: 457–72.

——(1952b) "Whitman's Knowledge of Shakespeare," *Studies in Philology*, 49: 643–69.

Suleri, Sara (1992) *The Rhetoric of English India*, Chicago: University of Chicago Press.

Sundquist, Eric. J. (1996) *The Oxford W.E.B. Du Bois Reader*, New York: Oxford University Press.

Sypher, Wylie (1942) *Guinea's Captive Kings: British Anti-Slavery Literature of the Eighteenth Century*, Chapel Hill, NC: University of North Carolina Press.

Takieddine-Amyuni, Mona (1980) "Tayeb Salih's *Season of Migration to the North*: An Interpretation," *Arab Studies Quarterly*, 2(1): 1–18.

Thaler, Alwin (1941) *Shakespeare and Democracy*, Knoxville, TN: University of Tennessee Press.

Tiffin, Helen (1987) "Post-Colonial Literatures and Counter-Discourse," *Kunapipi*, 9(3): 17–34.

Todorov, Tzvetan (1984) *The Conquest of America: The Question of the Other*, trans. Richard Howard, New York: Harper and Row.

Trachtenberg, Alan (1982) *The Incorporation of America: Culture and Society in the Gilded Age*, New York: Hill and Wang.

Van Sant, Gus (1993) *Even Cowgirls Get the Blues & My Own Private Idaho*, London and Boston: Faber & Faber.

Vaughan, Alden T. and Virginia Mason Vaughan (1991) *Shakespeare's Caliban: A Cultural History*, Cambridge: Cambridge University Press.

Vaughan, Virginia Mason (1994) *Othello: A Contextual History*, Cambridge: Cambridge University Press.

Viswanathan, Gauri (1989) *Masks of Conquest: Literary Study and British Rule in India*, New York: Columbia University Press.

Walcott, Derek (1970) *Dream on Monkey Mountain and Other Plays*, New York: Farrar, Straus and Giroux.

——(1980) *Remembrance and Pantomime*, New York: Farrar, Straus and Giroux.

Warren, George (1667) *An Impartial Description of Surinam*, London.

Weisbuch, Robert (1986) *Atlantic Double-Cross: American Literature and British Influence in the Age of Emerson*, Chicago: University of Chicago Press.

Wells, Stanley (1978) *Nineteenth-Century Shakespearean Burlesques*, 5 vols., London: Diploma Press.

Whitman, Walt (1907) *Complete Prose Works*, Boston, MA: Small, Maynard and Company.

Wilenz, Gay (1992) "English is a Foreign Anguish: Caribbean Writers and the Disruption of the Colonial Canon," in Karen Lawrence (ed.) *Decolonising Tradition: New Views of Twentieth Century "British" Literary Canons*, Urbana and Chicago: University of Illinois Press, 261–78.

Willis, Susan (1986) "Caliban as Poet: Reversing the Maps of Domination," in Bell Gale Chevigny and Gari Laguardia (eds.) *Reinventing the Americas: Comparative Studies of Literature of the United States and Spanish America*, Cambridge: Cambridge University Press.

Willson, Jr., Robert F. (1992) "Recontextualizing Shakespeare on Film: *My Own Private Idaho, Men of Respect*, and *Prospero's Books*," *Shakespeare Bulletin*, 10(3): 34–7.

Wynter, Sylvia (1990) "Beyond Miranda's Meanings: Un/Silencing the 'Demonic Ground' of Caliban's 'Woman'," in Carole Boyce Davies and Elaine Savory Fido (eds.) *Out of the Kumbla: Caribbean Women and Literature*, Trenton, NJ: Africa World Press, 355–72.

Yelin, Louise (1992) "Decolonizing the Novel: Nadine Gordimer's *A Sport of Nature* and British Literary Traditions," in Karen Lawrence (ed.) *Decolonizing Traditions*, Urbana and Chicago: University of Illinois Press, 191–211.

Zabus, Chantal (1985) "A Calibanic Tempest in Anglophone and Francophone New World Writing," *Canadian Literature*, 104: 35–50.

INDEX